CLASSICS

COMEDY

ARISTOPHANES was born, probably in Athens, *c.* 448–445 BC and died between 386 and 380 BC. Little is known about his life but there is a portrait of him in Plato's *Symposium*. He was twice prosecuted in the 420s for his outspoken attacks on the prominent politician Cleon, but in 405 he was publicly honoured and crowned for promoting Athenian civic unity in *The Frogs*. Aristophanes had his first comedy produced when he was about nineteen or twenty, and wrote forty plays in all. The eleven surviving plays of Aristophanes are published in the Penguin Classics series as *The Birds and Other Plays*, *Lysistrata and Other Plays* and *The Wasps/The Poet and the Women/The Frogs*.

MENANDER (*c.* 342–292 BC) was the most distinguished author of Greek New Comedy. An Athenian of good family, he wrote over a hundred plays, although only one survives intact today: *Dyskolos* or *Old Cantankerous*. This won the prize in 316 BC and was recovered from an Egyptian papyrus as recently as 1957. Many more fragments of his plays have since been discovered, and some sizeable pieces from *The Rape of the Locks*, *The Arbitration* and *The Girl From Samos* have been known since 1907. These confirm Menander's skill in drawing humorous or romantic characters and making good dramatic use of a limited range of plots with stock scenes of disguise and recognition. Menander's plays were revived in Athens after his death and some of them were adapted for the Roman stage by Plautus and Terence, through whom they strongly influenced light drama from the Renaissance onwards.

TITUS MACCIUS PLAUTUS was born in Sarsina, Umbria, in about 254 BC, and was originally named, after his father, Titus. Little is known of his life, but it is believed that he went to Rome when young and worked as a stage assistant. His potential as an actor was discovered and he acquired two other names: Maccius, derived perhaps from the name of a clown in popular farce, and Plautus, a cognomen meaning 'flat-footed'. Somehow Plautus saved enough capital to go into business as a merchant shipper, but this venture collapsed, and he worked (says the tradition) as a miller's labourer, and in his spare time studied Greek drama. From the age of forty onwards he achieved increasing success as an adaptor of Greek comedies for the Roman stage. Much of his work seems to be original, however, and not mere translation. He was rewarded by being granted Roman citizenship. According to Cicero he died in 184 BC.

TERENCE (c. 186–159 BC) was born at Carthage of Libyan parentage and was brought to Rome as a young slave. According to Roman tradition his talents and good looks won him an education, manumission and entry to a patrician literary circle, with whose encouragement he wrote six Latin plays modelled on Greek New Comedy, all of which survive. Only one, *The Eunuch*, was a popular success in his lifetime, but he was read and admired in Roman times and throughout the Middle Ages, and became the main influence on Renaissance comedy.

ERICH SEGAL has taught Classics at Harvard, Yale and Princeton and is currently an Honorary Fellow at Wolfson College, Oxford. He has published widely on Greek and Roman Comedy, and his latest book, *The Death of Comedy*, was published in 2001. He is also the author of nine best-selling novels.

NORMA MILLER was educated at the universities of Glasgow and Cambridge and spent her professional life as a teacher of Greek and Latin languages and literature at the Royal Holloway College. She is now Reader Emeritus at the University of London having retired a little early in order to concentrate on writing. Most of her published works are on Tacitus, but she has taught Greek Drama for many years, and has reviewed books on Greek Drama for the *Literary Review* and the *Journal of Hellenic Studies*.

DOUGLASS PARKER is Professor of Classics at the University of Texas at Austin. He previously taught at Yale University, the University of California at Riverside and Dartmouth College. In 1961–2 he was a Junior Fellow at the Center for Hellenic Studies in Washington, DC, in 1965–6 a Fellow of the California Institute of Arts and in 1984–5 a Guggenheim Fellow. He has translated plays by Aristophanes, Plautus, Terence, Aeschylus and Seneca, and is finishing versions of Ovid's *Metamorphoses* and Nonnus's *Dionysiaka*.

ALAN H. SOMMERSTEIN has been Professor of Greek at the University of Nottingham since 1988, and is Director of its Centre for Ancient Drama and its Reception. He has written or edited over twenty books on Ancient Greek language and literature, especially tragic and comic drama, including *Aeschylean Tragedy* (1996), *Greek Drama and Dramatists* (2002) and a complete edition of the comedies of Aristophanes with translation and commentary. For the Penguin Classics he has also translated Aristophanes' *The Knights*, *Peace* and *Wealth* in the volume *The Birds and Other Plays*.

Classical Comedy

Edited with an Introduction by
ERICH SEGAL

PENGUIN BOOKS

PENGUIN CLASSICS

Published by the Penguin Group
Penguin Books Ltd, 80 Strand, London WC2R ORL, England
Penguin Group (USA) Inc., 375 Hudson Street, New York, New York 10014, USA
Penguin Group (Canada), 90 Eglinton Avenue East, Suite 700, Toronto, Ontario, Canada M4P 2Y3
(a division of Pearson Penguin Canada Inc.)
Penguin Ireland, 25 St Stephen's Green, Dublin 2, Ireland
(a division of Penguin Books Ltd)
Penguin Group (Australia), 250 Camberwell Road, Camberwell, Victoria 3124, Australia
(a division of Pearson Australia Group Pty Ltd)
Penguin Books India Pvt Ltd, 11 Community Centre, Panchsheel Park, New Delhi – 110 017, India
Penguin Group (NZ), 67 Apollo Drive, Mairangi Bay, Auckland 1310, New Zealand
(a division of Pearson New Zealand Ltd)
Penguin Books (South Africa) (Pty) Ltd, 24 Sturdee Avenue, Rosebank, Johannesburg 2196, South Africa

Penguin Books Ltd, Registered Offices: 80 Strand, London WC2R ORL, England

www.penguin.com

This selection first published in Penguin Classics 2006

007

Editorial material new to this volume, copyright © Erich Segal, 2006
All rights reserved

The moral right of the editor has been asserted

The text and selected Notes of Aristophanes, *The Birds*, trans. by Alan Sommerstein,
reprinted by permission of Aris & Phillips, 1987
The text and selected Notes of Menander, *The Girl From Samos*, trans. by Norma Miller,
from *Plays and Fragments*, reprinted by permission of Penguin, 1987
The text and Notes of Plautus, *The Brothers Menaechmus*, trans. by Erich Segal, from
Plautus: Four Comedies, reprinted by permission of Oxford Worlds Classics, 1996
The text and Notes of Terence, *The Eunuch*, trans. by Douglass Parker, from *The Complete
Comedies of Terence*, ed. Palmer Bovie, Johns Hopkins Press, 1975

Set in 10.25/12.25 pt PostScript Adobe Sabon
Typeset by Rowland Phototypesetting Ltd, Bury St Edmunds, Suffolk
Printed in England by Clays Ltd, St Ives plc

ISBN-13: 978-0-140-44982-2

www.greenpenguin.co.uk

MIX
Paper from
responsible sources
FSC
www.fsc.org   FSC® C018179

Penguin Books is committed to a sustainable
future for our business, our readers and our planet.
This book is made from Forest Stewardship
Council™ certified paper.

Contents

CONTENTS

Chronology

Greece (BC)

c. 536–532 Founding of the tragic competition.

525/24? Birth of Aeschylus.

510 Democracy established in Athens (by Cleisthenes).

496 Birth of Sophocles.

490 Persian invasion under Darius; Greek victory at Marathon, which Pheidippides runs the twenty plus miles to Athens to announce.

486 Comedy admitted to the official programme of the Great Dionysia.

c. 480 Birth of Euripides.

480 Persian invasion of Athens by Xerxes, who even briefly captures the Acropolis. But later that year the Greeks enjoy a tremendous naval victory at Salamis.

456 Death of Aeschylus.

c. 448–445 Birth of Aristophanes.

445 Birth of the famous comic playwright Eupolis.

442–438 Building of the Parthenon, with frieze completed in 438.

431–404 Outbreak of Peloponnesian War between Athens and Sparta and their various allies.

430 Great plague in Athens.

429 Death of Pericles, greatest leader of Athens.

427 Aristophanes' *Banqueters*

426 Aristophanes' *Babylonians* (first prize), alas no longer extant.

425 Aristophanes' *Acharnians* (first prize).

424 Aristophanes' *Knights* (first prize).

423 Aristophanes' *Clouds*, his greatest failure.

422 Aristophanes' *Wasps* (second prize).

421 Aristophanes' *Peace* (second prize).

414 Aristophanes' *Amphiaraus*; *Birds* (second prize).

413 Athenians' naval expedition to Sicily ends in total disaster.

412 Euripides' *Helen, Iphigenia Among the Taurians* and a much-disputed third play.

411 Aristophanes' *Lysistrata*; *Thesmophoriazusae*. Death of Eupolis.

406 Death of Sophocles and Euripides.

408 Aristophanes' first *Wealth*.

405 Aristophanes' *Frogs*.

405–404 Blockade of Athens resulting in its surrender.

404 Athens defeated by Sparta.

399 Socrates is forced to commit suicide.

392 Aristophanes' *Ecclesiazusae*.

388 Aristophanes' second *Wealth*; destined to be his most popular play for centuries.

c. 386–380 Death of Aristophanes.

c. 342 Birth of Menander.

336 Philip of Macedon begins his attempt to conquer the world. It is rudely interrupted by his assassination. He is succeeded by his son Alexander who has similar global ambitions.

331 City of Alexandria founded in Egypt, named after the Emperor.

328 Alexander's eastward campaign. He gets beyond Persepolis where he founds yet another magnificent city in his own honour (often referred to as Alexandria-on-the-Tigris). One cannot help but think of the magnificent bombast of Marlowe's Tamburlaine, who aims to 'ride in triumph through Persepolis'. He subdues the many splendid cities that lay before him and makes his way to the banks of the Indus. Ultimately he claims divine status, regarding himself not only the ruler of the world, but divinely related to Heracles – and Zeus. His behaviour inspired tyrants of many subsequent ages. Even Napoleon claimed to be emulating his example.

326–323 Alexander the Great overthrows the Persian Empire, extending Greek control as far as Russia, Afghanistan, the

Punjab and Egypt. Death of Alexander marks the beginning of the Hellenistic age.

323 New Comedy begins.

321? Menander's first play, *Anger*, which has not survived.

316 Menander's *The Bad-Tempered Man* (first prize).

315? Menander's *The Girl From Samos*.

c. **292** Death of Menander.

Roman Republic (BC)

509 Fall of Tarquinius and the Monarchy. Establishment of two new magistrates – consuls to be elected every year. Dedication of the Capitoline temple. Treaty between Rome and Carthage which was then a major financial and military power.

508 War with Porsenna (who conquers Rome?).

501 First dictator appointed.

451–450 Decemvirates – usually composed of ex-consuls. Publication of the Twelve Tables acceding to popular pressure, ten men who compiled ten tables – listing basic principles of Roman law (two more were added later). This legislation marks a significant step towards wresting some of the monopoly of the legal power from the priests and the aristocracy.

357 Roman tax on manumission of slaves.

304 Repeal of reforms of Appius Claudius which accorded some legal powers to lower classes.

280–275 Third Macedonian War, against Pyrrhus who had come over from Greece in a mighty force. It was a long and hard slog. At its conclusion Rome's territory and power was increased by the acquisition of several states.

278 Rome's treaty with Carthage (itself a kind of joke).

272 Tarentum falls to Romans. Livius Andronicus, a captured slave, presents a tragic adaptation of a Greek play for next year's Roman Games.

271 Buoyed by his success, Livius introduces a comedy *and* a tragedy for the following year's Games. This begins a tidal wave of enthusiasm for the theatre and our first playwrights date from this time. All these plays except those of Plautus survive as fragments – they are mere scraps quoted by later scholars for academic purposes. The actors wore the *pallium* – Greek dress. Hence the term for the *fabula palliata* was used to designate these loose translations, some very loose, from the Greek which, despite their name, are known as Roman comedies. Volcatius Sedegitus, a critic of the early third century BC, has left us the closest estimations we have of the comic poets of the previous age. Curiously, in his list of ten he ranked Plautus as second only to Caecilius Statius, Terence as sixth best. And he only believed Ennius was worthy of mention by placing him tenth, 'for old time's sake' (*causa antiquitatis*).

264–241 First Punic War – Rome battling Carthage for the mastery of the Mediterranean world.

264 First Roman gladiatorial show.

c. 254 Birth of Titus Maccius Plautus, the first playwright to leave us anything substantial (see Gratwick, Further Reading). His twenty and a half surviving comedies – all ostensibly rendered from the Greek – represent the oldest extant literature of ancient Rome. The quality of his work has long been a matter of debate – until the late twentieth century, at which point Plautus dethroned Terence and became king of the stage once more. Audiences learnt once more that the object of all comedy is to make people laugh.

241 Roman naval victory against Carthage gives them not only Sardinia and Corsica, but a foothold in Sicily as well.

236 First play of Naevius produced.

227 Romans make Sicily and Sardinia provinces.

221 Hannibal, only twenty-five years old, given command of the Carthaginian forces in Spain.

219 Hannibal lays siege to Saguntum which he sacks brutally.

218 Hannibal crosses the Alps with a large army and – elephants. All but one of the beasts died during the winter.

218–201 Second Punic War.

213 Roman siege of Syracuse which falls, extending the Roman conquest.

211 Hannibal marches on Rome but the Romans succeed in recapturing Tarentum.

204 Plautus presents *The Braggart Soldier*, the first of many hits.

203 Hannibal is recalled to Carthage.

201 Peace with Carthage which becomes a client state; the aristocratic senator Terentius Lucanus brings Terence – a captured slave – home for his circle of upper-class friends, to be their intellectual plaything. Because of his talent – and good looks – he is freed and thereafter produces five comedies – and a theatrical revolution.

200 Plautus, *Stichus*. Aristophanes of Byzantium becomes the head of the Library in Alexandria.

191 Plautus' *Pseudolus*.

190 Plautus' *The Rope*.

188/7 Plautus' *Poenulus*.

c. **186** Birth of Terence (Publius Terentius Afer) at Carthage.

184 Death of Plautus.

166–159 Production of Terence's comedies.

166 *Andria*.

165 *The Mother-in-Law* (first failure).

163 *The Self-Tormentor*.

161 *The Eunuch* and *Phormio*.

160 *The Mother-in-Law* (second failure followed later by a third and final successful production).

159 Terence dies in a shipwreck en route towards Rome with many new plays.

55 Pompey the Great builds first stone theatre.

Introduction

The progression from Old to New Comedy and then on to Roman is actually the story of the long development of a single genre – modern comedy as we know it.

Extravagant Aristophanes made the theatre of Athens rock with his wild fantasies and complex melodies. The only writer of the New was Menander, though long regarded a mere anaemic echo of Aristophanes, he was later a model for the more muscular Roman Comedy. Plautus has bequeathed to us more than twenty comedies. Though based on Menander's plots and Aristophanes' exuberance, he did not really copy either of his predecessors. It was in its way a melding of the two Greek authors in this volume. Terence was another story altogether. His boisterous and rowdy Eunuch was a change of pace for the normally mild-mannered intellectuals who were his usual audience (and patrons). He cared only about pleasing the upper classes. It is curious that we have only one playwright from each of the significant different phases of Ancient Comedy.

While *The Birds* is the most hilarious and daring example of Old Comedy, Menander's *The Girl From Samos* appears to have been more typical of its author's usual dramaturgy. *The Brothers Menaechmus* is the only comedy of errors that has survived from the Greek and Roman treasure chest. We know Menander wrote at least four mistaken identity plays. And finally Terence, unfarcical as he may have been, is the father of comedy as we know it today. And that is quite an achievement.

ARISTOPHANES

I: The Birth of Laughter

In the beginning was the pun.

And in spite of snobbish denigration by some literati, this rhetorical device has been a favourite of man since time immemorial: we find it in various forms throughout the Old Testament as well as other ancient Semitic literatures like the Akkadian epic *Gilgamesh*. Even at the earliest moments of Genesis punning appears, where the author (or authoress) describes the fatal results of the serpent's persuasion of Eve, and then Adam, to eat the fruit of the Tree of Knowledge, the snake is described as *arom*, the most 'cunning' of animals (Genesis 3:1),[1] and after their sin both Adam and Eve have their eyes suddenly opened and both realize that they are 'naked', Hebrew *arommim* (same word, in the plural), and this pun signals a very grave crisis. The New Testament is similarly sprinkled with wordplay, for example the pun in the Aramaic edition of Matthew (23:25) where we find *qalmâ*, 'gnat', and *galmâ*, 'camel'. Placing themselves in the great literary tradition, the Romans eagerly adopted this practice, referring to it as *nomen omen*, 'The name's the game'. Thus the pun is ever present and plays an important role in all literature. And it does not lose its staying power through the ages.

Comedy evolved, says Aristotle, 'from the leaders of the phallic procession'.[2] Remnants of these pre-dramatic fertility rites celebrating the potency of the male member persisted and were still visible in the outsize comic replicas which dangled from the costumes of the 'Old Comedy' characters (from earliest times, the plays of Aristophanes and his contemporaries were known as Old Comedy). The Mega member plays an important role in the rejuvenation of the senescent chorus and an antique hero. Although we have no solid evidence other than vase paintings, it is still clear that in a very real sense Old Comedy was a celebration of the male member.

The first comedy on record is merely a single fragment from

the sixth century BC. It involves a certain Susarion of Megara
as both author and actor. He is somewhat hyperbolically
regarded as the 'inventor of comedy'. Here then is the complete
text of his epoch-making joke:

> O fellow citizens, O fellow citizens,
> A woman is the bane of life, your peace she wrecks,
> But face it guys, we just can't make a family without
>   their sex.[3]

Though brief, this mini-speech contains one fundamental
element of comedy: antagonism between men and women.
Susarion was clearly a modest beginner. The Golden Age of the
Old Comedy, the mini-genre defined by later critics, took place
in the latter half of the fifth century BC at Athens. Indeed, nearly
all the famous names I will cite lived in the same city at roughly
the same time, and no doubt lifted a cup together and ex-
changed jokes. Their *éminence grise* was undoubtedly Cratinus,
one of the three authors that the punctilious Roman poet and
critic Horace (65–8 BC) chose to laud by name in his discussion
of the ancient Greek theatre's special licence to satirize anti-
social elements in Athens. He gives us a useful description of
the genre in its heyday:

> Whenever Eupolis or Cratinus or even Aristophanes
> – real talents – not to mention the other authors of Old
> Comedy would come across someone who deserved satirizing
> as a villain, a no-good crook or a pervert or something else
> notorious, they would lambaste him with complete impunity.[4]

He is describing the fabled privilege enjoyed by these Athenian
comic poets of invoking the so-called *ius nocendi*, the special
holiday licence from censorship and censureship. Nevertheless,
there appear to have been some sort of legal limits which, if
overstepped, were punished at worst by a rap on the knuckles.
The demagogue Cleon tried to get young Aristophanes severely
punished for his sharp-tongued attack in his early *Babylonians*
(now lost). The reprimand must have been relatively innocuous

since the target, Cleon, could not succeed in keeping *Baby-lonians* from winning first prize.

Besides, the Old Comic attacks on notorious contemporaries had little effect beyond the festival stage. In the very same year that Aristophanes was prosecuted for satirizing Cleon, this rogue politician was elected one of the ten Athenian *strategoi* (generals). What use was Aristophanes' 'freedom of speech' if he could not keep a rogue from office or in 399 BC save a truly noble man from death. Socrates' fate was more worthy of tragedy than comedy. So much for the extra-dramatic political influence of Old Comedy.

Following Susarion's initial joke, we must hold our laughter until the mid fifth century, the heyday of these Old Comedy playwrights. It is interesting to note that the genre had only a brief flowering, and for reasons both dramatic as well as politi-cal was exhausted in less than half a century. It must be conceded that our judgement is inevitably skewed since only shards of Aristophanes' contemporaries' works remain – mostly those used by later scholars to illustrate grammatical anomalies. Though none of his colleagues has left a complete play, we can nevertheless distinguish themes common to all these other play-wrights, most of which are similar to those used by Aristophanes.

One example is the antagonism between man and wife (Susarion lives on!), used by Plato Comicus, an early playwright (427/4 BC–after AD 3), the similarity of whose name to that of the great philosopher has denied him some of the renown he deserves. But he was a major figure, and one of his female characters presents a familiar quip in his play *The Ants*: ''Tis right that we are pummelled now and then, especially when caught with other men.'[5] Plato uses the joke that it is necessary for a husband to beat his wife to keep her in line:

> Do beat your wife
> Throughout her life –
> She'll take a lot of beating,
> But let her loose and she'll vamoose
> And seek a secret meeting.[6]

Relatively speaking, we have more substantial fragments from
Eupolis. He has a high-ranking officer Alcibiades, more oppor-
tunist than patriot, quoted as threatening a man on stage: 'You
go home and bed your wife – or else I'll do it for you.'[7]

We also find the debut of our oldest and richest comic character, the boastful quack doctor. We can tell that this is a fantasy
because it shows a mock trial in which the doctor is being
indicted for overcharging. But the physician is not perturbed
by these accusations:

QUACK
  I don't care what happens after I get paid my fee.
PLAINTIFF
  Good Lord, Asclepius himself
  Would never charge as much
  For treating galumping diabetes or systolic emphysema –
  Not to mention psychopathic appendectomy!
JUDGE
  I say to you in closing, that you're guilty guilty guilty!
QUACK (disdainfully):
  I don't deny I've charged my patients through the nose.
  But then they're dead – and death's
  The most expensive malady of all.[8]

The reader might also find it interesting to learn that Aristophanes, a playwright who is commonly associated with naughty
language, was regarded in classical times as less foul-mouthed
than his colleagues. Eupolis and Cratinus were singled out for
being racy and taxed for their spicy wit and downright obscen-
ity. Cratinus is credited by some ancient scholars as an inno-
vator since he increased the number of speaking parts from two
to three. Although he is praised by later commentators for the
tightening of the plays' general looseness of structure, his own
works left much to be desired in that department. A great
many of the targets for the comic attack found throughout Old
Comedy involve the authors themselves. Aristophanes jokes
about his own baldness. Cratinus, who had retired from writing
to become a full-time boozer, suddenly revived from his stupor

in his ninety-eighth year for a last hurrah with what is clearly
an autobiographical comedy, *The Bottle*: the protagonist leaves
his wife Comedy to cavort with the lively Ms Drunkenness,
until sobriety returns and the hero goes back to his wife. To
the dismay of Aristophanes (who was then the hot new property), the old man won first prize.

These contemporaneous playwrights demonstrate all the
elements that were to become fixtures in ancient comedy. We
have already seen how even the mere three lines of the minuscule
legacy of Susarion contain elements that remain a part of comedy. Old Comedy's themes are in one way or another connected
with current problems. For example, several playwrights
brought Socrates on stage – as Aristophanes did in the *Clouds*.
This play was not a personal satire; it uses Socrates to epitomize
the eccentric philosopher – a new face on the Athenian intellectual scene.

The fragments we have of Aristophanic comedy are almost indis-
tinguishable from those of his fellow authors. Ancient critics
have noted that the only significant difference between his work
and that of his contemporaries is that the others seemed to be
'spicier'. It is amusing to imagine Aristophanes being outdone in
ribaldry. For example Pherecrates wrote some kind of Oedipus
tale in which Jocasta laments, 'I'm so confused I don't know what
to do / I've just found out I'm wife and mother too.'[9] On other
occasions Pherecrates can be downright lyrical; this is not an
ancient Greek version of 'Lucy in the Sky with Diamonds':

> Sweet mallow belching and hyacinth breathing
> Green clover wordlets and rose-smiles divine
> Peppermint kisses and celery thrusting
> Wild olive laughter and lovely blue lusting
> Whip out your pitcher, sing paeans for more wine![10]

It should not be surprising to learn that these theatrical comedies frequently use the same jokes, and often more than once.
Cratinus anticipates (or copies) Aristophanes' joke about old
men being in their second childhood.

Perhaps the most important feature of Old Comedy was that it *did not have a plot* – at least in the modern understanding of the term. Rather, it consisted of heterogeneous episodes, interspersed with choral songs. The material in Aristophanic comedy could best be described as the development of a 'Happy Idea'. The full evolution of a real story in the modern sense would have to wait for Menander and his New Comedy contemporaries. The one common feature was that they virtually all concluded with a revel (*komos* – the origin of the word 'comedy'). The partying at the finale traditionally includes a wedding (*gamos*) – or at least a coupling – of the rejuvenated hero and a young and sexy wife. An example is the facsimile wedding at the conclusion of Aristophanes' *Peace*.

It is also evident that Old Comedy is something midway between ritual and drama. There are many elements in its structure which are completely alien to modern expectations. For example, the *agon* (struggle), in which embodiments of the two conflicting thematic forces, such as War and Peace, Wealth and Poverty, engage in formal debate. This is perhaps why the comic chorus has twenty-four members – twice as many as a tragedy. This was convenient for dividing them into two teams of twelve, each to espouse opposing views. Another unique aspect of Old Comedy was the *parabasis* (literally, 'coming forward'). The chorus steps out of character and speaks directly to the audience, delivering what we would call today 'a message from our sponsor'. This was very often the author's view of the news of the day, castigation of the fools and follies of Athenian society, and there was almost always a plea for peace on earth. Furthermore, the actors and chorus were garbed in a manner quite alien to modern theatregoers' expectations. Like their tragic counterparts they wore masks. But instead of the high buskins of 'serious' drama actors, the comic actors wore the *soccus*, something akin to a ballet shoe, creating a graphic distinction between the comic and the heroic; in Aristophanes' *Lysistrata*, the naked women were played by padded men in female masks with exaggerated breasts and genitalia.

II: Strictly for Laughs

What we have extant from the plays of Aristophanes does not give an accurate picture of the evolution (and disintegration) of Old Comedy. Eight of his eleven surviving plays are from a thirteen-year period (425–411 BC). But in 405 he produced his masterpiece, the *Frogs*, which may very well be the last Old Comedy ever written. At this time Athens was in ruins after nearly a century of unending, exhausting warfare. Aristophanes' last two plays, *Wealth* (*Plutus*, 388) – and his now-lost *Cocalus*, represent a radical change in Greek theatre taste and the poet changed his style accordingly. His final plays demonstrated that even in his twilight years, Aristophanes was not too old to keep up with the times.

Aristophanes began his career at a precociously young age. So young in fact, that he did not dare put his real name on his first two offerings, the *Banqueters* (427) and the *Babylonians*, which actually won first prize at the Great Dionysia of 426. The poet continued his already glowing career with the first play he produced under his own name. In 425 his *Acharnians* won first prize. It also included a brief appearance of a character who would be one of Aristophanes' favourites – Euripides. For the hero, Dicaeopolis, turns to the comic portrayal of the tragic playwright for assistance, begging for the costume of one of his most notorious characters, the overdone 'hero in rags'. At one time or another, many of the playwrights make fun of avant-garde dramaturgic practice. As proof of the symbiosis of tragedy and comedy, critics are fond of quoting Cratinus' amusing verbal coinage (also an astute literary criticism), referring to a colleague as an 'Euripidaristophanizer'.[11]

The *Acharnians* presents the overriding theme of all the contemporary comic playwrights, the pain of the Athenians having to live in a constant state of war. Aristophanes' hero – like so many in the early plays – is an old man deracinated from his native village and forced into the crowded city. He longs for peace and exclaims in his opening speech, 'I loathe the town.' He dreams of his own country district which had some residual similarity to the Golden Age – no merchants selling coal or oil. Indeed, he says, 'I didn't even know the word "buy".'[12]

In short, he is so desperate to end the war that he undertakes a trip to Sparta as an ambassador for himself. Since Old Comedy is the most far-fetched fantasy, he actually succeeds in this quixotic quest and does in fact return with a private and entirely personal thirty-year truce in the form of a skin of wine. We should note here that another characteristic of the Aristophanic hero is his unabashed selfishness. The conclusion finds the hero a successful merchant with a joyous finale in the offing. As Dicaeopolis exits to roister, the General Lamachos goes off to do battle. The play ends with a duet that says it all, a debate between the injured General and the sozzled hero. At the conclusion we also find another familiar comic element: Dicaeopolis becomes a 'bridegroom', with two juicy young 'brides'. With typical comic amnesia he somehow 'forgets' that he already has a wife. Or perhaps the dalliance with these dancing girls does not constitute any breach of the marriage vows?

Aristophanes' subsequent plays are idealistic and lunatic in equal measure. At the conclusion of the *Knights*, the hero, elderly Demos – 'the people' – is boiled and rejuvenated, expelling the bellicose Cleon. The lovely maiden Peace is rescued (Cleon had been keeping her hidden all this time) and 'gets together' with the newly reinvigorated Demos. Peace on Earth – and in bed. Demos and his partner go off to celebrate, and the ending could not be happier.

Unhappily in 423 it all went wrong. Aristophanes produced the *Clouds*, which he believed was his masterpiece. But the judges and audience thought it was a disaster, an outrage, or perhaps both. His embarrassing last place in the competition absolutely broke his heart and he spent the rest of his career trying to get his revised version presented. Yet even with his 'improvements', it was never performed again. The play that has come down to us contains some elements of the second draft: specifically the *parabasis*, which vented the poet's anger at having been unfairly judged the previous year. Later critics

tell us that at least the *agon* and the angry conclusion of the
hero burning down Socrates' so-called Thinkatorium were later
additions. Uncharacteristically – and more to the point, un-
comically – the play ends on a note of anger. As Socrates'
students scatter, the hero Strepsiades urges the chorus to beat
them up: 'Chase them, hit them, pelt them – for a hundred
causes – but most of all remembering how they wronged the
gods!'[13] Yet in theory, *Clouds* had a lot going for it: the conflict
of generations, the antagonism between country and city, mari-
tal discord (the hero is a rustic who married a posh lady and
lived to regret it). Then there is the unforgettable character of
eccentric philosopher Socrates, whose ideas and pedagogy were
mercilessly mocked.

It is a battle of the generations. The old man enrols himself
in the Thinkatorium and has a very amusing private tutorial-
cum-psychiatric session with the great teacher. But alas the old
man has an old brain which cannot fathom the subtleties of
Socratic thinking, so inevitably the principal has to expel him.
Socrates suggests that if the old man has a young son, he should
send him along as he would do rather better at mastering the
subtleties of Socratic dialectic. The young man does too well.
In fact, when he finishes his course he is able not only to
rationalize the aggressing of their debtors, but also the beating
up of his own father and mother. This is too much for the
country bumpkin. Strepsiades, in a rage, rushes to burn down
Socrates' Thinkatorium. The unhappy ending was quite unlike
the sort of thing the Athenian public had come to expect. No
doubt the audience agreed wholeheartedly with the judges'
decision to rank the play third and last.

But this fiasco at least opened Aristophanes' eyes to recognize
the kind of crowd he was dealing with. He changed his tune
and took first place again the following year with the *Wasps*,
which in many ways bore great similarity to the *Clouds*, but
with the significant omission of the anger and pyromania in the
finale. Instead, the protagonist attends a party and returns with
the best-looking girl (nude), and despite the strictures of son to
father to behave himself, again a comic reversal of roles. The
son attempts to teach the father how to behave, but Philocleon

will have none of it and moments later the slave Xanthias frantically reports his elder master's gross behaviour. The old man struts home with his exquisite prize, venting his renewed youthful energy by punching spectators en route and promising the pretty lady that as soon as *his* son dies he will inherit enough money to make an honest woman of her. 'I'm not yet in charge of my own affairs – because I'm too young.'[14] *That* was more like it – typical Aristophanic topsy-turvydom.

Athens was at war for most of the fifth century BC, first with Persia then with their one-time ally Sparta. The strife seemed endless. Is it any wonder that Old Comedy hungered for happy endings? To some comic dramatists this could only have been accomplished if the great leaders of the past were still alive. The comic dream of restoring the good old days was not new. Aristophanes exploited this theme in his *Frogs* (405). Dionysus, the Theatre God, makes a 'heroic' journey to the Underworld to bring back Euripides, the audience's favourite playwright. But he is soon convinced that the man Athens really needs is Aeschylus. By choosing the older playwright, Dionysus ignores the vociferous objection of the younger dramatist, whom he had promised to bring back to Athens. Aristophanes shows his true conservative colours by choosing to revive the older man, for Aeschylus represented a golden age when all was right with Athens. And then of course there is the ultimate wish fulfilment: bringing back the heroes of Athens past in order to solve the crisis of Athens present. Indeed, variations of the theme of resurrecting some of the noblest heroes of the past – Pericles et al. – grew more intense as the situation in Athens worsened. In reviving Aeschylus, a classic as opposed to his avant-garde rival, he symbolized the good grand old style of tragedy as opposed to all the trendy innovations of Euripides. In any case the *Frogs* was such an overwhelming success that it became the only Greek comedy on record to be given an immediate second performance.[15]

And yet the invocation of past heroes is not unique to our playwright. At about the same time as the *Frogs*, Eupolis produced the *Demes*, a comedy on a similar theme. This dramatist brings to life a quartet of dead worthies from the glorious

Athenian past, the only ones that can save the city: Pericles, Miltiades, Solon and Aristides. An early imperial critic remarked, 'even as a dead man, Pericles triumphed over his enemies.'[16] Whether it be one resurrected hero or four, the fact remains that the fantastic plots of the Old Comedy playwrights reflected the woes of the city. But there is a significant difference between a theme of rejuvenation, which we have found often in early Aristophanes, and his later theme of resurrection. The latter is a somewhat grimmer phenomenon, with no happy ending possible.

Aristophanes' *Lysistrata* was a landmark play in ancient Greek theatre. For many critics believe that it was the first comedy to have a female protagonist. Until *Lysistrata*, heroines were almost unknown in Greek comedy, although they were disproportionately prominent in Greek tragedy: Medea, Antigone, Clytemnestra, Cassandra, Electra, to name but a few. Just as her male comic counterparts, the heroine is temporarily freed from logic. Indeed, how did women from all over Greece in wartime get to the meeting called by Lysistrata with which the play begins? Lysistrata's plan to have all the women in Greece rise as one and deny their military husbands sex until they came to their senses and made peace had a flaw to it: the husbands were all away at war.

But comedy ignores such minor matters. In any case her plan succeeds and very soon all of Greece, as exemplified by the two half-choruses, one Athenian the other Spartan, is 'aroused' against her conspiracy. But she holds firm and fiction triumphs, at least on the comic stage.

The play has touching moments. For example, when the mothers bemoan giving birth to sons, whom they must sacrifice to the god of War. Whereas the soldiers, however old they may be, come home from the fighting and quickly find a girl to wed: 'But a woman's flowering is brief, if she lets it pass her by, no one will want to marry her, and she will sit alone, waiting in vain. Her future will be bleak and lonely.'[17] The audience would no doubt be surprised to hear Lysistrata argue that there are more important things for a woman than caring for her husband and children. In those days such attitudes bordered on heresy.

Further indication of how much Old Comedy had begun to undergo a metamorphosis can be seen in Aristophanes' *Ecclesiazusae* (*c.* 392), a comedy both similar to *Lysistrata* and yet radically different. A glance at the differences displays the changes in theatrical style. It was played before an audience with vastly diverse expectations. The chorus is all but silent and there are some new elements that distinguish it from the Old Comedy tradition. To begin with, anticipating the New Comedy conventions, the setting is a city street. There seem to have been few (if any) choral interludes apart from the entrance and exit of the chorus.

Ecclesiazusae presents the revolt of the Athenian women who this time steal and dress up in their husbands' clothes in order to masculinize themselves further as they occupy the Acropolis. The play once again concludes with women 'still on top'. But this is where the similarity with *Lysistrata* ends. Most of the *Ecclesiazusae* is curiously unsatisfying. Part of the reason may be because of the unappealing sub-plot, which follows the fortunes of Blepyrus, an old codger who is desperate to find a place to relieve himself, and ultimately decides to do it right on stage. The plot is to say the least disgusting and distasteful. Still, more curiously, he continues his dialogue with his neighbour while he is 'doing his business'. The scene is anything but refreshing. Most important of all, the play, unlike *Lysistrata*, does not end with the women returning to their homes. It leaves society unsettled and uncomfortable. And even though *Ecclesiazusae* does end with a sort of *gamos* it is hardly a joyous one. New legislation has declared that sexual priority must go to the older, uglier women in the city. We are very far from the kind of happy endings we found in early Aristophanic comedies, like the *Acharnians*, *Birds* and *Frogs*.

The transitional period between 'Old' and 'New' is now referred to as 'Middle Comedy', a designation invented by the third/second-century BC polymath, Aristophanes of Byzantium. The genre is very domestic and we recall Gilbert Murray's observation that New Comedy dealt with 'private people living in town'.[18] This is already evident in *Wealth*, Aristophanes of Athens' last extant play. This common theme – with endless variations – enabled comedy to stretch beyond the walls of Athens to the whole Greek-speaking world. Terracotta statuettes of their characters have been found in places as distant as modern Barcelona and southern Russia. This encouraged an enormous production of these bourgeois plays. Unlike Old Comedy they had no *ad hominem* attacks. But the plays had a recognizable philosophical background. We have some glimpse of this in an extraordinary work by Athenaeus (third century AD) entitled *The Dinner of Intellectuals*, a lengthy description of a party among professionals of philosophy, literature, law and medicine, from which we owe some of our extant scraps of lost third-century BC Greek authors.

In the plays themselves we find a character quite close to the cheeky slave who would become so prominent in the next phase of comic development. The slender plot involves relatively mundane problems like abandoned babies discovered, intoxicated man raping girl at nocturnal festival, etc. Afterwards by chance, she becomes engaged to the very man who raped her. On the wedding night he discovers she is pregnant and rejects her. Yet the lad discovers that he himself is the guilty rapist and the forthcoming child is his own. He makes amends by welcoming his new wife and child into the family. All's well that ends well. This happy ending is stage-managed by the goddess of Chance, who is also operating in *Wealth*. This is as different from Old Comedy as can be. There are no fantastic ascents to heaven or descents to hell.

Instead, Aristophanes' last extant play follows the fortunes of a bourgeois Athenian family struggling in their own bourgeois way to cope with the contemporary economic crisis. It all takes place in a city square where, in the first scene, the protagonist Chremylus enters, intent on following a ragged beggar and he in turn is followed by his own saucy slave. We soon discover that the grungy old man is – or at least claims to be – the blind god of Wealth. Chremylus undertakes to cure him. He is a generous community man, not a typically selfish Aristophanic hero who cares only for himself. His plan is to take this stranger to spend the night in the Temple of Asclepius, the god of Healing. Their strategy is interrupted by the appearance of Poverty, another abstract character. In a debate, the hero counters her claims that the world *needs* poverty. He literally intends to share the wealth. Poverty's argument makes some good points. Chremylus argues that when Plutus can again see the gods, he will reward only good people. Poverty replies that if all the good is rewarded with money there will be no slaves. So she is chased away.

The next morning they wake to find the blind god of wealth has been cured. He suddenly sees who the honest people in Athens are. This is good for the good and bad for the bad. The naughty language is practically absent from the play, an exception being the duets between the naughty slave, whose topic is 'shitcakes', and the chorus. In any case *Wealth* introduces an element that we had not seen before on the Athenian stage: Money, Cash. While earlier plays had depicted lowly people gaining triumphant heights, there were never any bankers involved. But Aristophanes had astutely sensed the direction in which the comic muse was heading and tried to keep pace. We also cannot fail to notice that the characters are all 'civilians' in the true etymological sense of the word – city folk.

This is, in short, an *hors d'oeuvre* of the feast that is Aristophanes' legacy to modern conventional comedy. First-time readers may find the plays to be somewhat strange, but they should simply sit back and enjoy them – which is what Aristophanes intended in the first place.

MENANDER

Polite Comedy

The road from Aristophanes to Menander was long and winding, the seventy or so years between *Wealth* and *Old Cantankerous* (*Dyskolos*) was not a single arid stretch. The most successful of these writers of Middle Comedy was Antiphanes,[19] who began in the 380s within a year or so of Aristophanes' death and was active until a decade before Menander's dramatic debut in 321 BC. We know 134 titles by this author, but more than 300 fragments of his comedies suggest an even larger output. According to an ancient biographer, the number of his plays is closer to 260. He seemed to have had an affinity for satirizing myth, one of the few distinguishing characteristics of Middle Comedy in general.

A fragment from one of his comedies shows traces of the romantic atmosphere that would typify so much of Menander. Antiphanes' character in *Poetry* describes his friend's first encounter with the heroine: it turned out that she was living right next door to him (of course), and it was love at first sight (of course). At first she is thought to be a slave but later she was discovered to be freeborn, and therefore eligible to marry an Athenian. At the outset there seemed to be no one to save her from a life of shame, but she was a good girl and not a concubine and therefore the outcome of the play is predictable. It was, after all, only following tradition.

But Antiphanes is perhaps best remembered for his oft-quoted argument that, compared to the authors of comedy, the tragedians had it easy. They dealt with the same few plots again and again. They did not have to invent anything. In fact, after the first words of the prologue, the audience would be completely clued in.[20] By contrast, everything in comedy has to be freshly baked. The jokes could be old but the circumstances had to be new. To the Middle Comedy playwright, structure was everything, they took extreme care with their plots. At first glance, the plays do not seem overtly sexual. But the reader should not be misled. Sex was always there percolating beneath the neat folds of the hero's tunic.

One of most conspicuous differences between Aristophanes' early plays and his later ones was the further diminution of the role of the chorus. The *parabasis* totally disappeared and the formal *agon* is half of what it was in the full flower of Old Comedy. In fact, few manuscripts had original lyrics to the choral songs, and on the rare occasions when present, they were mostly unrelated to the play itself. The diminishing of lyrical elements must to some extent account for the flatness of dialogue found in the fourth-century fragments. An ancient

critic even discerned a pattern which characterized very late
Aristophanes. The comedies included 'rape and recognition and
all the other things Euripides loved'.[21] This important remark
acknowledges the playwright's debt to both Comedy and
Euripides.

Furthermore, Aristotle and other ancient critics noted the
drastic diminution of political and personal satire. But in the
finality of this development, the Greeks unwittingly handed
the baton to the Romans, those upstart, unsophisticated people
now occupying a good portion of mainland Italy, and the picture changed drastically in the third century BC when the
conquering of Italy and the end of the First Punic War brought
the Romans into contact with real Greek culture, and with their
ethos of 'conquer something and then make it your own', the
Romans embraced the theatre. As the poet Horace would later
put it so neatly, 'Captured Greece took captive her captors and
brought Greek arts to rustic Italy.'[22]

The plays of Menander played an important part in this
cultural transfer. Paradoxically, the celebrated virtuoso of New
Comedy was only a success after his death. Notwithstanding
that, the test of time proved that he had been the best and most
enduring New Comedy playwright. The sad part was that he
himself always knew it. There is an anecdote of his meeting
Philemon, a far more successful contemporary whom he chided:
'Don't you feel ashamed when the judges choose your plays
over mine?'[23] But when Menander finally came into vogue he
did so with a vengeance. Hellenistic critics were so infatuated
with his dramaturgy that one of them, ranked the 'newly discovered' genius second only to Homer.[24] It is certainly un-
deniable that Menander played a crucial role in the evolution
of Comedy. What first strikes the modern reader is the proxi-
mity of New Comedy to Euripidean tragedy.

For the imperial Roman scholar Quintilian, for example,
Menander was perfection itself, in speech, in character analysis
and in his portrait of life. Plutarch regards him as the only
reason for a civilized man to go to the theatre and enthusiasti-
cally lauds the playwright and his 'salt'.[25] Once again we notice
that Menander was the paragon. Quintilian in the first century

AD added to his eulogy a reverent praise of his remarkably subtle characterizations:

> The careful study of Menander alone would, in my opinion, be sufficient to develop all those qualities with the production of which my present work is concerned; so rich is his power of invention and his gift of style, so perfectly does he adapt himself to every kind of circumstance, character and emotion.[26]

I am sure that when Menander at last lay dead in the ground, his post-mortem success came as cold comfort. And yet Homer never went out of style, but Menander simply disappeared. Thus when Goethe and his eighteenth-century contemporaries praised the 'unattainable charm' of Menander's dramaturgy, it was literally unattainable. They could only judge from books of choice quotations. The plays were irretrievably lost – or so it seemed. But around the turn of the twentieth century, archaeologists unearthed ample selections from Menander.[27] The fragments were large enough to be read as dramatic works and not just eloquent sound bites. It was still a small percentage of the dramatist's total output, but there was now sufficient to fill one Loeb Library volume.

And then in the middle of the twentieth century came a landmark event, the appearance of an undreamed of treasure: an entire play by the master: *Dyskolos*, published in 1957 by Martin Bodmer. The papyrus also contained substantial portions of *The Shield* (*Aspis*) and almost all of *The Girl From Samos* (*Samia*). This proved to be a mixed blessing, for not every critic was able to discern the poet's 'unattainable charm'. To begin with, Menander's comedies were rigidly formulaic. Perhaps the primary quintessential characteristic of New Comedy was its sameness. One wonders how theatregoers could watch endless variations on the same bourgeois themes: kidnapped girls, lost parents found (mothers, fathers, or even both). Yet close analysis of Menander's plots reveals a complexity not immediately visible. There was a fixed cast of characters but in essence the family supplants the state as the focal point of the drama. It all takes place – the *Dyskolos* being a notable exception – on the same city street in Athens. The players are usually neighbours – two families, sometimes one family and a neighbouring pimp with his attractive . . . proté-gées, one of whom may turn out in the end to be the long-lost daughter of the family next door.

Mistaken identities are another familiar theme. Take as an extreme example, Menander's *Shield*. Here, the slave returns home with his master's armour, leaving no doubt that the young man is dead. This sets off a race for the hand of the dead soldier's fiancée. Smelling money, the miserly Uncle Smikrines avails himself of his legal priority to marry her first. Clearly they will not live happily ever after. She mourns the dead young hero as his greedy old uncle proceeds with preparations for the wedding. All ends well and the young man turns out to be very much alive after all. There was a mix-up of shields on the battlefield. Another soldier was wearing his armour and died in it. The 'delayed prologue', spoken by Tyche, the goddess Chance, who has been called the presiding deity of New Comedy plots, gives the advantage of keeping the audience in the dark like the players themselves.

There is one element for which Menander was most cele-brated. As Ovid remarked in the early years of the Roman Empire: 'Never did charming Menander write a play without love in it.'[28] This practice in New Comedy often involved lost people wandering in error, all of whose problems are solved by recognition that one or both of them is a relative.

At first glance, these civilized bourgeois seem more sedate than their predecessors. Certainly their costumes have become more 'respectable'. Gone is the oversized phallus – it is discreetly back where it belongs. Yet this does not mean that sex itself has disappeared. It is merely presented in a more civilized form. Costumes may become more conservative, but youthful libido remains as frisky as ever underneath. In fact, it was also a commonplace for one of Menander's characters to come peril-ously close to incest.[29]

Greek tragedy very strictly adheres to a kind of 'privacy'. The actors live wholly in their own noble world, taking no notice of the audience, never addressing them directly. By contrast, comedy has an easy-going atmosphere where characters are forever breaking the theatrical illusion. One keeps the audience out, the other opens the gates of laughter so that everyone can enter. The age of political satire had been long over and contemporary political allusions were not encouraged. And so playwrights had to restrict their subjects to more pedestrian topics. Thus the plots revolved around the kind of domestic complications that still survive in modern sitcoms. Nonetheless, these domestic comedies do offer a window onto the political world of Menander's Athens, as Lape observes:

> [New] Comedy offers important evidence of the interconstitutive relationship between the public and private in democratic Athens, the role of gender and sexual ideology in sustaining the norms and ideology of democratic citizenship, and the immanent tensions and instabilities within the citizenship system.[30]

Menander may seem sedate, but his subtext is highly erotic and – for lack of a better word – titillating. We get some idea of the process of New Comedy if we examine two of Menander's plays which ostensibly deal with the same subject, premarital rape. Seven months before *The Arbitration* (*Epitrepontes*) begins, in the darkness of an evening festival, Charisios has raped Pamphile, a nice young girl who, it will turn out, is the next-door neighbour. Alas, she cannot see her assailant because of the lack of light. And subsequently she discovers she is pregnant as a result of this dastardly deed.

Meanwhile there has been a prior arrangement between the neighbouring fathers that their children should marry. But Charisios is blissfully unaware that his new bride was his old victim. On their wedding night, he is shocked to discover that his bride is damaged goods. He doesn't touch her and not long afterwards he leaves her. While he is out of town, the lass gives birth to a son. Ashamed, she asks her nurse to expose the child. The moment Charisios returns, he is upset to learn that his wife has given birth to a baby, which she has instructed her nurse to abandon. He is once again in a fury and leaves the house to begin a wild and conspicuous affair with Habrotonon, a harp girl, to whom he pays a lot of money each day. Meanwhile, the infant has been discovered by a shepherd, who in turn gives it to Mr and Mrs Charcoal-Burner who long for a child. Yet the fellow holds onto the infant's trinkets. Tempers flare as the two disputants fight over the jewellery.

The crisis is probably set forth in a delayed prologue – now lost – spoken by the goddess Misunderstanding. She no doubt reveals to the audience that Pamphile is the victim of Charisios' rape. In other words, the child is *his*! And now the audience can watch the other characters wander in error. The shepherd enters with a large bag of trinkets and the Charcoal-Burner comes in to demand his property. Since they cannot agree they seek an independent arbitrator to solve their quarrel. The arbitrator they choose is, of all people, Smikrines. The irony is heavy. The old man rules for Mr and Mrs Charcoal-Burner, unaware that he is signing away his own grandson. At that moment, young Charisios' slave notices his master's ring among the trinkets – the very one he lost when he had drunkenly misbehaved. Unaware of this high drama, Charisios leaves with his fancy lady to attend a friend's party.

Later, when the hero's chum Chairestratos' slave, Onesimos, discusses what he has discovered with Habrotonon, she urges him to tell his master. After all, the baby might be freeborn and therefore should not be raised by a slave. The truth is starting slowly to emerge. Habrotonon protests that 'If mother is free-born, why keep this all in secret?'[31] Charisios' good reputation has been just thrown away. Onesimos gives the infant to Smikrines, who discovers the ring to be his son's. But the problem remains – who is the baby's mother? Habrotonon is talking straight: 'Who is the father of the baby?' To their mutual astonishment, the husband and wife learn that they are *both* the child's parents. The rest of the play – at least the fragments we have of it – unites both families in typical Menandrian harmonious moods and the comedy concludes with a universal celebration which may even include a happy outcome for

Habrotonon, the noble demi-mondaine. Editor Stanley Ireland
has theorized that, in the now-lost Act V, Habrotonon is probably freed so she can marry Chairestratos.[32]

Menander may seem tame to the first-time reader, but he is
master of quiet outrage. Incest is omnipresent. Consider for
example the all-too-fragmentary *The Farmer* (*Georgos*). Here
the young lad named Moschion has compromised the girl-next-
door and, of course, made her pregnant. The young hero has
just returned from Corinth and bemoans the fact that in his
absence his father has decided he should marry his own half-
sister. This was not considered incest in Athens; at the time that
kind of union was legally permissible. Young Moschion is not
only upset about the proposed marriage but is more troubled
by the possible consequences for his neighbour Myrrhine's
daughter, the young girl he has wronged. He is especially upset
because the victim is living all alone with her poor widowed
mother and brother. She is outraged, but helpless. The extant
fragments begin with a lament of young Moschion expressing
shame for what he has done. For if he obeys his father,
Myrrhine's daughter will be left 'seduced and abandoned'. He
sneaks out of the house to avoid the wedding.[33]

Meanwhile, in a far-away field, Kleainetos, the farmer, by
whom her brother Gorgias is employed, has hurt himself. His
slaves take this opportunity to run away, leaving their master
to bleed to death. But Gorgias stays and nurses the farmer for
three days, saving his life. During this time the injured old farmer
has begun to chat amicably, questioning his young saviour
about his family. The young lad tells him about an outrage committed on his sister by Moschion, his next-door neighbour.
Whatever happens, the old and lonely man is so grateful to young
Gorgias that he promises to marry his dowry-less sister.

But now the original premise, the pseudo-incest of Moschion
and step-sister palls when it is at last discovered that Kleainetos
is the long-lost father of *both* Gorgias and his sister. And was
about to marry his own daughter! Such things could occur in
Greek mythology, but not in New Comedy. Menander saves
the day by having the affable and older Kleainetos, who it turns
out is father of the twins he had deserted so long ago, decide

instead to marry Myrrhine. This sudden stroke of romance leaves the way open for Moschion to marry his sweetheart. There is honour for all – and a baby for the young bride and groom, as families past, present and future are reunited at the play's end and another near-miss is narrowly avoided. These Menandrian comedies are a mere fraction of familiar and infinite New Comedy variations of man rapes girl, girl gives birth, big scandal till the truth emerges. There are no surprises. But of one thing the audience may be sure: if the girl was freeborn, in the end he will *always* make an honest woman of her. Characters of New Comedy all keep their feet firmly rooted on the ground. The names in Aristophanes and Menander may differ, but in the end, to quote Shakespeare's famous piece of doggerel: 'Jack shall have Jill, / Naught shall go ill.' This is certainly true of Menander.

PLAUTUS

The Laughing Writer

In his second-century AD study of the great Latin authors, the polymath Aulus Gellius compared the works of Roman playwrights and their Greek antecedents. At one of his literary soirées, he and his learned friends so much enjoyed the reading of Caecilius' Latin adaptation of Menander's *Necklace* (*Plokion*) that they decided to look at the Greek original. They were astonished: 'My God, what a difference!' the scholars exclaimed, almost in one voice. Suddenly, by comparison, Menander's flawless dialogue was in a class by itself. The Greek original had been 'Romanized', and not only did Caecilius omit some elegant lines, 'he threw in some cheap gags of his own'.[34]

Gellius reminded his guests of the golden age critic Horace's judgement of the verses of Plautus. The classical critic complained that the playwright is 'just anxious to put a penny in his pocket. After that, he doesn't give a damn whether the play stands up or falls on its face!'[35] To counter this rather snobbish judgement we could adduce Molière's famous judgement that the supreme achievement is to make the theatregoers happy (*le grand art est de plaire*); Plautus definitely was master in this domain.

Since all the dramatists who preceded Plautus – including Livius Andronicus, the so-called 'founding father' of Roman drama – come down to us only in fragments, Titus Maccius Plautus has the distinction of being the earliest extant Latin author. We still have twenty of his comedies more or less complete (he may have composed as many as 130 and 'doctored' others). Plautus made his debut at some unknown occasion after 215 BC.

In 254 BC, the generally accepted date for the master playwright's birth, Rome was becoming a significant nation. But she was in the midst of the first of her three wars with Carthage, the powerful Phoenician colony in North Africa. By the time Plautus was in his teens, the Romans had conquered most of modern Italy. Through the cities of Etruria and Magna Graecia, especially Tarentum, came an extra benefit: culture. From at least the sixth century BC, all the arts had flourished here, especially drama. And for the very first time, the Romans met theatre. It was love at first sight.

We know nothing about the details of Plautus' life but there are hints that when he was young he toured with one of the native improvisatory Atellan farces, named after the Campanian village where the genre was believed to have originated.

Certainly his name was a professional coinage, for what mother would name her own child Titus Maccius Plautus, in other words 'Dick O'Fool McSlapstick' or even 'Floppy Dick McFool'. That is a stage name if ever there was one. Plautus must go down in history as the most successful playwright of the ancient world. By the second century AD, George Duckworth reports, no fewer than 130 'Plautine' manuscripts were circulating among producers – at least *some* of which were genuine. Despite differences of opinion about the authenticity of the twenty (and a half) surviving plays, this is the canon we have today.

The First Punic War ended in 241 BC. The very next year, the first plays – a comedy and a tragedy – were produced in

Rome at the *ludi Romani* (Roman public games). They were Latin adaptations of a Greek tragedy and comedy, the work of a captured slave named Livius Andronicus. It became an instant tradition. Each year at this time the holidaying Romans would savour stage plays rendered into Latin from their originals. Not surprisingly, their Greek tragic models were based on Sophocles and Euripides. Their comedies were not inspired by the boisterous Old Comedies, perhaps unsurprisingly given that these stopped being performed in the early fourth century BC. They rather preferred the quiet domestic comedies of Menander and his colleagues.

Like their Hellenistic forebears, Roman comedies presented stock characters in stock situations. Their setting was the city, their people the bourgeoisie, their plots romantic and utterly predictable: boy meets/wants/has previously raped girl. Or else a girl is discovered to be freeborn and therefore respectable marriage material. The whole milieu was at once realistic, and yet is still removed from reality. Reading these plays, we have no notion that during the time of their composition the Hellenistic world was torn constantly by war and strife.

Plautus, like his contemporaries, may have based his plays on Athenian originals, yet they have a character uniquely their own. The Roman playwright refashioned the subdued dialogue of New Comedy into something rich and strange with the inventive cornucopia of complex lyrics. But most conspicuous was what Elaine Fantham has described as 'the kaleidoscopic brilliance of Plautine language'.[36] It is further enhanced by striking coinages, both verbal and imagistic. Some are colourful metaphors such as 'you are babbling boulders' in his *Pot of Gold* (*Aulularia*).[37] Others are more surreal. For example, in *The Captive* (*Captivi*), the slave, who typically exists in a violent atmosphere of menace with dire threats of punishment, is punningly referred to as *statua verberea*, 'whipped-up statue'.[38]

Scholars have long debated the precise nature – and worth – of Plautus' alterations to his Greek originals. It is fairly safe to say that he poured on a plenitude of puns (there are virtually none in Menander). He did not always change the plots, but he would at least emphasize those aspects and figures that amused him most. His *Casina* illustrates this dramatic *modus operandi*. Perhaps the strongest irony is the dramaturgical in-joke of the title itself. We know from internal evidence that this is one of the plays which has been renamed by Plautus. Thus he has deliberately called it after a person who does not appear, the ultimate thumb of the nose to Greek New Comedy. The prologue explains the Roman playwright's intent: the lovely 'title character', the maiden Casina, will not arrive on stage during the play. Nor will the young man who is in love with her. The reason? 'Plautus didn't want them to.'[39]

This is not merely an exercise of will in order to bring the misadventures of a libidinous old codger to the fore, it is also a deliberate subversion of the cardinal feature of his Athenian predecessor. Youthful romance? 'Plautus didn't want them to.'

Scholars had no Greek original which could provide a comparison between a Plautine play and its Greek model. Then, in 1968, Eric Handley's Inaugural Lecture reported the discovery of an extraordinary papyrus which contained a brief passage from Menander's *Double Deceiver*, the model for Plautus' *Sisters Bacchis*.[40] We could now see precise changes wrought by Plautus and his colleagues. After two millennia we could once again put the Latin and its Greek original side by side to make a very specific, detailed comparison and to see precisely what Plautus had done with the original. Handley's work opened a new scholarly window through which we could now see 'on a very small scale but by direct observation how [Plautus] likes his colours strong, his staging more obvious, his comedy more comic'.[41] Subsequent interpreters have unanimously agreed that Plautus characteristically preferred the broader strokes of farce over Greek New Comedy elements of realism, irony, pathos and subtle characterization.

These comparisons demonstrated the playwright's metatheatrical practice – his works abound in references to 'the play as play and the performers as players and playwrights'.[42] Indeed, perhaps the cleverest of clever slaves, Pseudolus, in the play which bears his name, compares his scheme to swindle his master to the creative act of writing for the theatre:

> Just like a playwright when he's starting to compose,
> Seeking what is nowhere in the world – yet finds it,
> Transforming baseless lies into a semblance of the truth,
> Thus, I shall now become a playwright.[43]

Both text and context glance at once forward and back. Even as they recall a famous fragment by the Greek Middle Comedy playwright Antiphanes in which he describes how much greater the comic poet's creative effort/challenge is compared to that of the tragedian's. Like his contemporaries, Plautus appears to have used the Greek models as a mere springboard, a process he called *vortere* ('to convert, adapt'). The playwright describes his techniques in the prologue to the *Trinummus*: 'Philemon wrote it. Plautus made the "barbarian version".'[44] This was a favourite joke. Plautus adapted a Greek play into a language the original author would have considered barbarian.

But Plautus is much too modest. His method totally transformed the Greek works into something entirely 'rich and strange'. He seasoned the bland fodder of Attic Comedy with the piquant sauce of native Italian farce, refurbishing the sedate originals into brash musical comedies by using his innate operatic sense to recast simple iambic dialogue into eminently singable, polymetric Latin songs (*cantica*).

That he knew Greek well is unquestioned. That he translated faithfully is out of the question. Indeed, like the Old Comedy poets of Athens, Plautus' language is so colourful and idiosyncratic that there can be no doubt that he took great liberties. Plautine style became synonymous with neologisms and verbal virtuosity.

He is also the first known professional dramatist in the modern sense of the word. Neither Aristophanes nor Menander had to write for a living. For Plautus, however, the notions of his next play and his next meal were inextricably intertwined. The Romans were a puritan folk, at once fascinated and suspicious of the theatre and make-believe. To them, playing was a kind of free-thinking, a trespassing into forbidden territory. In a deep way they feared they might be punished by the Gods. So for at least two centuries they did not dare build a permanent theatre. And so to soothe their ambivalent psyches they performed their annual dramas on makeshift wooden stages. It was not until 55 BC, when Pompey the Great built his stone theatre, that Rome had a permanent playhouse. Here as well, the superstitious Romans could not tolerate such a structure unless it was used for some utilitarian as well as theatrical purpose. Thus, when they were not seating an audience, rows of seats served as steps to the temple of Venus Victrix. And even here the comedies played on their conscience. As one dour church father later remarked, it was still the playhouse – a site for sinners. And it would not be long before the church closed down the theatres completely.

Plautus normally disparaged women, but there is one glittering exception – Alcumena, the legendary wife of Amphitryon. She is the mythological heroine with whom Zeus falls in love but is unable to seduce except in one unusual manner. Since she is unshakeably and immovably loyal to her husband, the only way the great god can enter her bed is by disguising himself as . . . her husband. But then the *Amphitryon* is itself an exception. This is Plautus' only play on a mythological theme and yet even it could be a backhanded way of proving his point. The only faithful wife is herself a myth. In this serious, unusual play, one where the prologue coins the term Tragic-Comedy (*tragicomoedia*), Alcumena remains steadfast and makes an eloquent defence of her own purity. When she is accused of infidelity she responds proudly:

> I don't believe a 'dowry' is what most people mean by that
>   word.
> To me it means speaking your heart
> with honesty, quiet, and a cordial sense of friendship with
> my husband's family.
> I only want to remain a dutiful wife to you, generous to your
> family and be – to everyone we know forever honest.[45]

It is impossible to imagine that speech coming from any other character on the Plautine stage. Quite the contrary, the general attitude is more like the quip at the very end of *The Brothers*

Menaechmus (Menaechmi): when their slave is auctioning off the local Menaechmus' belongings, he adds, 'and if there's any bidder for the thing – his wife will go.'[46] The records do not show if there were any offers. Perhaps the biggest irony of all is that the Romans referred to their renditions of the plays into Latin as *fabulae palliatae*, plays in Greek dress. Perhaps it was another way of saying, 'those decadent Greeks always behave this way'.[47]

TERENCE

Tears and Laughter

Publius Terentius Afer was a slave, probably born in Carthage, during the last decade of the second century BC. He was brought to Rome by the distinguished senator Terentius Lucanus. Enthused by the young man's mind (*ingenium*) – as well as his outward beauty (*forma*) – the law-maker had him educated and then freed. At his formal release from slavery, the young man took the nomen Terentius from his benefactor. Although his cognomen 'Afer' is attested for ordinary Roman families, Suetonius' description of the young man as 'dark-skinned' (*fuscus colore*) has fuelled speculation that Terence might be the first black African author in the classical world.

In any case, Terence holds a special place in Western theatrical tradition as 'the father of modern comedy'. Astonishingly, the entire Western comic tradition depends upon a mere half-dozen plays written by this freed slave. But perhaps the greatest error is the critics' tendency to link Plautus and Terence as if they were a double-act like Simon and Garfunkel. They are two completely different dramatists who viewed the theatre with different eyes. Plautus, for example, was obliged to play down to his audiences' farcical expectations – his livelihood depended on the commercial success. Terence, by contrast, had noble patronage and was supported by a group of aristocrats, the semi-mythical literary coterie gathered around the philhellenic aristocrat Scipio Aemilianus.

He was writing for their pleasure and their pleasure only. And they were a fastidious group. Thus the two playwrights have different perspectives on the same subject-matter. Plautus' characters are purely in search of fun. But the young men of Terence are in search of love. Marriage to them is 'a consummation devoutly to be wished'. Plautus' view of matrimony is encapsulated in the scene where 'the repentant boy apologizes to his father for his misbehaviour, offering to marry not only the girl he had in mind but as many other women he wants him to.' To which his father responds, 'Come on my boy, one wife is more than enough for any man.'[48]

The essential difference between Plautus and Terence can be seen even at a relatively microscopic level. In a single word, Terence's characters always seem to be on the verge of tears, (the verb or noun *lacrima*) the words for crying or its cognates appear more times in Terence's half-dozen extant plays than in *all* of the twenty and a half comedies by 'his colleague'. In short, Terence cries where Plautus laughs.

Plautus' theatre is self-conscious: 'Hurry up,' one character complains, 'the spectators are getting thirsty.'[49] By contrast Terence almost never breaks the dramatic illusion, or the 'Greek illusion' for that matter. Whereas the older playwright will drop in sly – and some not so sly – illusions to things Roman and still protest that 'It all takes place in Athens, folks',[50] Terence strives to keep the Hellenic impression intact.

Throughout the centuries Plautus and Terence have each gone in and out of favour. But since the Middle Ages, thanks to medieval schoolmasters who deemed Plautus' language and subject-matter to be inappropriate for young minds, Terence has been dominant for a longer time. Terence has been worshipped by literati like Julius Caesar who deemed him 'puri sermonis amator', a lover of pure speech.[51] If this were the only criterion for theatrical success, then Plautus would have been long forgotten. Terence's Latin was exceptionally good, as are the many illustrated manuscripts which have survived the centuries. This is why the medieval schoolmasters delighted in teaching the young playwright how to write neat Latin plays. Indeed, 'neat'[52] appears to be a favourite compliment paid to the playwright. Ben Jonson in his epistle dedicatory to the complete works of Shakespeare (1623) refers to Terence: 'The merry Greeke, tart Aristophanes, neat Terence . . .'

We will never know the real secret of Terence's unprecedented success. But we do know it did not go unrewarded. Some of the changes are subtle; for example his title character Hecyra is a theatrical innovation: a *sympathetic* mother-in-law. Sostrata is so sensitive a parent that, upon learning that she is the cause of the newly-weds' unhappiness, offers to retire to the country and give them peace. In contrast to Plautus, whose characters can make sardonic quips like 'you mean you actually think a pimp is a human being?', Terence lives up to his own credo – first articulated in *homo sum humani nil a me alienum puto* (I am a man and nothing to do with human beings is alien to me).[53]

In his brief but tumultuous career, Terence was involved in numerous literary feuds – some no doubt inspired by jealousy of his association with Roman aristocrats such as Amelius Paullus. In any case his enemies accused him of lifting several familiar characters – like the parasite or leech and the Braggart Soldier, from Menander's play the *Yes-Man* (*Kolax*) – to enhance his anaemic adaptation. By some inexplicable rule of thumb, Latin authors were not supposed to use something from the Greek that had already been used before.

He defends himself through his prologue, arguing that he had no intentions of 'stealing' Menander's play, by insisting to the audience,

> If our author slipped, it was ignorance, void
> Of any intent to steal. Here, judge for yourselves:
> Menander wrote the original *Yes-Man*, containing
> A leech (the title role) and a blowhard soldier.
> Terence admits that he borrowed both from the Greek
> For the cast of his *Eunuch*, but flatly denies any knowledge
> Of their previous Latinization.[54]

In fact when you think about it by this rule, all comedy must be plagiarism wherever you find running slaves, big fat matrons,

braggart soldiers, evil hookers, gluttonous parasites, kidnapped
children, cranky masters bamboozled by their tricky slaves and
love, hate, jealousy and so forth. Face it, 'There's nothing to
say that hasn't been said before.'[55]

Indeed, as so often in Roman comedy, the 'compromised'
Greco-Roman lady is poor and dowryless – a tough sell to the
hero's father. Not only is she reunited with her family at the
end but has proof of her Athenian citizenship. One example of
this is the *Brothers* whose duplex argumentum presents two
contrasting styles of love – the second of which is ostensibly
unsuitable for marriage but turns out in the end to be extremely
suitable – an Athenian citizen who has lost her parents, or at
least can't find them.

Everything always ends happily in Terence even though the
question of parentage looks glum at the beginning. Even the
much-neglected title character in *The Mother-in-Law* (*Hecyra*)
is treated kindly, and in contrast to tradition is kind to her
daughter-in-law. Other unusual characters include a kindly
pimp and a tame braggart soldier; this is pure Terentian
invention.

All of which contributes to the happy union in the end.

Terence has another innovation: playing on the precon-
ceptions of the audience. He creates suspense through a bit of
surprise characterization.

And yet the play was a singular disaster. Perhaps 'double
disaster' would be more accurate. For the *Mother-in-Law* is
notorious: it was unable to hold the audience on the first two
occasions the actors tried to present it. Its maiden performance
in 165 BC was rudely interrupted by an announcement to the
'unwashed mob' that a tightrope walker was about to perform
outside. Again, when it was restaged five years later in 160, a
similar disturbance once again chased the actors from the stage.
It was later that year at the *ludi Romani* that it finally won a
full hearing, if not a prize.

The long prologue to the third production is spoken by
Ambivius Turpio, the veteran actor-producer who was a lumi-
nous legend for discovering new talent. He pleads with the
audience to give Terence's play a chance to be heard in its

entirety. It might make the play's rejection a bit more under-
standable – and a little less humiliating for the playwright. In
his peroration, the impresario begs for the audience's goodwill
on this the third effort, arguing cryptically that the Roman
theatregoers should not allow the 'creative arts to be dominated
by a select few'.[56] This time, in any case, they made it to the
end. Some naive critics have rationalized that there is a lost
prologue, an error in the transcription or transmission of the
play which may have confused the audience. Stanley Ireland,
for example, believes that this is what possibly puzzled the
second audience. And made them susceptible to the more exciting attractions of the gladiatorial show. He theorizes that to
'audiences accustomed to the often blatant transparency of
Plautine comedy, the depth of misapprehension which Terence
imposes upon those that viewed the *Mother-in-Law* must have
come as no small dramatic shock.'[57] This is a highly suggestive
theory because – as Ireland concedes – the brighter mind of the
spectators had already caught on to the fact that the playwright
was experimenting with a new literary technique which nowa-
days we refer to as suspense.

Whatever drew the audiences away from the first two aborted
stagings of the *Mother-in-Law*, the third group of spectators
who saw it all would have had the unique pleasure of tasting
some new wine in old bottles, spiced by irony. The play at once
sports with old conventions and canonizes a new form, one
that will dominate the stage for millennia to come.

It remains a puzzle what it was about the *Mother-in-Law*
that caused the otherwise successful playwright so much grief.
At first glance the play seems to have all the stereotyped
trappings of the genre, especially the violation of the heroine
by an unknown assailant ten months earlier, culminating in a
cognitio which makes both mother and child perfectly legal.
All ends well, and they live happily ever after. There is, however, a significant exception here. Although everything in the
Mother-in-Law happens according to formula, there is *no
advance prediction* by the prologue, nor any dramatic clue that
convention is being flouted. Perhaps the instinct of the cleverer
members of the audience could sense the playwright's intention,

but it is nowhere clearly indicated in the text. Only later critics like Donatus in the fourth century argued that Terence had created a 'new dramatic scheme'.

Cicero, among Terence's greatest admirers, describes the young playwright's style as 'Menander with a Latin voice'. But translator Douglass Parker cautions: 'The fun may be Plautine, the characters and plot may be Menandrean, but the totality is Terence's own.' And as Mikhail Bakhtin argued, the Romans taught the whole world how to laugh.[58]

NOTES

1. *Soncino Books of the Bible.*
2. Aristotle, *Poetics* 1449a10. Apart from three of the plays presented in this volume, translations of classical quotations are my own.
3. Susarion fragment 1 Kassel–Austin (K–A below).
4. Horace, *Satires* 1.4.1–5.
5. Aristophanes fragment 9 K–A.
6. Plato Comicus fragment 105 K–A.
7. Eupolis fragment 171 K–A.
8. Ibid. 99.90–7 K–A.
9. Pherecrates fragment 138 K–A.
10. Ibid.
11. Cratinus fragment 307 K–A.
12. Aristophanes, *Acharnians* 33–5.
13. Aristophanes, *Clouds* 1507–8.
14. Aristophanes, *Wasps* 1342ff.
15. The only other analogous phenomenon on record is the triumph of Terence's *Eunuch*, which also was repeated the same day it was performed (161 BC).
16. Aristides 2.342d.
17. Aristophanes, *Lysistrata* 595–8.
18. G. Murray, *Aristophanes: A Study* (Oxford, 1933).
19. E. Handley, *Menander and Plautus: A Study in Comparison* (London, 1968).
20. 'He had merely to say "Oedipus" and everybody knew the rest', quoted by Athenaeus 6.22ff.
21. *Vita Aristophanis* 28.65, ed. Dübner = Testimonia 1.49–51 K–A.

22. Horace, *Epistles* 2.1.156–7.
23. Aulus Gellius 17.4.1.
24. *Inscriptiones Graecae* 14.1183c = Testimonia 170 K–A.
25. Plutarch, *Moralia* 853–4.
26. Quintilian 10.1.69.
27. The 'Cairo Codex' of Menander, containing major portions of *Arbitration, Rape of the Locks* and *The Girl From Samos*, was discovered and published in 1907.
28. Ovid, *Tristia* 2.369.
29. While everyone knows that New Comedy is essentially about marriage, its respectability goes back to Aristophanes and beyond. As S. Lape remarks: 'When the social dynamics of comedy's matrimonial unions are considered, Menander's place in the history of Greek political thought emerges more clearly. The modification of the family and the use of marriage strategies to abolish economic inequalities and the attendant social ills of greed and self-interest have a long history in political philosophy and Old Comic political commentary', *Reproducing Athens* (Princeton, 2004), p. 28.
30. Ibid., pp. 38–9.
31. Menander, *Arbitration* 498.
32. Menander, *The Bad-Tempered Man (Dyskolos)*, ed. with a translation and commentary by S. Ireland (Warminster, 1995).
33. Menander, *The Farmer* 1–21.
34. Aulus Gellius, *Attic Nights* 2.23.
35. Horace, *Epistles* 2.1.175–6.
36. E. Fantham, *Comparative Studies in Republican Latin Imagery* (Toronto, 1972), p. 96.
37. Plautus, *The Pot of Gold* 151.
38. Plautus, *The Captives* 151.
39. Plautus, *Casina* 65.
40. Handley, *Menander and Plautus*.
41. Ibid., p. 18.
42. N. W. Slater, *Plautus in Performance: The Theatre of the Mind* (Princeton, 1985), p. 9.
43. Plautus, *Pseudolus* 401–4.
44. Plautus, *Trinummus* 19.
45. Plautus, *Amphitryon* 839–43.
46. Plautus, *The Brothers Menaechmus* 1160.
47. Slater, *Theatre of the Mind*, discusses various hypotheses/theories about the prologue of *The Brothers Menaechmus* being by a later hand.

48. Plautus, *Trinummus* 1184–5.
49. Plautus, *Poenulus* 1225.
50. Plautus, *The Brothers Menaechmus* 8.
51. *Carmen* 1.1 = Suetonius, *Vita Terenti* 7.
52. The adjective 'neat' was still current coin in Dickens's day.
53. Terence, *Self-Tormentor* 77.
54. Terence, *Eunuch* 28–34.
55. Ibid. 41.
56. Terence, *The Mother-in-Law* 46–7.
57. *Hecyra*, ed. S. Ireland (Warminster, 1989), p. 9.
58. Cicero, *Limon* = Suetonius, *Vita Terenti* 7; *The Complete Comedies of Terence*, trans. D. Parker, ed. P. Bovie (Baltimore, 1974), p. 152; and see M. Bakhtin *Rabelais and his World*, trans. H. Iswolsky (Bloomington, 1984), pp. 1–58.

Further Reading

Bain, D., *Actors and Audience: A Study of Asides and Related Conventions in Greek Drama* (Oxford, 1977)

Beare, W., *The Roman Stage*, 3rd edn (London, 1964)

Bieber, M., *The History of the Greek and Roman Theatre*, 2nd edn (Princeton, 1961)

Boardman, J., J. Griffin and O. Murray, *Greece and the Hellenistic World* (Oxford, 1988)

—, *The Roman World* (Oxford, 1988)

Brown, Peter G. McC., 'Plots and Prostitutes in Greek New Comedy', Papers of the Leeds International Latin Seminar, 6:241–66

—, 'Love and Marriage in Greek New Comedy,' *Classical Quarterly* 43 (1993), pp. 189–205

Dover, K. J., *Aristophanic Comedy* (Berkeley and Los Angeles, 1972)

Fraenkel, E., *Elementi Plautini in Plauto* (Florence, 1960)

Goldberg, S. M., *The Making of Menander's Comedy* (London, 1980)

—, *Understanding Terence* (Princeton, 1986)

Gratwick, A. S., 'Titus Maccius Plautus', *Classical Quarterly* (ns 1973), pp. 78–84

—, 'The Early Republic', in *The Cambridge History of Classical Literature*, vol. 2 (Cambridge, 1982)

Green, J. R., *Theatre in Ancient Greek Society* (London, 1994)

Gruen, E. S., 'Plautus and the Public Stage', in *Studies in Greek Culture and Roman Policy* (Leiden, 1990), revised and reprinted in Segal, *Oxford Readings in Menander, Plautus and Terence*

Handley, E., *Menander and Plautus: A Study in Comparison*, Inaugural Lecture, University of London (1968)

—, 'Comedy', in P. E. Easterling and B. M. W. Knox (eds.), *The Cambridge History of Classical Literature*, vol. 1 (Cambridge, 1985), pp. 355–425

Henderson, J., *The Maculate Muse: Obscene Language in Attic Comedy*, 2nd edn (Oxford, 1991)

Hunter, R. L., *The New Comedy of Greece and Rome* (Cambridge, 1985)

Janko, R., *Aristotle on Comedy: Towards a Reconstruction of Poetics* II (London, 1984)

Konstan, D., *Roman Comedy* (Cornell, 1983)

—, *Greek Comedy and Ideology* (New York and Oxford, 1995)

Lape, S., *Reproducing Athens: Menander's Comedy, Democratic Culture, and the Hellenistic City* (Princeton, 2004)

Ludwig, W., 'The originality of Terence and his Greek models', *Greek, Roman and Byzantine Studies* 9 (1968), pp. 169–82

McCarthy, Kathleen, *Slaves, Masters and the Art of Authority in Plautine Comedy* (Princeton, 2000)

Segal, C. P., 'The Character and Cults of Dionysus and the Unity of the *Frogs*', *Harvard Studies in Classical Philology* 65 (1961), pp. 207–42

—, 'Aristophanes' Cloud-Chorus', *Arethusa* 2 (1969), pp. 143–61

Segal, E., *Roman Laughter: The Comedy of Plautus*, 2nd edn (Oxford, 1987)

— (ed.), *Oxford Readings in Aristophanes* (Oxford, 1996)

— (ed. and trans.), *Plautus in Four Comedies* (Oxford, 1996)

—, *The Death of Comedy* (Cambridge, Mass., 2001)

— (ed.), *Oxford Readings in Menander, Plautus and Terence* (Oxford, 2002)

Silk, M. S., *Aristophanes and the Definition of Comedy* (Oxford, 2000)

Slater, N. W., *Plautus in Performance: The Theatre of the Mind* (Princeton, 1985)

Taplin, O., 'Fifth-Century Tragedy and Comedy: A Synkrisis', *Journal of Hellenic Studies* 106 (1986), reprinted with minor revisions by permission of the author

—, *Comic Angels and Other Approaches to Greek Drama through Vase-Painting* (Oxford, 1993)

Webster, T. B. L., *Studies in Later Greek Comedy* (Manchester, 1953)

—, *Studies in Menander*, 2nd edn (Manchester, 1960)

Whitman, C. H., *Aristophanes and the Comic Hero* (Cambridge, Mass., 1964)

Wiles, D., *The Masks of Menander* (Cambridge, 1991)

Zagagi, N., *Tradition and Originality in Plautus* (Göttingen, 1980)

A Note on the Texts

The texts of the plays by Aristophanes, Menander and Terence have been house-styled: single quotation marks and spaced en-rules are used; speech-prefixes and stage directions are standardized. The American spelling in Terence's *The Eunuch* has been anglicized. In *The Birds*, ⟨ ⟩ indicate conjectural text.

Line numbering follows the standard editions for ancient Greek and Latin originals and does not always match the English translation.

Notes are from the editions from which the plays have been taken, sometimes augmented by the present editor.

ARISTOPHANES

THE BIRDS

PREFACE

The Birds is not merely a literary masterpiece; it is the fullest expression of the comic dream. And it was composed at a significant moment in Athens' history. The Athenians had launched a massive armada, regarded by some as the most magnificent force ever raised by a Greek city. This was intended to conquer Sicily (and its fabled riches), and more importantly, sever Sparta from her Western allies. Before the fleet sailed, there was an ominous event which shook every citizen to the core. Athenians were wont to place a statue of Hermes *erectus* outside their doors to ward off evil spirits. The night before they sailed, some unknown vandals had mutilated the shafts of all such statues' sexual organs. This was not mere capricious damage; it was viewed by many as an omen which sent chills up their spines. Thucydides describes the Athenians' mood as they watched the fleet sail off as 'drunk with dreams'.[1] In fact, Aristophanes has appropriately named one of his two wandering tramps Euelpides ('Hopefulson').

In keeping with the familiar Aristophanic pattern, the heroes first enter as broken-down tramps who are fleeing the pressures of the city in search of some paradise, 'soft as a woolly mantle to go to sleep in' (121–2). This is certainly a modest aspiration, but it is only the beginning of Peisetaerus' ultimate rise to godhead. Their aim, curiously enough, is to become birds and be able to fly away from their urban troubles. They encounter Tereus, a notorious mythological villain who has been transformed into a bird as punishment for seducing his sister-in-law. His wife, Procne, in turn was transformed into another bird for her brutal act of revenge – serving their son Itys to Tereus in a stew.

Both dropouts from society lack adult sexual feelings. They are childish and regressed. An idea of the dual level at which much of the dialogue is pitched can be seen in Tereus' description of life in Birdland as a kind of sexual paradise: 'we feed in gardens on white sesame, myrtle-berries, poppies and bergamot' (160–61).

These plants are not merely aphrodisiacs, they are also double entendres for female sexual parts. Given the two levels on which the playwright is operating, it is no surprise that the Greek word 'wing' is also a euphemism for 'phallus'. In many modern languages this remains true. Indeed, the winged phallus is depicted on various artefacts from the earliest times.[2] As will become clear, the two vagabonds are not only worn out from urban troubles but their libido has withered as well. This is not an overly subtle message, in fact as W. Arrowsmith observed, 'no other play of Aristophanes, not even *Lysistrata* is so pervaded, so saturated by the language of desire.'[3] Even one of the Homeric apocrypha mentions a god who was known as a very naughty bird, emphatically phallic: winged Eros (*Pteros*). The permeating sexuality of the play reflects the erotic arousal of the Athenians for conquest as they sailed off on the Sicilian expedition. The tone is set by one of the tramps: in the very first line of dialogue, one of them asks the other, 'Are you telling us to go straight on, along where we can see that tree?'

The prologue starts on a journey to kingship which includes other infantile birdlike pleasures, such as flying in the air and being able to vent their hostility on an unsuspecting audience by ignoring toilet training and 'dumping their loads' on their heads. They ingratiate themselves with the avian population, arguing that the birds antedated Zeus and were deposed by him. They then establish Birdland, midway between Earth and Olympus. This will enable them to set up a blockade stopping the gods from eating the mortals' sacrifices and preventing them from sleeping with their earthly mistresses.

Very soon, the Olympians are dying of hunger and can do nothing but abjectly sue for peace with the heroes. They send an embassy which includes Hercules, Poseidon and a bizarre foreign god, Triballian. The negotiation is swift since Hercules, the strongest and the hungriest, is anxious to eat, and he muscles his colleagues into agreement. When at last the gods capitulate, the final *komos* is the greatest celebration in Old Comedy. But not before the victorious Peisetaerus exacts all his 'impious' demands. Earlier he has been forewarned by Prometheus, always a friend of man, to hold out for the ultimate prize, the hand in marriage of Basileia, who is described as Zeus' constant companion (*paredros dios*, 1753). There is plenty of precedent in Greek mythology for the conquering young god taking the deposed king's wife. He not only aims to dethrone the King of the Universe, though his name is not mentioned, it seems as if he is also demanding the hand of his Queen. What is most amazing, he gets it. Or at least, as close as propriety would allow.

In the early twentieth century, Gilbert Murray posed a rhetorical question: 'Greek doctrine is full of punishment of those who make themselves equal to even the lowest order of the Gods – yet Peisetaerus dances off in triumph. What did the audience feel?'[4] The question is its own answer. From the safety of their seats and privacy of their imaginations, the audience will enjoy the vicarious thrill of marrying the Mother of the Gods. The universal Oedipal yearning is consummated. It was arguably the boldest comedy ever written. And it is possible that this is the reason that the judges did not accord it the first prize. Perhaps it was too close for comfort. Although *The Birds* is a product of the uncensored imagination, it has not proved to be the most popular play of Aristophanes; curiously enough that honour goes to the feeble second-rate *Plutus* (*Wealth*), which survives in no fewer than 148 manuscripts as opposed to a mere eighteen of *The Birds* and eight for *Lysistrata*. It is a curious literary puzzle. The only possible explanation is that the schoolmasters had a text from which to teach their charges Ancient Greek without having to resort to the naughty language of many Aristophanic plays.

NOTES

1. Thucydides 1.70, 4.10, 6.24, 6.31.
2. J. Henderson, *The Maculate Muse* (New Haven and London, 1975), p. 128.
3. W. Arrowsmith 'Aristophanes' *Birds*: The Fantasy Politics of Eros', *Arion* 1/1 (1973), pp. 164ff.
4. G. Murray, *Aristophanes: A Study* (Oxford, 1933), p. 155.

CHARACTERS

PEISETAERUS
EUELPIDES } *two elderly Athenians*

SERVANT *of Tereus*

TEREUS, *now a hoopoe*

CHORUS *of birds**

CHORUS-LEADER

A PRIEST

A POET

AN ORACLE-MONGER

METON

AN ATHENIAN INSPECTOR

A DECREE-SELLER

FIRST MESSENGER
SECOND MESSENGER } *from the city walls*

IRIS

FIRST HERALD (*of the city of Cloudcuckooville*), *returned from a mission to mankind*

A YOUNG MAN *who wants to kill his father*

CINESIAS

AN INFORMER

PROMETHEUS

POSEIDON

HERACLES

A TRIBALLIAN GOD

SECOND HERALD (*of Peisetaerus*)

---

*The birds forming the chorus are individually identified in lines 297–304.

Silent Characters

XANTHIAS
MANODORUS (*also*   } *slaves of Peisetaerus*
called MANES)   *and Euelpides*

A FLAMINGO

A MEDE-BIRD

SECOND HOOPOE, *grandson to Tereus*

A GOBBLER-BIRD

PROCNE, *now a nightingale*

A RAVEN *as piper*

SLAVES *acting as archers and slingers*

PRINCESS, *a heavenly maiden*

The scene is a rocky, wooded landscape, to which PEISETAERUS *and* EUELPIDES *enter by a side passage.* PEISETAERUS *has a jackdaw perched on his wrist,* EUELPIDES *a crow; one man carries in his free hand a ritual basket and some myrtle wreaths, the other a fire-pot. They are followed by two* SLAVES *carrying the rest of their luggage, including cooking equipment and bedding.*

PEISETAERUS [*to his jackdaw*]: Are you telling us to go straight on, along where we can see that tree?

EUELPIDES [*to his crow*]: Oh, blast you! [*To* PEISETAERUS] *This* one's croaking to go back the way we came.

PEISETAERUS: Why are we traipsing back and forth like this, you idiot? This aimless to-and-fro of a journey will be the death of us!

EUELPIDES: To think, wretched me, that I've gone around and about for more than a hundred miles of travelling, at the bidding of a crow!

PEISETAERUS: To think, hapless me, that I've pounded the nails off my toes, at the bidding of a jackdaw!

EUELPIDES: I just don't know any longer where on earth we've got to.

PEISETAERUS: Do you think you could find our own country, starting from here?

EUELPIDES: I'm sure that from here even Execestides couldn't! [PEISETAERUS *begins to move on, in the same direction as before*]

PEISETAERUS [*nearly losing his footing*]: Help!

EUELPIDES: *You* can go that way, chum. [*He sets out in a different direction*]

PEISETAERUS: He really has swindled us, that man from the bird-market, that loony tray-vendor Philocrates, who told us that these two birds would show us where to find Tereus, the hoopoe,[1] who was turned ⟨once upon a time from a man⟩ into a bird. He sold us this bird – Jackdaw, son of Tharreleides – for an obol,[2] and this other one for three obols; and we've found that all they really know is how to nip us! [*By now both men have reached the foot of the stage-platform, at*

10

20   *opposite ends of it. The jackdaw is showing signs of excite-*
        ment] Now what's making you gape like that? Are you going
        to lead us on right into these cliffs somewhere? There's no
        way through here.
        EUELPIDES: And there's certainly no path anywhere here,
        either.
        PEISETAERUS: What, is the crow saying something about the
        route?
        EUELPIDES: It's certainly now croaking something different
        from before.
        PEISETAERUS: Well then, what's it saying about the route?
        EUELPIDES: All it's saying is, it's going to bite my fingers off
        me!
        PEISETAERUS [*to the audience*]: Isn't it dreadful that when
        we're ready and eager to go to *birdition*,[3] we're then unable
30   to find the way? The thing is, you gentlemen who are listen-
        ing, that we're suffering from the opposite affliction to Sacas.[4]
        He's a non-citizen trying to force his way in. *We*, having the
        full status of tribe and clan membership, citizens among
        citizens, and without anyone trying to shoo us away, have
        upped and flown out of our country on two swift feet. It's
        not that we hate that city as such, or don't wish it to be really
        great and happy and open to all the world to come and pay
40   fines in. That's the thing: the cicadas chirp on the branches
        for a month or two, the Athenians chirp away at lawsuits
        continually all their lives long. That's why we're trekking this
        trek; with a basket, a pot and some myrtle-wreaths,[5] we're
        wandering in search of a trouble-free place where we can
        settle and pass our lives. Our journey now is to see Tereus
        the hoopoe, wanting to find out from him if he's seen a city
        of that kind anywhere he's flown over.
        EUELPIDES: I say!
        PEISETAERUS: What is it?
50   EUELPIDES: The crow has been trying for some time to show
        me something that's up above.
        PEISETAERUS: This jackdaw too is gaping upwards as if it
        was showing me something. It must be that there are birds
        hereabouts. [*They climb the steps to where rocks and bushes*

conceal the stage-house[6] *door*] We'll soon know, if we make a noise.

EUELPIDES: Do you know what you should do? Kick the rock with your leg.

PEISETAERUS: You hit it with your head – that'll make twice the noise.

EUELPIDES: All right, take a stone and knock.

PEISETAERUS: By all means, if you like. [*He picks up a stone and begins to knock with it*] Boy, boy!

EUELPIDES: What are you saying, man? Calling the hoopoe 'boy'? Surely instead of 'boy' you ought to be calling 'hoop-ho'!

PEISETAERUS [*continuing to knock*]: Hoop-ho! You'll force me to knock again, you know. Hoop-ho!   60

SERVANT [*within*]: Who's there? Who's shouting for my master?

> [*The* SERVANT *comes to the door and opens it. He is a bird, with an enormous gaping beak. Both men are terrified at the sight of him*]

PEISETAERUS [*staggering backwards*]: Apollo preserve us, the size of that gape! [*Meanwhile* EUELPIDES *has fainted, and both have lost hold of their guide-birds, which fly away*]

SERVANT [*who is equally frightened*]: Heaven help us, these are a pair of bird-catchers!

PEISETAERUS [*recovering himself*]: I say, what are you frightened of? Can't you even speak a bit more nicely?

SERVANT [*recovering himself*]: You shall perish!

PEISETAERUS: But we're not men.

SERVANT: What are you, then?

PEISETAERUS: I'm a Fearfowl, a Libyan bird.

SERVANT: You're talking nonsense.

PEISETAERUS: Just you ask my lower half![7]

SERVANT [*turning to* EUELPIDES, *now back on his feet*]: And what bird may this be? Answer, won't you?

EUELPIDES: I'm a Shitterling, from the land of Phasis.

PEISETAERUS: But in heaven's name, what animal may *you* be?

SERVANT: I am a slave bird.   70

PEISETAERUS: Were you beaten by some cock in a fight?

SERVANT: No; the thing was, at the time when my master turned into a hoopoe, he prayed then that I might become a bird, so that he could have an attendant and servant.

PEISETAERUS: Does a bird actually need a servant?

SERVANT: *He* does – I suppose because he once used to be a man. At one moment he gets a longing to eat Phalerum whitebait: I take the bowl and run for whitebait. Or he wants pea-soup – we need a stirring spoon and a pot; I run for a stirring spoon.

80 PEISETAERUS: This fellow's a runner-bird. Well, runner-bird, do you know what we want you to do? Call your master for us.

SERVANT: But, by Zeus, he's just gone to sleep after eating some myrtle-berries and gnats.

PEISETAERUS: All the same, wake him up.

SERVANT: I know very well he'll be annoyed, but for your sake I'll wake him up. [*He goes off inside, closing the door*]

EUELPIDES [*calling after him, though not too loudly*]: Damn and curse you! How you killed me with fright!

PEISETAERUS: *And*, dash it, the fright made my jackdaw flit!

EUELPIDES: You utterly cowardly creature! you were so frightened you let your jackdaw go?

PEISETAERUS: And what about you, may I ask? Didn't you let go of your crow when you fell down?

90 EUELPIDES: By Zeus, I did not.

PEISETAERUS: Where is it, then?

EUELPIDES: It flew off.

PEISETAERUS [*ironically*]: So you didn't let it go? My good friend, how brave you are!

TEREUS [*within, to his* SERVANT]: Open the glade, so I can come out some time.

[*The door opens and* TEREUS *comes out. He has the head and wings of a hoopoe, but few if any feathers on his body*]

PEISETAERUS: Heracles, what kind of animal might this be? What's this plumage? What kind of triple crest is that?

TEREUS: Who is it that are looking for me?

EUELPIDES [*who, like* PEISETAERUS, *is too overcome by*

laughter to be able to answer properly]: You look as though
the Twelve Gods had blasted you!

TEREUS: You're not making fun of me, are you, just because you
see this plumage? I was once a man, you know, gentlemen.

PEISETAERUS: It's not you we're laughing at.

TEREUS: What is it, then?

PEISETAERUS: It's your beak we think looks funny.

TEREUS: This is just the sort of indignity that Sophocles inflicts   100
on me, Tereus, in his tragedies.

PEISETAERUS: You're Tereus, are you? Are you a bird or a
peacock?

TEREUS: I am a bird.

PEISETAERUS: Then where are your feathers?

TEREUS: They've fallen off.

PEISETAERUS: What, because of some disease?

TEREUS: No; all birds shed their feathers in winter, and later
we grow new ones. But tell me, who are the two of you?

PEISETAERUS: We? We're humans.

TEREUS: Where do you come from by birth?

PEISETAERUS: Where the fine warships come from.

TEREUS: You're not jurors, are you?

PEISETAERUS: Oh, no, quite the other way; we're juror-   110
phobiacs.[8]

TEREUS: Does that crop grow in those parts?

PEISETAERUS: You can find a little of it in the countryside, if
you look hard.

TEREUS: And what, pray, is the thing you have come here in
want of?

PEISETAERUS: We want to have a talk with you.

TEREUS: What about?

PEISETAERUS: It's because you were originally a man, once
upon a time, like us; and you owed people money, once upon
a time, like us; and you liked to avoid paying them, once
upon a time, like us. Then later you changed to the shape of
a bird, and you've flown over land and sea in every direction;
and you have all the knowledge that a man has and that a
bird has. That's why we've come here to you, to beseech you   120

if you could tell us of some city that's nice and fleecy, soft as
a woolly mantle[9] to go to sleep in.

TEREUS: Then you're looking for a city that's greater than the
city of the Cranaans?[10]

PEISETAERUS: Greater? Not at all; just one that suits us better.

TEREUS: Obviously you're hoping to live under an aristocracy.

PEISETAERUS: Me? Certainly not; even the son of Scellias
makes me feel sick!

TEREUS: Well, what kind of city would you most like to live
in?

PEISETAERUS: One where my greatest troubles would be of
130   this sort: one of my friends would come to my door of a
morning and say this: 'In the name of Olympian Zeus, make
sure you give your children a bath and come with them early
to my place; I'm going to be celebrating a wedding. Do this
without fail; if you don't, you needn't come to me when the
time comes that I'm in trouble!'

TEREUS: By Zeus, you do love a toilsome life! [To EUELPIDES]
What about you?

EUELPIDES: I fancy the same sort of thing.

TEREUS: What sort of thing?

EUELPIDES: A place where the father of an attractive boy
would meet me and complain to me like this, as if I'd done
140   him wrong: 'A fine thing you did to my son, old sparkler! You
met him coming away from the gymnasium after bathing, and
you didn't kiss him, you didn't greet him, you didn't draw
him close, you didn't finger his balls – and you an old family
friend of mine!'

TEREUS: You poor little thing, what troubles you yearn for!
Well, there is a happy city of the sort you're talking about,
beside the Red Sea.

PEISETAERUS: Help! Nowhere beside the sea for us, on any
account – where the *Salaminia*[11] can pop up one morning
with a summons-server on board! Do you have a Greek city
you can tell us of?

150   TEREUS: Why don't you go and settle at Lepreus in Elis?

PEISETAERUS: Because, by the gods, even though I haven't seen
it, I abhor Lepreus because of Melanthius.

TEREUS: Well, there are also the Opuntii in Locris; you can settle there.

PEISETAERUS: I wouldn't become an Opuntius for a talent of gold!

EUELPIDES: But what's this life here with the birds like? You'll know all about it.

TEREUS: Not a disagreeable life to spend. Here, in the first place, you have to live without a purse.

EUELPIDES: You've taken a lot of humbug out of life!

TEREUS: And we feed in gardens on white sesame, myrtle-   160
berries, poppies and bergamot.

EUELPIDES: Why, you live the life of newly-weds![12]

PEISETAERUS [suddenly]: Ah, ah! I see in the bird race what could be a grand design and a mighty power, were you to be persuaded by me.

TEREUS: What do you want us to be persuaded of?

PEISETAERUS: What you should be persuaded of? First of all, don't fly about all over the place with gaping beaks, because doing that wins you no respect. For example, back there with us, if you ask about those flighty people and say 'Who is that Teleas?', the reply will be this: 'The man's a bird – unstable, flighty, unpredictable, never ever sticking in one place.'   170

TEREUS: By Dionysus, you're right to make that criticism. Well, what can we do about it?

PEISETAERUS: Establish a single city.

TEREUS: But what kind of city can we birds establish?

PEISETAERUS: Are you serious? What an utterly stupid thing to say! Look down.

TEREUS [doing so]: There, I'm looking.

PEISETAERUS: Now look up.

TEREUS [doing so]: I'm looking.

PEISETAERUS: Turn your head round.

TEREUS [doing so]: This'll do me good, by Zeus, if I twist my neck!

PEISETAERUS: Did you see anything?

TEREUS: Yes, the clouds and the sky.

PEISETAERUS: Well, this is surely a stage for the birds, isn't it?

TEREUS: A stage? In what way?   180

PEISETAERUS: A place for them, as one might say; but because
it's the scene of activity, and everything passes through it, it
is at present called a stage. But if once you settle and fortify
it, then instead of being called your stage it will be called
your State. The result will be that you'll rule over men as if
they were locusts, and as for the gods, you'll crush them by
starvation like the Melians.

TEREUS: How?

PEISETAERUS: Well, the air, surely, is between them and the
earth. So then, just as when we want to go to Delphi we have
to ask the Boeotians for the right of transit, in the same way,
when men sacrifice to the gods, you won't let the aroma of
the thigh-bones pass through unless the gods pay you tribute.

TEREUS: Wowee! Holy Earth! Holy snares, gins and nets, but
I've never heard a cleverer idea! So much so that I'll found
this city with you, should the other birds agree.

PEISETAERUS: Then who's going to explain the idea to them?

TEREUS: You. They used to be inarticulate, but I've lived with
them a long time and I've taught them language.

PEISETAERUS: So how are you going to call them together?

TEREUS: Easily. I'll go into my thicket here right away, then
wake up my nightingale, and we'll summon them. If they
hear our voice, they'll come running.

PEISETAERUS: Dearest of birds, don't just stand there now!
Come on, I beg you, as fast as you can, go into the thicket
and wake up the nightingale.

    [TEREUS *goes inside*]

TEREUS [*within, singing*]:
    Come, my consort, leave your sleep
    and let forth the melodies of sacred song
    with which from your divine lips you lament
    your child and mine, the much-bewailed Itys,
    quavering with the liquid notes
    of your vibrant throat.
    [*The song of the nightingale is now heard, played by the
    piper*]
    Through the leaf-clad green-brier comes
    the pure sound, reaching the abode of Zeus,

where golden-haired Phoebus hears
and in response to your elegies plucks
his ivoried lyre and stirs the gods
to make music together; and from immortal lips   220
issues as one voice the harmonious
swelling divine refrain of the Blest Ones.
[*The piper plays on, solo*]

EUELPIDES: Lord Zeus, what a voice that bird has! How she
filled the whole thicket with her sweetness!

PEISETAERUS: I say –

EUELPIDES: What is it?

PEISETAERUS: Keep quiet, won't you?

EUELPIDES: Why?

PEISETAERUS: The hoopoe's getting ready to sing again.

TEREUS [*within*]:
Epopoi, popopopopoi, popoi!
Io, io, ito, ito, hither, hither,
hither let all my feathered fellows come!
All who dwell in the country plough-lands   230
rich in seed, the myriad tribes of barleycorn-eaters
and the races of seed-gatherers
that fly swiftly and utter soft notes,
and all who in the furrows often
gently twitter over the turned soil
with joyful voices, like this,
tio tio tio tio tio tio tio tio!
And all of you who find their food
in gardens on the ivy branches,
and you of the hills, the oleaster-eaters and the arbutus-   240
    eaters,
hurry, come flying to my call:
trioto trioto totobrix!
And you who in the marshy valleys swallow
the sharp-biting gnats, and all you who inhabit
the well-watered regions of the land and the lovely meads
    of Marathon,
and the bird of patterned plumage, francolin, francolin!
And you whose tribes fly with the halcyons[13]   250

over the swell of the open sea,
come hither to learn the news;
for we are assembling here all the tribes
of long-necked fowls.
For a sharp-witted old man has come here,
novel in his ideas
and an attempter of novel deeds.
Come to the meeting, all of you,
hither, hither, hither, hither!

260   Torotorotorotorotix!
Kikkabau, kikkabau!
Torotorotorolililix!

[PEISETAERUS *and* EUELPIDES *watch expectantly for the birds to arrive*]

PEISETAERUS: Do you see any birds?

EUELPIDES: No, by Apollo, I don't, though I'm staring open-mouthed at the sky.

PEISETAERUS: Then it looks as though the hoopoe was wasting his time going into the bushes, after the fashion of a thickknee, and crying 'popoi'.

TEREUS [*within*]: Torotix, torotix!

[*Enter* FLAMINGO, *taking his stand on a hillock in front of the stage-house*]

EUELPIDES: Well, anyway, old chap, look, there's a bird coming here.

PEISETAERUS: By Zeus, a bird it is! What on earth is it? Not a peacock, is it?

[TEREUS *re-enters from the thicket*]

270   EUELPIDES: Our friend here will tell us himself. [*To* TEREUS] What is that bird?

TEREUS: That's not one of those everyday birds that you see all the time; it's a bird of the marshes.

EUELPIDES: Whew, it's pretty – and it's flaming red!

TEREUS: Naturally, because its name is Flamingo.

[*Enter a* MEDE-BIRD *and posts himself on a second hillock*]

PEISETAERUS [*to* EUELPIDES]: I say – hey, you there!

EUELPIDES: What are you calling me for?

PEISETAERUS: Here's another bird.

EUELPIDES: By Zeus, there *is* another, and he too is aberrantly located. [*To* TEREUS] Who may this prophetic bard be, this outlandish bird, this hill-walker?

TEREUS: His name is Mede.

EUELPIDES: Mede? Lord Heracles, but then if he's a Mede how has he flown here without a camel?

[*Enter* SECOND HOOPOE. *He stands on a third hillock*]

PEISETAERUS: Here's yet another bird who's occupied a crest.

EUELPIDES [*to* TEREUS]: What extraordinary sight is this? So 280 you're not the only hoopoe – there's also this other one?

TEREUS: He's the son of Philocles' hoopoe, and I'm his grandfather – just as you might say Hipponicus was the son of Callias and Callias the son of Hipponicus.

EUELPIDES: So this bird is Callias. What a lot of feathers he's lost!

TEREUS: Yes: being a pedigree bird, he gets plucked by prosecutors,[14] and in addition to that the females pull out his feathers.

[*Enter a* GOBBLER-BIRD. *He stands on a fourth hillock*]

PEISETAERUS: Poseidon! here's still another gaudy bird. [*To* TEREUS] What might the name of this one be?

TEREUS: This one? Gobbler.

PEISETAERUS: You mean there's another Gobbler besides Cleonymus?

EUELPIDES: Well, if he were Cleonymus, surely he'd have 290 thrown away his ... crest?

PEISETAERUS [*to* TEREUS]: But tell me, what are the birds all crested for? Have they come to run in the four hundred?[15]

TEREUS: No, my dear fellow, they make their homes on crests for the sake of security, like the Carians.

PEISETAERUS [*pointing off-stage*]: Poseidon! can't you see what a plaguy great mob of birds has assembled?

EUELPIDES: Lord Apollo, what a cloud of them! Whew! with the way they're flocking, you can't even see the wing-entrance now!

[*The twenty-four birds of the* CHORUS *are now entering*

the orchestra. As they mill around in a noisy throng, PEIS-
ETAERUS *and* EUELPIDES *try to identify each one*]

PEISETAERUS: That one's a partridge.

EUELPIDES: And *that* one, by Zeus, is a francolin.

PEISETAERUS: And that one's a widgeon.

EUELPIDES: And that one's a halcyon.

PEISETAERUS: And what's the one behind her?

EUELPIDES: What is he? A barbur.

300   PEISETAERUS: What, is there a bird that's a barber?

EUELPIDES: Well, there's barber Sparrow, isn't there? And that
one's an owl.

PEISETAERUS: What do you say? Who's been bringing owls to
Athens?[16]

EUELPIDES: Jay –

PEISETAERUS: Turtledove –

EUELPIDES: Lark –

PEISETAERUS: Marsh-warbler –

EUELPIDES: Wheatear –

PEISETAERUS: Pigeon –

EUELPIDES: Vulture –

PEISETAERUS: Hawk –

EUELPIDES: Ringdove –

PEISETAERUS: Cuckoo –

EUELPIDES: Stockdove –

PEISETAERUS: Firecrest –

EUELPIDES: Porphyrion –

PEISETAERUS: Kestrel –

EUELPIDES: Dabchick –

PEISETAERUS: Bunting –

EUELPIDES: Lammergeyer –

PEISETAERUS: Woodpecker.

EUELPIDES: Whew! Look at these birds!

PEISETAERUS: Whew! Look at these fowl! How they cheep,
how they screech as they run about, each louder than the
other!

EUELPIDES: Are they – threatening us?

PEISETAERUS: Help! they're certainly staring at the two of us
with gaping beaks.

EUELPIDES: That's how it seems to me too.

CHORUS: 310
    To-to-to-to-to-to-to where has he gone, he who
      summoned me? In what place may he be abiding?

TEREUS [*coming forward*]: Here am I; I have been here all the
time, and have not deserted my friends.

CHORUS:
    Twa-twa-twa-twa-twa-twa-twa-twa-t-what friendly
      news, pray, do you have for me?

TEREUS: News that concerns you all: something safe, honest,
pleasurable and to your advantage. Two men, subtle
reasoners, have come here to me.

CHORUS: Where? How? What are you saying?

TEREUS: I am saying that two old men have come here from   320
the land of humans, and they have come bringing with them
the stem of a stupendous scheme.

CHORUS-LEADER: You've done the greatest wrong I've known
since I was fledged! What *are* you saying?

TEREUS: Don't be frightened so soon at what I'm telling you.

CHORUS-LEADER: What *have* you done to me?

TEREUS: I have welcomed here two men who are enamoured
of our society.[17]

CHORUS-LEADER: You have actually done that?

TEREUS: And I'm glad I've done it.

CHORUS-LEADER: And they are already somewhere among us?

TEREUS: As sure as I'm among you.

CHORUS:
    Ah, ah!
    We have been betrayed, we have been wickedly treated!
    He who was our friend, who fed beside us
    in fields that nourished him and us alike,   330
    has violated our ancient ordinances,
    has violated the sworn covenants of the birds.
    He has invited me into a trap, he has left me at the mercy
    of a wicked race, which ever since its creation
    has been brought up to be my enemy.

CHORUS-LEADER [*turning, together with his fellows, towards*
   PEISETAERUS *and* EUELPIDES]: Well, we'll have a reckoning

with *him* later; but my opinion is that these two old men should pay their penalty now and that we should tear them to pieces.

PEISETAERUS: We've had it, then.

EUELPIDES: You know, it's you alone that's responsible for getting us into this mess. Why did you bring me here from back home?

PEISETAERUS: So you could come with me.

EUELPIDES: You mean, so I could bleed and weep.

PEISETAERUS: Now you really are going and talking rubbish. How will you weep, once you've had your eyes pecked out?

CHORUS:
Aho, aho!
Advance, attack, deliver a murderous
battle-charge, lay wings on them
from every side, encircle them completely!
For both these two are doomed to howl
and to provide fodder for my beak.
For there is no wooded mountain, nor heavenly cloud,
nor grey sea, that shall harbour these two
so that they escape me.
[*By now the two men are trapped between the menacing ring of birds and the front of the stage-house*]

CHORUS-LEADER: Now let's wait no longer to pluck and peck these two. Where's the taxiarch? Let him bring the right wing forward.

EUELPIDES: This is it. [*Looking desperately about him*] Where can I get away, wretched me?

PEISETAERUS: Here, stay where you are, can't you?

EUELPIDES: To be torn in pieces by these creatures?

PEISETAERUS: Well, how do you think you're going to escape from them?

EUELPIDES: I've no idea how.

PEISETAERUS: Well, what I say to you is that we must stand and fight and take up . . . one of the pots. [*He searches among the luggage, which has been left on the ground close by, and finds a pot*]

EUELPIDES: What good will a pot do us?

PEISETAERUS: Well, no owl will come near us.

EUELPIDES: But against these crook-taloned creatures?

PEISETAERUS: Grab the spit and plant it in the ground in front   360
of you.

EUELPIDES [as he does so]: And what about protecting our
eyes?

PEISETAERUS: Take a saucer or plate from there, and put it on.

EUELPIDES: You brilliant fellow, what a fine contrivance, what
military expertise! In resourcefulness you've already shown
you outclass Nicias.[18]

[The two men have now completed 'arming' themselves]

CHORUS-LEADER: Eleleleu! Forward! Level your beaks! No
hanging back! Pull them, pluck them, hit them, flay them!
Strike the pot first!

[As the birds begin to charge in upon PEISETAERUS and
EUELPIDES, TEREUS rushes forward in an attempt to stop
them]

TEREUS: Here, tell me, you vilest of all creatures, why are you
trying to murder and tear apart two men who have done you
no harm – men who are relations and fellow-tribesmen of
my wife?

CHORUS-LEADER: Should we show any more mercy to these
men than we would to wolves? Or what other beings are   370
there who are even more our enemies than these, whom we
could take revenge on?

TEREUS: But suppose that they're enemies by birth and yet
friendly by intention? Suppose they've come here to give you
some valuable instruction?

CHORUS-LEADER: How could these men ever give us any valuable instruction or advice? They are the enemies of our
feathers and our forefeathers!

TEREUS: Why, the wise learn a great deal from their enemies.
It is precaution, after all, that keeps everything safe. Now
you can't learn that from a friend; but your enemy compels
you to, right away. For example, it was from foemen, and
not from friends, that human communities learned to con-
struct high walls and acquire long ships; and that knowledge   380
keeps children, home and property safe.

[*The* CHORUS-LEADER *glances round the circle of his com-
rades, who nod their assent to giving the two men a
hearing*]

CHORUS-LEADER: Well, in our opinion it's to our advantage
to listen first to what they have to say; one *can* learn some
wisdom even from one's enemies.

PEISETAERUS [*aside to* EUELPIDES]: They seem to be slacken-
ing their anger. Foot by foot,[19] withdraw. [*The two men
retire a little towards the stage-house*]

TEREUS [*to the* CHORUS]: Besides that, it's only fair, and also
you ought to oblige me out of gratitude.

CHORUS-LEADER: Well, certainly we've never opposed you in
anything before.

PEISETAERUS [*to* EUELPIDES]: They're behaving more peace-
ably, so lower the pot. Now we must mount a patrol, holding
390   our spear – our spit – within the camp perimeter, right by
the pot, keeping a lookout far and near; because we mustn't
run away.

[EUELPIDES *has now put down his pot-shield, as instructed, and is marching back and forth like a sentry*]

EUELPIDES: And tell me, if we do get killed, where on earth
are we going to be buried?

PEISETAERUS: Why, Potters' Town will welcome us. In order
to get a state funeral, we'll tell the generals that we died
fighting the enemy at Orneae!

CHORUS-LEADER [*to the* CHORUS]:
400   Return to your ranks, as you were before,
and bend down and ground your spirit
beside your anger, like a hoplite;
and let us discover who these men may be
and whence they have come
and what is the idea that they have.
[*The birds withdraw to their original position and formation in the orchestra, and perform the drill movements of
grounding imaginary arms*]
Ho, hoopoe, 'tis thee I call!

TEREUS:
And, calling, what wouldst thou hear?

CHORUS-LEADER: Who may these men be, and whence?
TEREUS:
    Travellers from Greece, the land of wisdom.
CHORUS-LEADER: And what chance may it be   410
    that has brought them to come
    to the birds?
TEREUS:
        A passionate desire[20]
    for your life and your lifestyle
    and to share your home, too,
    and your whole existence.
CHORUS-LEADER [amazed]:
    What do you say? –
    And what is the tale he tells?
TEREUS:
    A tale incredible, and more than incredible, to hear!
CHORUS-LEADER:
    Does he see any worthwhile gain in staying here,
    which gives him confidence that by living with me
    he may be able either to overcome his enemy
    or to help his friends?   420
TEREUS:
    He speaks of great felicity, too great
    to speak of or to credit; for
    he will argue, and convince you,
    that all this expanse is yours,
    in this direction, and in that, and in this.
CHORUS-LEADER: Is he insane?
TEREUS:
    He's unspeakably shrewd!
CHORUS-LEADER: Is there some wisdom in his breast?
TEREUS:
    He's the sharpest of foxes,
    all ingenuity, a dead-shot, an old hand, the   430
        sieved meal of subtlety.
CHORUS-LEADER:
    Tell him to speak, to speak, I beg you!
    On hearing the words you've spoken to me

my heart has taken wing!

TEREUS [*to the two* SLAVES]: Here now, you and you, take this suit of armour back inside, and hang it in the kitchen next to the trivet – and may it bring us good fortune. [*To* PEISETAERUS] And you explain and inform these birds about your plan, for which I've called them together.

[*The* SLAVES *go over to* PEISETAERUS *and* EUELPIDES *to take away their 'armour', but* PEISETAERUS *halts them*]

PEISETAERUS: By Apollo, I will *not*, not unless they make a
440   pact with me, the pact that that monkey of a knife-maker made with his wife: that they're not to bite me, or to pull at my balls, or to poke me –

EUELPIDES: You don't mean in the –?

PEISETAERUS: Certainly not. No, I'm saying in the eyes.

CHORUS-LEADER: I agree to the pact.

PEISETAERUS: Then please swear to it.

CHORUS-LEADER: I swear; my reward to be, that I shall be victorious by the verdict of all the judges and all the audience –

PEISETAERUS: You will be!

CHORUS-LEADER: But should I break my oath, then let me win by just one vote.

PEISETAERUS: Hear ye, O people! The hoplites may now take
450   up their arms and go back to their homes, but they should look out for any notices we may post on the boards. [*He and* EUELPIDES *hand over their 'armour' to the two* SLAVES, *who take it within and return to the stage*]

CHORUS:
Ever deceitful, in every way,
is the nature of man; but nonetheless, speak to me.
For you may well succeed
in revealing some quality that you see in me, or
some superior potential
which my dull-witted mind has overlooked.
    This thing
that you perceive, explain it to us all;
for whatever benefit you succeed
in providing for us shall be common to us all.

CHORUS-LEADER: Now tell us the matter for which you have   460
   come here to persuade us to your way of thinking, and have
   no fear; for we shall certainly not be the first to violate the
   treaty.

PEISETAERUS: I'm positively bursting to tell you, by Zeus, and
   I've got the dough of my speech well mixed; there's nothing
   to stop me kneading it to perfection. [*Turning to the two*
   SLAVES] Boy, bring me a garland; and will somebody quickly
   fetch water to pour over my hands. [*The* SLAVES *go inside*]

EUELPIDES: Are we going to have a dinner, or what?

PEISETAERUS [*as he takes a garland from one of the* SLAVES,
   *who have by now re-entered, and has his hands washed by
   the other*]: No, no, but I've been aiming for a long time to
   say something, a great big fat speech that will shatter these
   birds to the very soul. [*Addressing the birds*] So grieved am I
   for your sake, you who once upon a time were kings –

CHORUS-LEADER: Us kings? What of?

PEISETAERUS: Yes, you, kings over everything that exists, over
   me here to begin with, and over Zeus himself; you who are
   senior in birth and antiquity to Cronus and the Titans and   470
   to Earth!

CHORUS-LEADER: And to Earth?

PEISETAERUS: By Apollo, yes.

CHORUS-LEADER: I certainly never had *that* information
   before!

PEISETAERUS: That's because you've an unintelligent, un-
   inquisitive nature, and haven't studied your Aesop. He said
   in his tale that the Lark was born first of all birds, before the
   Earth came to be. Then her father fell sick and died; there
   was no earth, he'd been lying unburied for four days, she had
   no idea what to do, and finally in desperation she buried her
   father in her own head.

EUELPIDES: And so now the father of the Lark lies dead in
   Headcrest cemetery!

PEISETAERUS: Well then, if they were born before the Earth
   and before the gods, isn't the kingship theirs by right as the
   eldest?

CHORUS-LEADER: By Apollo, it is.

EUELPIDES [*to the audience*]: So you'd jolly well better grow a
480   beak in future – Zeus is surely soon going to hand his sceptre
         back to the woodpecker!

PEISETAERUS: Now then, to show that it was not the gods but
the birds who governed and reigned over men in olden times:
there are many proofs of this. For example, I shall first show
to you that the Cock was the first monarch and ruler of the
Persians, long before all those Dariuses and Megabazuses –
so that in memory of that rulership he is still called the
Persian Fowl.

EUELPIDES: Ah, that's why even now, alone among birds, he
struts about like the Great King, wearing his headgear erect!

PEISETAERUS: And he was so powerful then, so great and
mighty, that even today, in memory of that old power of his,
490   when he just sings his song of dawning everybody jumps up
         and starts work – smiths, potters, tanners, cobblers, bathmen,
         corn-dealers, lyre-turning shield-makers; and men put on
         their shoes and go out in the night –

EUELPIDES: I'm the one to ask about *that*! I, poor me, lost a
Phrygian wool cloak thanks to him. I'd been drinking a
bit one time in town, where I'd been invited for a baby's
naming-day party, and I'd just fallen asleep; and before the
others had begun dinner, that bird went and crowed! I
thought it was early morning, and set off for Halimus; and
I'd just poked my nose out of the city walls, and a clothes-
snatcher hits me from behind with a cudgel. I fall down and
I'm just about to cry out, and he's whipped off my cloak!

PEISETAERUS: Well, anyway, the Kite in those days was ruler
and king over the Greeks.

500   CHORUS-LEADER: Over the *Greeks*?

PEISETAERUS: Yes, and he as king was the first to institute the
custom of grovelling before kites.

EUELPIDES: Yes, I for one, by Dionysus, rolled on the ground
when I saw a kite; and then on my back, with my mouth
open, I swallowed an obol,[21] and so I had to trail my bag
home empty.

PEISETAERUS: The Cuckoo, again, was king of all Egypt and
Phoenicia; and whenever the Cuckoo said 'cuckoo', then all

the Phoenicians would get down to the job of harvesting their
wheat and barley in their fields.

EUELPIDES: Ah, so that's the real meaning of the expression
'Cuckoo! Cocks skinned and down to the job!'

PEISETAERUS: And they held their sway so strongly that if in
the cities of the Greeks some Agamemnon or Menelaus did
rule as king, there was a bird sitting on their sceptres, taking   510
a share of any presents they received.

EUELPIDES: Well, I didn't know *that*. And actually I used to
be amazed when a king like Priam, in the tragic plays, came
on stage with a bird; but I see – it was perching there keeping
an eye on Lysicrates[22] to see what . . . presents he received.

PEISETAERUS: And what is the most dreadful thing of all, is
that Zeus, who is king now, is shown standing with an eagle
on his head because he's king, and his daughter likewise with
an owl, and Apollo, like a servant, with a hawk.

CHORUS-LEADER: By Demeter, you're right about that. What
might the reason be for their having them?

PEISETAERUS: It's so that when someone's sacrificing and then
puts the offals, as the custom is, into the god's hand, *they*
can take the offals before Zeus can! Again, no man in those   520
days would swear by a god – they all swore by birds; even
today Lampon swears 'by Goose'[23] when he's trying to put
one over on you. That's how great and holy everyone held
you to be in the old days: now they treat you as slaves,
imbeciles, dummies. They've come now to throwing stones
at you, like they do at madmen; and in the very sanctuaries,
every fowler sets things to catch you – nooses, springes, limed
twigs, snares, light nets, heavy nets, traps. Then, when they've
caught you, they sell you by the batch, and the customers   530
feel you over when they buy you. And what is more – granted
they're determined to do so – but they don't even just have
you roasted and served up: they grate on cheese, oil, silphium,
vinegar, and they mix another dressing, a sweet and oily one,
and then sprinkle it over you hot, just as if you were carrion
meat!

CHORUS:
    Very painful, very painful indeed is the tale

540   you have brought before us, human! How I bewail
the sloth of my fathers, who
in my own time have cast away
these privileges that my forebears handed down to them!
But you, by the grace of fate and a happy turn of fortune,
have come to be my saviour;
for I shall entrust to you
my nestlings and myself, and join your following.

CHORUS-LEADER: Now stay here and instruct us what we should do; because life won't be worth living for us, unless by hook or by crook we can recover our kingship.

550   PEISETAERUS: Very well then, I instruct you first of all that there should be a single City of the Birds; and then you should completely encircle the whole of the air, and all this space between heaven and earth, with a wall of great baked bricks, like Babylon.

EUELPIDES: Oh, Cebriones and Porphyrion! what a formidable fortress of a city!

PEISETAERUS: And when that's been set up, you demand the rulership back from Zeus; and if he says no and is unwilling and doesn't immediately concede defeat, you proclaim a holy war against him, and prohibit the gods from passing to and fro through your territory with their cocks up, in the way they used to come down previously to debauch[24] their Alc-menas and their Alopes and their Semeles.[25] And if they do

560   violate your borders, then put a seal on their skinned pricks, so they can't screw those women any more. And I suggest you send another bird as a herald to the human race, telling them that the birds are kings and so in future they should sacrifice to the birds and then afterwards, secondly, to the gods. They should assign appropriately to the gods, one by one, that bird which matches each of them. If one is sacrificing to Aphrodite, one should offer barleycorns to the Coot bird; if one is offering a sheep to Poseidon, one should make a burnt offering of wheat grains to the Duck; if one is sacrificing something to Heracles, then honeyed stuffed loaves should be offered to the Seagull; while if one is sacrificing a ram to Zeus the King, why, the Wren is the King bird, and to him,

in advance of Zeus himself, an uncastrated gnat must be immolated.

EUELPIDES [*laughing*]: I like that – immolating a gnat! Now   570
let great Zan thunder away!

CHORUS-LEADER: And how are men going to get the notion that we're gods and not masquerading jackdaws – we who fly about and have wings?

PEISETAERUS: What a silly thing to say! Hermes too, surely, flies and wears wings, and he's a god; and so do lots and lots of other gods. Victory, for example, flies on golden wings, and so does Eros too; and Iris was said by Homer to be 'like to a tremulous dove'.

EUELPIDES: And Zeus – won't he thunder and send down upon us his *winged* lightning-bolt?

PEISETAERUS: Anyway, if in ignorance they think that you're nobodies and those characters on Olympus are gods, then a great cloud of sparrows and rooks must rise and gobble up   580
their seed in the fields. And then in their hunger let Demeter dole out wheat to them!

EUELPIDES: She won't be prepared to, by Zeus; you'll see, she'll just make excuses!

PEISETAERUS: And the ravens, for their part, by way of a test, should knock out the eyes of their sheep, and of the teams with which they plough their land. Then let Apollo, Healer that he is, heal them; he draws a salary for that!

EUELPIDES: Don't do that till I've first sold *my* two poor little oxen!

PEISETAERUS: But if they regard *you* as god, *you* as their life, *you* as Mother Earth, *you* as Cronus, *you* as Poseidon, then every blessing will be theirs.

CHORUS-LEADER: Tell me one of the blessings.

PEISETAERUS: To begin with, the locusts won't eat up their vine-blossoms; one troop of owls and kestrels will crush   590
them. Again, the ants and gall-wasps won't always be eating up their fig-trees; one flock of thrushes will make a clean sweep of the lot of them.

CHORUS-LEADER: But how will we give them wealth? Because that's something they're very much in love with.

PEISETAERUS: When they consult a diviner, these birds will show them which are the good mining sites, and they'll also reveal to the diviner which trading voyages will be profitable, so that no shipowner will perish.

CHORUS-LEADER: How do you mean, none will perish?

PEISETAERUS: When he consults the diviner about his voyage. one of the birds will always proclaim 'Don't sail now; there'll be a storm' or 'Sail now; you'll earn a profit'.

EUELPIDES: I'm buying a cargo-boat and turning shipowner; I'm not going to stay with you!

600   PEISETAERUS: And they will reveal to men the hoards of money which were buried by their forebears – because they know about them, at any rate people always say, 'Nobody knows where my treasure lies – except maybe some bird.'

EUELPIDES: I'm selling that cargo-boat and getting a mattock, and digging up crocks of gold.

CHORUS-LEADER: And how will they give men health? Health dwells with the gods.

PEISETAERUS: If they're prospering, isn't that great good health?

EUELPIDES: I can tell you it is; certainly no man who's fallen on hard times has a healthy life!

CHORUS-LEADER: And how will men ever reach old age? That too is in the gift of Olympus. Or must they die when they're little children?

PEISETAERUS: Not at all; the birds will add an extra three hundred years to their lives.

CHORUS-LEADER: Where will they get them from?

PEISETAERUS: Where from? From their own. Don't you know that 'five human ages lives the raucous crow'?[26]

610   EUELPIDES: Good grief, these birds are much better for us as rulers than Zeus is!

PEISETAERUS: Yes, aren't they much better? In the first place we don't have to build them temples of stone or to furnish the temples with golden doors; they will live under bushes and saplings, while for the prouder birds an olive tree will be their temple. Nor shall we go to Delphi or to Ammon[27] and
620   sacrifice there; we shall stand among the arbutus and the

oleasters, holding barley or wheat grains, and pray to them
with upstretched hands to give us a share of blessings – and
these we shall immediately receive, just by throwing them a
few grains of wheat.

CHORUS-LEADER: Old man, transformed from my worst
enemy into my dearest friend by far, there is no way that I
would ever again of my free will separate myself from your
policy!

CHORUS:
   And, exulting in your words,
   I give notice and I make oath   630
   that if you join thoughts with me in unity of purpose,
   honestly, sincerely, piously, to attack the gods,
   thinking in harmony with me, then
   not for much longer shall the gods
   be abusing *my* sceptre!

CHORUS-LEADER: Well then, whatever tasks need to be done
by brawn, we're ready to be assigned to; whatever needs to
be planned by brain, that all rests with you.

PEISETAERUS: Very well then, it's no time now for us, by Zeus,
to nod off, or to get the shilly-shallies like Nicias; we must   640
get something done as soon as possible.

TEREUS: Yes, but first come into my nest – within my sticks
and twigs, such as they are – and both of you tell us your
name.

PEISETAERUS: That's easy. My name's Peisetaerus.

TEREUS: And this man here?

EUELPIDES: Euelpides of Crioa.

TEREUS: Pleased to meet you both.

PEISETAERUS *and* EUELPIDES: Thank you.

TEREUS: Now then, come inside, this way.

PEISETAERUS [*to* EUELPIDES]: Let's go in. [*To* TEREUS] You
lead the way and take us inside.

   [TEREUS *moves towards the door;* PEISETAERUS *and*
   EUELPIDES *begin to follow him, but* PEISETAERUS *sud-*
   denly stops]

TEREUS: Come on!

PEISETAERUS: But – er, the thing is – hey, put back here again!

[TEREUS *retraces his steps*] Look here, tell us, how will I and
650   my friend here be able to live with you when you can fly and
we can't?

TEREUS: Oh, quite well.

PEISETAERUS: Take care now, because in Aesop's fables there's
some story told about the fox, how she went into partnership
with an eagle with unhappy results.

TEREUS: Have no fear. There's little root that you can chew,
and you'll have wings.

PEISETAERUS: In that case, let's go in. [*To the two* SLAVES]
Come on then, Xanthias and Manodorus, pick up the
luggage.

CHORUS-LEADER [*to* TEREUS, *as the party are again about to
go inside*]: I say – I want you – I said *you*!

TEREUS: Why are you calling?

CHORUS-LEADER: Take these men with you, and give them a
660   good lunch; but bring out here the nightingale, the sweet-
voiced fellow-songstress of the Muses, and leave her with us,
so that we can disport ourselves with her.

PEISETAERUS: Oh, yes, by Zeus, do do this as they ask; bring
the little birdie out of the sedges.

EUELPIDES: Yes, in the gods' name, bring her out, so that we
two also can have a look at the nightingale.

TEREUS: Well, if that's what the two of you want, that's what
we must do. [*Calling into the stage-house*] Procne! come
outside and show yourself to our visitors.

[PROCNE *comes out. She has a woman's body with a bird's
head, and is equipped as a piper*]

PEISETAERUS: Holy Zeus, what a lovely birdie! How fair, how
tender!

EUELPIDES: Do you know, I'd have great pleasure in spreading
her legs for her?

670   PEISETAERUS: And what a lot of gold she's wearing, like a real
young miss!

EUELPIDES: *I* think I'd like to kiss her.

PEISETAERUS: But, you silly fool, she's got a pair of spits for a
beak!

EUELPIDES: Why, then, we'll just have to peel her like an egg – strip the shell off her head and then kiss her like that.

TEREUS [*firmly, before* EUELPIDES *can put his idea into practice*]: Let's go.

PEISETAERUS: You lead the way for us, with fortune's blessing.
[TEREUS *leads* PEISETAERUS, EUELPIDES *and their* SLAVES *into the stage-house, leaving* PROCNE *outside*]

CHORUS:
O beloved one, O vibrant-throated one,
O dearest of birds,
partner of all my songs,
Nightingale my companion,
you have come, you have come, you have appeared,   680
bringing your sweet voice to me!
Now, you who play the notes of springtime
on the fair-sounding pipe,
introduce our anapaests.

CHORUS-LEADER: Come now, you men whom nature gives but feeble life, like to the race of leaves, weaklings modelled from clay, shadowy strengthless tribes, flightless creatures of a day, suffering mortals, men like the figures of dreams – pay attention to us, the immortal, the everlasting, the celestial, the ageless, whose counsels are imperishable, so that you may hear correctly from us all about the things on high, and   690 with accurate knowledge of the birth of birds and of the origin of gods and rivers and Erebus[28] and Chaos may tell Prodicus from me that in future he can get lost! In the beginning[29] there was Chaos and Night and black Erebus and broad Tartarus,[30] and there was no earth or air or heaven; and in the boundless recesses of Erebus, black-winged Night, first of all beings, brought forth a wind-gotten egg,[31] from which, as the seasons came round, there sprang Love the much-desired, his back sparkling with golden wings, Love like to the swift eddies of the wind. And he, mating by night with winged Chaos in broad Tartarus, enchicked our own race and first caused it to see the light. But of old there   700 was no race of immortal gods, until Love blended all things together; then, as one thing blended with another, Heaven came to be, and Ocean, and Earth, and all the imperishable race of blessed gods. Thus we are far the oldest of all the blest ones. That we are the children of Love is clear by many tokens. We fly, and we associate with those who are in love; and there are many pretty boys, who had sworn they wouldn't, but whom, when they were nearing the end of their bloom, their men lovers managed to screw thanks to our power, one giving a present of a quail, another a porphyrion, another a goose, another a Persian fowl. And mortals get all their greatest blessings from us birds. In the first place we make known the seasons of spring, of winter, of autumn: the time to sow, when the crane departs noisily for Africa; at that time it also signals to the shipowner to hang up his steering-paddle and go to sleep, and to Orestes[32] as well to weave himself a warm cloak, so he won't feel cold when he's out stripping other people. After that, again, the kite appears to herald another season, when it's time to shear the spring wool from the sheep; and then the swallow, when you ought to be already selling your winter cloak and buying a thin one. And we are your Ammon, your Delphi, your Dodona,[33] your Phoebus Apollo; for you embark on all your activities only after first going to consult the birds – on a trading voyage, on the acquisition of assets, on man's wedlock. And everything that has decisive significance in relation to divination you classify as a 'bird': an ominous utterance is a 'bird' in your terms, and you call a sneeze a 'bird', a chance encounter a 'bird', a sound a 'bird', a servant a 'bird', a donkey a 'bird'. Is it not plain that we are your prophetic Apollo? So, if you recognize us as gods, you will have musical prophets to consult at all seasons, in the winter, in the summer, in the moderate heat. And we won't flit away and sit snobbishly up there among the clouds, like Zeus; no, we will be with you and will give to you, to your children, to your children's children, health-and-wealth, happiness, life, peace, youth, laughter, dances, festivities – and birds' milk. In fact you'll find it possible to tire yourselves out with good things, so wealthy will you all be.

CHORUS:

> Muse of the thickets –
> tiotiotiotiotinx! –
> Muse of intricate song, with whom I,
> among the mountain glens and peaks –   740
> tiotiotiotiotinx! –
> perched on a leaf-clad ash tree –
> tiotiotiotiotinx! –
> bring forth from my vibrant throat
> sacred melodies of song for Pan
> and holy choral strains for the Mountain Mother –
> totototototototototinx! –
> from whence, like a bee,
> Phrynichus[34] was ever sucking the nectar of deathless   750
>   music
> to produce his honeyed songs –
> tiotiotiotiotinx!

CHORUS-LEADER: If any of you, spectators, wants to complete
the rest of his days pleasantly among the birds, let him come
to us. Everything which here by 〈human〉 custom is disgraceful, among us birds is creditable. For instance, if here custom
considers it disgraceful to strike one's father, away there with
us it's creditable if someone rushes at his father and hits him
and says 'Put up your spur, if you're fighting'. And if one of
you happens to be a tattooed runaway slave, among us he'll   760
be called a mottled francolin; and if someone happens to be
a Phrygian[35] – as thoroughly Phrygian as Spintharus – he'll
be a *pigeon* of Philemon's stock; and if he's a slave and a
Carian like Execestides, let him grow papas with us, and a
citizen kin-group will come to light for him. And if the son
of Peisias wants to betray the gates to the exiles, let him
become a partridge, a chick of the old cock; because with us
there's nothing disgraceful in playing partridge tricks!

CHORUS:

> In strains like these the swans –
> tiotiotiotiotinx! –   770
> all together sounding with their wings
> a harmonious note hymned Apollo –

tiotiotiotiotinx! –
sitting on the banks by the river Hebrus –
tiotiotiotiotinx!
Their cry pierced the clouds of heaven;
the many-hued tribes of beasts were spellbound,
and the windless, crystal air lulled the waves to rest –
totototototototototinx!

780 And all Olympus resounded,
and amazement seized its lords, and the Olympian
     Graces and Muses
sang out their joyous response –
tiotiotiotiotinx!

CHORUS-LEADER: There's nothing more advantageous or
more agreeable than to grow wings. For instance, if one of
you spectators were winged, and if he was hungry and bored
with the tragic performances, he could have flown out of
here, gone home, had lunch, and then when he'd filled himself
790 up, flown back here again to see us. And if some Patrocleides
among you happens to feel he needs to crap, he wouldn't
have had to ... exude into his clothes; he'd have upped and
flown off, let off a fart, taken a deep breath and flown back
here again. And if there's any of you who happens to be
having an affair with a married woman, and he sees the lady's
husband in the Councillors' seats, he again could have taken
wing from among you and flown off, then after screwing her
flown from her place back here again. So you see it's worth
any price to make yourself winged. After all, Dieitrephes,
who has only the 'wings' on his wicker flasks, was chosen
800 phylarch, then hipparch,[36] and then now, having started from
nothing, he's managing great affairs – he's become a tawny
horsecock!

[PEISETAERUS *and* EUELPIDES *re-enter; they are now
winged, and have feathers instead of hair on their heads*]

PEISETAERUS: Well, so much for that.

EUELPIDES [*laughing*]: By Zeus, I've never ever seen anything
funnier!

PEISETAERUS: What are you laughing at?

EUELPIDES: Those pinions of yours. Do you know what you look most like in your feathered state?

PEISETAERUS: Well, *you* look like a goose painted on the cheap.

EUELPIDES: And *you* look like a blackbird with a bowl pluck.

PEISETAERUS: We have been subjected to these comparisons, in the words of Aeschylus, 'not at the hand of another, but by our own feathers'![37]

CHORUS-LEADER: Come now, what have we got to do?

PEISETAERUS: First of all to give our city some great and noble name, and then after that to sacrifice to the gods. 810

EUELPIDES: That's what I think too.

CHORUS-LEADER: Well, let's see, what shall we have as our city's name?

PEISETAERUS: Do you want us to call it by that great Lacedaemonian name – Sparta?

EUELPIDES: Heracles! Do you think I'd use Sparta as a name for my city? I wouldn't even use esparto cords for a bedstead – no indeed – not if I had linen girths.

CHORUS-LEADER: Well, what name *shall* we give it?

EUELPIDES: Something from these parts – from the clouds and the regions of upper air – something very bombastic.

PEISETAERUS: Do you like 'Cloudcuckooville'?

CHORUS-LEADER: Wowee! You *have* found an absolutely great, beautiful name! 820

EUELPIDES: Ah, so *this* is the Cloudcuckooville where most of Theogenes' riches are, and all of Aeschines'!

PEISETAERUS: No, even better than that: it's the plain of Phlegra, where the gods got the better of the Children of Earth at bragging.

CHORUS-LEADER: A splendid sort of city, this! Now what god shall be our city's guardian? For whom shall we prepare the sacred robe?

PEISETAERUS: Why not leave Athena Polias[38] with the job?

EUELPIDES: And how, pray, can a city still be regarded as well ordered, where a god who's a woman stands with a suit of 830 armour on, and a Cleisthenes with a weaver's shuttle?

CHORUS-LEADER: Well, who *is* to possess the Storkade of our city?

PEISETAERUS: A bird from among yourselves, of the Persian breed, he who is spoken of everywhere as a most fearsome chick of the War-god.

EUELPIDES: O Chick our Lord! And how well suited the god is to living on rocks!

PEISETAERUS [*to* EUELPIDES]: Come on now, you go off to the air and do some odd jobs for the wall-builders: fetch them
840   up rubble, strip off and mix mortar, carry up a hod, fall off the ladder, post sentries, keep the fires covered, run the rounds with a bell, and spend the night there. And send one herald up to the gods, and also another from up here down to mankind, and then to return from there to me.

EUELPIDES: And *you* can stay right here and – go to blazes for me!

PEISETAERUS [*as* EUELPIDES *leaves*]: Go where I've sent you, my good friend. None of these things I've spoken of will get done without you. – As for myself, I'll summon the priest to organize the procession, so that I can sacrifice to the new
850   gods. [*Calling through the central stage-house door*] Boy, boy! pick up the basket and the lustral water.

[PEISETAERUS *goes into a wing of the stage-house. The* CHORUS *are joined by a* RAVEN *to act as their piper. During their ensuing song* XANTHIAS *and* MANODORUS *come out of the central door, one carrying the ritual basket, the other a basin of lustral water and other requisites for the sacrifice*]

CHORUS:
I agree, I concur,
I hereby join in recommending
that great and solemn processional hymns should rise
to the gods, and at the same time as well, to win
their favour, we should sacrifice a sheep or so.
Let it rise, rise, rise, the Pythian cry,[39]
and let Chaeris pipe an accompaniment to our song.
[*The piper plays on, solo, but untunefully.* PEISETAERUS

*comes out again, accompanied by a priest who leads a
small and scrawny billygoat]*
PEISETAERUS [*calling angrily to the piper*]: You, stop your
blowing! [*Coming closer to him*] Heracles, what's this? By   860
Zeus, I've seen plenty of strange things, but this I've never
seen, a raven in a piper's muzzle! – Priest, it's over to you;
sacrifice to the new gods.
PRIEST: I shall do so. Now where's the boy with the basket?
[*The basket and basin are carried round the stage-altar by
the two slaves. The* PRIEST *then raises his hands towards
heaven*] Pray ye to the Hestia⁴⁰ of the birds, and to the Kite
guardian of the hearth, and to each and all of the Olympian
birds and birdesses –
PEISETAERUS [*aside*]: Hail, O Hawk of Sunium, Lord of the
Great Bluethroat!
PRIEST: – and to the Swan of Pytho and Delos, and to Leto
the Quail Mother, and to Artemis the Goldfinch –
PEISETAERUS [*aside*]: Artemis isn't Colaenis any more, she's a   872
goldfinch, Acalanthis!
PRIEST: – and to Sabazius the Frigate-bird, and to the Great
Ostrich Mother of gods and men –
PEISETAERUS [*aside*]: O Lady Cybele the Ostrich, mother of
Cleocritus!
PRIEST: – to grant to the Cloudcuckoovillians health and safety
from all harm, both for themselves and for the Chians –
PEISETAERUS [*aside, laughing*]: I like the way the Chians get   880
tacked on everywhere!
PRIEST: – and also to the bird Heroes and Heroes' children, to
Porphyrion and White Pelican and Grey Pelican and Marsh
Harrier and Grouse and Peacock and Reed Warbler and Teal
and Skua and Hern and Tern and Marsh Tit and Great Tit –
PEISETAERUS [*breaking in*]: Stop, damn you! Stop invoking!
Whew! You wretched fool, what sort of victim are you invit-   890
ing ospreys and vultures to share? Can't you see that a single
kite could snatch this and make off with it? Leave us, you
and your wreaths; I'll sacrifice this beast all on my own. [*Exit
PRIEST*]

CHORUS:
>So now, I see, once again
>I must sound you out a second song,
>a holy and pious one for your ablution, and summon
>the Blest Ones – just *one* of them, if
900 >you want to have enough meat;
>for the sacrifice we've got here is nothing
>but beard and horns.

PEISETAERUS [*who has washed his hands during the song*]: As
we sacrifice, let us pray to the feathery gods –
[*He is interrupted by the arrival of a long-haired, ill-clad*
POET, *who enters singing*]

POET:
>Cloudcuckooville
>the blest O celebrate,
>Muse, in the strains of thy hymns!

PEISETAERUS: Where does this thing come from? [*To the* POET]
Tell me, who are you?

POET:
>I? One who pours forth a strain of honey-tongued words,
>a punctual servant of the Muses
910 [*speaking*] – to quote Homer.

PEISETAERUS: You mean you're a *slave*, with that long hair?

POET:
>Nay, all we songmasters
>are punctual servants of the Muses
[*speaking*] – to quote Homer.

PEISETAERUS: No wonder you've got such a *punctural* thin
cloak to match. But look, poet, what have you damn well
come up here for?

POET: I have composed many fine songs in honour of your
Cloudcuckoovilles, dithyrambs and maiden-songs and songs
à la Simonides.

920 PEISETAERUS: When did you compose these? Beginning when?

POET: Long, yea, long have I been celebrating this city.

PEISETAERUS: But look, I've only now begun making its
naming-day sacrifice, and it was just now that, as with a
child, I gave it its name!

POET:

Ah, the Muses' word is one that flies swiftly,
like the twinkling of horses' feet.
But do thou, O father, O founder of Aetna,
namesake of hieratic sanctities,
give to me whatsoever
thou art pleased by thy nod
graciously to grant me.   930

PEISETAERUS: This pest is going to be a real nuisance to us,
unless we can escape from him by giving him something. [*To
one of his* SLAVES] Here, you! you've got a jerkin and a tunic;
strip off and give it to the learned poet. [*The* SLAVE *takes off
his jerkin and hands it to* PEISETAERUS, *who presents it to
the* POET] Have the jerkin; you certainly seem to me to be
freezing.

POET:

Not unwillingly doth my loving
Muse accept this gift;
but do thou learn in thy heart
a word of Pindar's[41]

PEISETAERUS: The fellow just won't leave us!   940

POET:

'For among the Scythian nomads an outcast from the
      host is he
who possesses no shuttle-woven garment:
inglorious goeth' – a jerkin without a tunic.
Understand what I say to thee!

PEISETAERUS: I understand that you want to have that short
tunic! [*To the* SLAVE] Take it off; we must help the poet!
[*Giving the tunic to the* POET] Take this, and be off.

POET: I'm going – *and*, moreover, when I've gone, I shall
compose, in honour of your city, something like this:
      'O golden-throned one, glorify thou the shivery, icy land: 950
o'er snowswept plains with many pathways have I gone.'
[*As he departs*] Alalai!

PEISETAERUS [*calling after him*]: Why, by Zeus, you've already
escaped from that iciness, now you've got that little tunic! –
Really, that was a nuisance I never expected, that he should

have found out about our city as fast as that! [*To one of the* SLAVES] You take the lustral water and go round again. [*The* SLAVE, *who already has the ritual basket, takes the basin also, and carries both round the altar*] Let all speak fair!

[*Enter an* ORACLE-MONGER,[42] *carrying a scroll*]

ORACLE-MONGER [*urgently*]: Don't start sacrificing the goat!

960 PEISETAERUS: Who are you?

ORACLE-MONGER: Who am I? A collector of oracles.

PEISETAERUS: Then be damned to you!

ORACLE-MONGER: My dear sir, don't treat matters of religion lightly. There is an oracle of Bacis directly referring to Cloud-cuckoovilles.

PEISETAERUS: Then how come you weren't already quoting this oracle *before* I founded this city?

ORACLE-MONGER: I was restrained by the godhead.

PEISETAERUS: Well, there's nothing like hearing the verses.

ORACLE-MONGER [*unrolling scroll*]:
'But when wolves and steel-grey crows shall dwell
together in the parts between Corinth and Sicyon –'

PEISETAERUS: So what have I got to do with the Corinthians?

970 ORACLE-MONGER: By that expression Bacis was alluding to the air.
'First sacrifice to the Giver of All Gifts a white-fleeced
ram;
and whosoever cometh first as proclaimer of my words,
to him give a clean cloak and new sandals –'

PEISETAERUS: The sandals are in there too?

ORACLE-MONGER [*showing him the scroll*]: Here, have the book.
'– and give him the libation-bowl, and fill his hands with
offals –'

PEISETAERUS: It's also in there to give him offals?

ORACLE-MONGER [*as before*]: Here, have the book.
'And if, inspired youth, thou doest this as I enjoin thee,
thou shalt become an eagle 'midst the clouds; but if thou
givest not,
then shalt thou not be a turtledove, not a blue thrush, not
a woodpecker.'

PEISETAERUS: That's in there as well?   980
ORACLE-MONGER [*as before*]: Here, have the book.
PEISETAERUS [*producing a scroll of his own*]: The oracle, I see,
   doesn't at all resemble this one, which I wrote down from
   the words of Apollo:
      'But when a quack of a fellow shall come uninvited,
      annoy the sacrificers, and desire to share the offals,
      even then must thou strike him in the parts between the
      ribs –'
ORACLE-MONGER: I think you're making it up.
PEISETAERUS [*showing him the scroll*]: Here, have the book.
      ' – and show no mercy even to an eagle 'midst the clouds,
      not if he be Lampon nor if he be the great Diopeithes.'
ORACLE-MONGER: That's in there as well?
PEISETAERUS: Here, have the book! [*Beating him with the
   scroll*] Get to blazes out of here, will you?   990
ORACLE-MONGER [*turning to flee*]: Help! poor me! [*He runs
   off*]
PEISETAERUS [*calling after him*]: So run off, will you, and
   southsay somewhere else!
      [*Before* PEISETAERUS *can continue with the sacrifice,*
      METON *enters. He is a slightly effeminate-looking man,
      wearing high, soft boots and carrying some outsize geo-
      metrical instruments*]
METON: I come to you –
PEISETAERUS [*aside*]: Here's another pest! [*To* METON] What
   have *you* come to do, now? Of what form is your intention?
   What is the idea of your buskin'd journey?
METON: I want to measure out the air for you and divide it into
   street-blocks.
PEISETAERUS: And in heaven's name, who on earth are you?
METON: Who am I? Meton,[43] well known in Greece and ...
   Colonus.
PEISETAERUS [*pointing to his instruments*]: And tell me, what
   are these things you've got?
METON: Air-rulers. In the first place, you see, the whole of the   1000
   air is very similar in shape to a baking-cover. Well – [*here he
   begins to use his instruments to make a diagram on the*

ground] I will apply from above this curved ruler, insert dividers – you understand? –

PEISETAERUS: I *don't* understand!

METON: – and apply a straight ruler and take the measurement, so that your circle may become square, with an Agora in the middle and straight streets leading to it, right to the very centre, which will be circular and from which, as from a star, rays will beam straight in every direction.

1010 PEISETAERUS: The man's a Thales!⁴⁴ Meton –

METON: What's the matter?

PEISETAERUS: Please understand that I'm your friend, and take my advice and skip it out of the way.

METON: What's the danger?

PEISETAERUS: Like in Sparta, they're expelling foreigners, and there are large numbers of buffets on the march through town.

METON: You're not having a civil conflict, are you?

PEISETAERUS: No, indeed.

METON: Then what's it about?

PEISETAERUS: There's a unanimous decision to bash up all quacks!

METON: Then, you know, I think I'll beat a retreat. [*Preparing to go*]

PEISETAERUS: Yes, indeed, because I don't know if you can get away in time. They're close, and attacking – here! [*Striking him*]

METON: Help! poor me! [*He runs off*]

PEISETAERUS [*calling after him*]: Didn't I tell you long ago? Go
1020   somewhere else, will you, and take your *own* measurements!

[PEISETAERUS *turns to find that an* ATHENIAN INSPECTOR *has entered from the other side. He is fat and luxuriously dressed, and carries a pair of voting-urns*]

INSPECTOR: Where are the honorary consuls?

PEISETAERUS: Who is this Sardanapallus?

INSPECTOR: I have been chosen by lot to come here to Cloud-cuckooville as inspector.

PEISETAERUS: Inspector? And who sent you here?

INSPECTOR [*with obvious disgust*]: Some wretched paper of
    Teleas's.

PEISETAERUS: Well then, would you like to take your pay and
    just leave without being put to any trouble?

INSPECTOR: Yes, by the gods, I would. At least, I wanted to
    stay at home and speak in the Assembly; there's been some
    negotiations with Pharnaces that I've been handling.

PEISETAERUS: Take your pay, then, and go; here it is! [*Striking
    him*]

INSPECTOR [*angrily*]: What was that meant to be?   1030

PEISETAERUS: An Assembly meeting about Pharnaces. [*He
    strikes him again*]

INSPECTOR: Witness, everyone! I'm being assaulted – I, an
    inspector! [*Exit with all dignified speed*]

PEISETAERUS [*calling after him*]: Shoo off, will you – and
    take your voting-urns with you! – Isn't it dreadful? They're
    actually sending inspectors to our city already, before we've
    even sacrificed to the gods!

    [PEISETAERUS *moves to resume the sacrifice, only to find
    that a* DECREE-SELLER *has entered, carrying a large scroll*]

DECREE-SELLER [*reading*]: 'And if the Cloudcuckoovillian be
    guilty of an offence against the Athenian –'

PEISETAERUS: What sort of nuisance is *this*, now, this scroll?

DECREE-SELLER: I'm a decree-seller, and I've come here to you
    to sell you some brand-new laws.

PEISETAERUS: Like what?

DECREE-SELLER [*reading from another part of the scroll*]: 'The   1040
    Cloudcuckoovillians shall use ⟨Athenian⟩ measures, weights
    and decrees, in like manner as the Olophyxians.'

PEISETAERUS: *You'll* be using the same ones as the *Asphyxians*
    in a minute! [*Setting upon him*]

DECREE-SELLER: Here, what's the matter with you?

PEISETAERUS [*chasing him off with blows*]: Take your laws
    away, will you? I'll give you a law or two today!

INSPECTOR [*re-entering, behind* PEISETAERUS]: I summon
    Peisetaerus to appear in the month of Munichion on a charge
    of wanton outrage.

PEISETAERUS [*turning*]: Really, you! Were you *still* here?
[*Chasing him off*]

DECREE-SELLER [*re-entering, behind* PEISETAERUS, *reading*]:
1050   'And if any person expel the officers and fail to admit them
according to the decree –'

PEISETAERUS [*turning*]: Dash it all, were *you* still here as well?
[*Chasing him off*]

INSPECTOR [*re-entering, as before*]: I'll ruin you! I'll write
down you're ten thousand drachmas –

PEISETAERUS [*turning and rushing at him*]: And *I'll* scatter
those voting-urns of yours. [*He knocks the urns out of the*
INSPECTOR's *hands; the* INSPECTOR *flees*]

DECREE-SELLER [*re-entering, as before*]: Do you remember
when you used to soil the pillar of the law, of an evening?
[*He lifts up his clothes and breaks wind at* PEISETAERUS]

PEISETAERUS: Ugh! Grab him, someone! [*One of the* SLAVES
attempts to seize the DECREE-SELLER, *but he manages to*
escape. PEISETAERUS *calls after him*] Here, stay here, will
you? [*To the* SLAVES] Let us get away from here as fast as
we can, to sacrifice the goat to the gods inside. [PEISETAERUS
and the SLAVES *go inside, taking the goat and sacrificial*
equipment with them]

CHORUS:
    Henceforth to me, the all-seeing
    and all-ruling, will all mortals
1060   sacrifice with prayerful prayers.
    For I survey all the earth,
    and I preserve the flourishing crops.
    slaying the brood of all tribes
    of animals, which with all-devouring jaws
    feeds both upon all that swells from a seed-pod on the
        ground
    and, sitting in the trees, upon their fruit;
    and I slay them that with most hostile injury
    ravage sweet-scented gardens;
    and all creeping and biting things, as many
1070   as exist, perish in slaughter
    beneath my wing.

CHORUS-LEADER: On this day in particular, as you know, the
   proclamation is repeated that if any of you kills Diagoras the
   Melian[45] he'll receive a talent, and if anyone kills one of the
   long-dead tyrants, he'll receive a talent. So we too now want
   to make the same proclamation here: If any of you kills
   Philocrates the Sparrovian, he will receive a talent, and if he
   brings him in *alive*, four talents; because he strings together
   siskins and sells them at seven for an obol, then also abuses
   thrushes by blowing air into them and putting them on dis-   1080
   play, and fills blackbirds' nostrils with their own feathers,
   and likewise captures pigeons, keeps them imprisoned, and
   forces them to act as decoys, confined in a net. That's the
   proclamation we want to make. And if any of you keeps
   birds caged up in your courtyard, we order you to release
   them; and if you don't obey, you'll be arrested by the birds
   and *you* in your turn will be imprisoned to act as decoys on
   our estates.

CHORUS:

   O happy tribe of winged
   birds, who in winter
   need wear no cloaks!   1090
   Nor in summer does the hot
   far-shining ray stifle us;
   for I dwell among the leaves
   in the bosom of the flowery meadows,
   when the divine-voiced cicada, drunk with the sunshine,
   in the noonday heat sounds out his high-toned song.
   And I winter in cavern hollows,
   sporting with the mountain nymphs;
   and in spring we feed on the virginal
   white-swelling myrtle-berries and   1100
   the fruits of the Graces' garden.

CHORUS-LEADER: We want to say something to the judges on
   the subject of our victory – all the good things we'll give them
   all if they vote for us, so that they'll get rewards far surpassing
   those offered to Paris. In the first place – what every judge
   most yearns for – the owls of Laureium will never desert you;
   they'll dwell in your houses, nest in your purses and hatch

out small change. Then in addition to that, you'll live in
1110   houses like temples, because we'll roof your homes eagle-
fashion. And if you're allotted some little public office and
want then to do some plundering, we'll put a sharp hawkbill
in your hands. If you're dining out somewhere, we'll send
you each a crop. But if you don't vote for us, then make
yourselves metal crescents to wear over you, like the statues
have; because anyone among you who doesn't have a crescent
– well, when you're wearing your best white clothes, that's
just when we'll use them to punish you as all the birds cover
you with their droppings!

[*Re-enter* PEISETAERUS]

PEISETAERUS: Birds, our sacrifice has been successful. But how
1120   odd that no messenger is here from the walls, from whom
we could learn what's been happening there. Ah, here comes
someone running, panting like an Olympic athlete!

[*Enter* FIRST MESSENGER, *running and breathless*]

FIRST MESSENGER: Where-where is he, where-where-where
is he, where-where-where is he, where-where is Governor
Peisetaerus?

PEISETAERUS: Here I am.

FIRST MESSENGER: The construction of your wall is finished.

PEISETAERUS: Very good.

FIRST MESSENGER: A most splendid and magnificent piece of
work; so broad that Proxenides of Boaston and Theogenes
could drive two chariots past each other in opposite directions along the top of it, with horses under their yokes as big
as the wooden horse of Troy.

PEISETAERUS: Heracles!

1130   FIRST MESSENGER: And its height – I actually measured it
myself – is a hundred fathoms.[46]

PEISETAERUS: Poseidon, what a height! Who built it to such a
size?

FIRST MESSENGER: Birds, no one else – no Egyptian brick-
carrier was there, no mason, no carpenter – they did it with
their own hands, so that I was amazed. From Africa there
came some thirty thousand cranes, who had swallowed
stones for the foundations; these were shaped by the corn-

crakes with their bills. Another ten thousand storks made
bricks. Water was brought to the air from below by the 1140
thickknees and the other river-birds.

PEISETAERUS: And who brought the clay for them?

FIRST MESSENGER: Herons, in hods.

PEISETAERUS: But how did they get the clay *into* their hods?

FIRST MESSENGER: That, my good sir, was really the cleverest
idea they'd devised. The geese used their feet like shovels to
dig into the clay and pitch it into the hods for them.

PEISETAERUS: Is there, then, anything that *feet* can't do?

FIRST MESSENGER: And there were the ducks too, I assure you,
with aprons on, laying the bricks; and behind them, like 1150
bricklayers' lads, flew the swallows, carrying in their beaks
the mud for the plaster topping.

PEISETAERUS: After that, why should anyone take on hired
labour any more? Let me see now, what else? Who made the
woodwork to finish off the walls?

FIRST MESSENGER: Birds were the carpenters, and very skilful
ones – the nuthatches, who hatcheted away making the gates
– and the noise of their hatcheting was like in a shipyard!
And now the whole place there is furnished with gates, 1160
bolted, guarded all round, patrolled by men with bells; everywhere there are watches and signal-fires in place on the
towers. – But I'll be nipping off to have a wash; you do the
rest now yourself. [*Exit*]

CHORUS-LEADER [*to* PEISETAERUS, *who seems to have been
struck speechless*]: Here, what's up with you? Are you
amazed that the fortification's been completed so quickly?

PEISETAERUS: Yes, by the gods, I am; it *merits* amazement. It
seems to me truly tantamount to – a pack of lies. [*Another
MESSENGER is seen approaching*] But now here's a guard
running on, come to us to report what's happening away
there, with a war-dance look on his face.

SECOND MESSENGER [*running up to* PEISETAERUS]: Help, 1170
help! Help, help! Help, help!

PEISETAERUS: What's the matter here?

SECOND MESSENGER: Something most appalling has been
done to us! One of the gods from Zeus has just flown through

the gates into the air, evading the jackdaw guards on daytime
sentry duty.

PEISETAERUS: The fearful, the audacious act to be guilty of!
Which one of the gods?

SECOND MESSENGER: We don't know. He had wings, that we
do know.

PEISETAERUS: Well, shouldn't you have sent a border patrol
after him straight away?

SECOND MESSENGER: But we have – we've sent thirty thousand
1180   mounted Hawk Archers, and every one of them is on the
move, with talons bent – kestrel, buzzard, vulture, great owl,
eagle – and the sky is awhir with the rush and whistle of
wings as the god is hunted for. And he's not far away – in
fact he's already hereabouts somewhere!

[*He runs off*]

PEISETAERUS: Then we must take up slings and bows! [*Calling
within*] Come here, all the orderlies! sling and shoot! And
someone give me a sling!

[XANTHIAS, MANODORUS *and other* SLAVES *come out,
with bows and slings, one of which is given to* PEIS-
ETAERUS]

CHORUS:
War is unleashed, war beyond description,
1190   between me and the gods! Now, everyone, guard
the cloud-girt air, which Erebus childed,
that none of the gods pass through this way
unseen by you –

CHORUS-LEADER [*speaking through music*]: – and be on the
watch, everyone, looking out in every direction; for already
the sound can be heard close at hand of the whirling wings
of an airborne god.[47]

[IRIS *is swung into view, aloft, by the theatrical crane. She
sports a large pair of wings and her light gown billows out
like a sail*]

PEISETAERUS [*to* IRIS]: Hey, you, where, where, where are you
1200   flying? Stay still! Keep where you are and don't move! Halt!
Stop running away! [IRIS *at last comes to a halt, suspended
in mid-air*] Who are you? Where are you from? [IRIS *remains*

silent] You should be saying where on earth you've come from!

IRIS: I am from the gods, the Olympian gods.

PEISETAERUS: And what's your name? *Paralus* or *Salaminia*?

IRIS: Iris the fast.

PEISETAERUS: Do you mean a fast boat, or a fast bitch?

IRIS: What is this?

PEISETAERUS: Won't a buzzard fly up and arrest this person?

IRIS: Arrest *me*? What on earth is this awful nonsense?

PEISETAERUS: You are really going to howl! [*He lashes out at her, hitting the cage in which she rides and setting it swinging and rocking*]

IRIS: This is an extraordinary business!

PEISETAERUS: By what gate did you enter the fortress, you utter villain?

IRIS: By Zeus, I've no idea [*mimicking his tone*] 'by what gate'.   1210

PEISETAERUS [*to one of his* SLAVES]: Did you hear her, how she dissembles? [*To* IRIS] Did you make an approach to the Chief Jackdaws? Aren't you answering? Have you had a seal from the storks?

IRIS: What's the matter with you?

PEISETAERUS: You *haven't* had one?

IRIS: You *are* sane, are you?

PEISETAERUS: Wasn't there any Chief Bird there, either, to stick an entry-pass on you?

IRIS: I can assure you, my man, nobody's been *sticking* me!

PEISETAERUS: And so you fly like this, do you, without a word, through a city which is not yours and through the void?

IRIS: What other route should the gods fly by?

PEISETAERUS: By Zeus, I've no idea – but not *this* one. Anyway,   1220
you're committing a crime right now. Do you know this, that if you got your deserts you'd have had the strongest claim of any rainbow to be seized and put to death?

IRIS: But I'm immortal!

PEISETAERUS: No matter, you'd still have been put to death. Because, I tell you, it'll be a quite intolerable slight to us, in my opinion, if when we rule over all else, you gods are going to persist in your insubordination and still won't recognize that you in your turn have now got to obey your superiors. Now tell me, I say, where you're sailing on those wings of yours.

1230   IRIS: Me? I'm flying from my Father to mankind, to tell them to sacrifice to the Olympian gods, to slaughter sheep at sacrificial hearths, and to fill the streets with the savour of oblations.

PEISETAERUS: What are you talking about? What gods?

IRIS: What gods? Us, the gods in heaven.

PEISETAERUS: You think you're gods?

IRIS: Why, what other god is there?

PEISETAERUS: Birds are men's gods now, and to them men must sacrifice – and not, by Zeus, to Zeus!

IRIS [declaiming in tragic style]:
O fool, O fool, provoke not thou the hearts
Of gods, most terrible, lest all thy race
1240   Be overthrown by Justice, with the mattock
Of Zeus, and smoky flame do calcinate
Thyself and all the enclosure of thy house
With bolts Licymnian!

PEISETAERUS: Listen, you! Stop your spluttering! And keep still! Tell me, do you think it's a Lydian or a Phrygian you're trying to scare, talking like that? Do you know that if Zeus annoys me any further, I'll calcinate his palace 'and the halls
1250   of Amphion'[48] with incendiary eagles, and I'll send porphyrion-birds to heaven to attack him, dressed in leopard-skins, over six hundred in number? And once upon a time just one Porphyrion[49] caused him some trouble! And if you annoy me at all, then I'll take on the servant first – raise up her legs and screw her, yes, Iris herself, so as to amaze her how at my age I'm still hard enough to stand three rammings![50]

IRIS: Blast you to pieces, mister, you and your language!

PEISETAERUS [waving his arms at her]: Shoo off, won't you? Quickly, now! [Clapping his hands] Away! Shoo!

IRIS [as the crane slowly begins to swing her off]: I swear my Father will put a stop to your insolence!

1260   PEISETAERUS: Oh, dash it all, can't you fly off somewhere else and calcinate some younger fellow? [IRIS disappears]

CHORUS:
We have shut out the gods of the race of Zeus
so that they will no longer pass through my city,
nor yet will any mortal upon earth any more
send the smoke of holy sacrifices by this way to the gods.

PEISETAERUS: This is terrible! The herald who went to man- 1270
kind – is he never going to come back again?

[Enter FIRST HERALD *(a bird), carrying a golden crown*]

FIRST HERALD: O Peisetaerus, O blest one, O most wise one,
O most renowned one, O most wise one, O most astute one,
O thrice blest one – oh, do give me my cue!

PEISETAERUS: What is it you're saying?

FIRST HERALD [*presenting the crown*]: All the peoples honour
you for your wisdom, and crown you with this golden crown.

PEISETAERUS [*allowing the crown to be placed on his head*]: I
accept it. Why do the peoples honour me so?

FIRST HERALD: Founder of the most renowned City of the Sky,
do you not know what great honour you have won among
men, and how many of them you have who are passionate
lovers of this country? Before you founded this city, in those 1280
days all men were Spartan-mad, all hairy and hungry and
dirty and Socrates-y and carrying clubbed sticks. But now
they've made a complete about-turn and they're bird-mad,
and out of delight they're doing, in faithful imitation, all the
things that birds do. First of all, when they got out of bed in
the morning, right away they'd all fly together, just like us,
to forage ... among the laws; and then they'd swoop down
together upon the bookstalls, and there browse through
decrees. And they were so blatantly bird-barmy that many of 1290
them had actually had the names of birds given to them.
There was one, a lame tavern-keeper, who was called 'Partridge'; Menippus had the name 'Swallow'; Opuntius, 'Raven
minus an eye'; Philocles, 'Lark'; Theogenes, 'Sheldrake';
Lycurgus, 'Ibis'; Chaerephon, 'Bat'; and Syracosius, 'Jay'.
And Meidias, he was called 'Quail'; because he really looked
like a quail who'd been hit over the head by a quail-tapper.[51] 1300
And from love of birds, they were all singing songs where
there was a swallow in the lyrics, or a duck, or a goose, or a

pigeon, or a pair of wings, or even a tiny bit of feather tacked on. Well, that's what the news is like from down there. But I tell you one thing: there'll be more than ten thousand people coming here from down there, wanting wings and a crook-taloned life-style; so you'd better get wings from somewhere for your new settlers. [*Exit*]

PEISETAERUS: Well then, by Zeus, we've no business now standing about. You [*to* XANTHIAS] go as fast as you can and fill up all the baskets and hampers with wings, and let Manes bring the wings out here to me; and I'll receive those from down there who come to us.

[XANTHIAS *and* MANES (MANODORUS) *go inside. During the ensuing song* MANES *goes back and forth, bringing out basket after basket full of wings*]

CHORUS:
Very soon all mankind
will call this city populous.

PEISETAERUS: Only let fortune be with us!

CHORUS: My city is the prevailing passion –

PEISETAERUS [*to* MANES, *who is with difficulty bringing out a large basket*]: Bring it quicker, I tell you!

[MANES *puts down the basket and hurries back inside*]

CHORUS:
For what does this city not have
that is good for a man to settle amidst?
Wisdom is here, Desire, the immortal Graces,
and the happy countenance
of gentle-hearted Tranquillity.

PEISETAERUS [*to* MANES, *as before*]: What lazy service! Hurry faster, won't you? [MANES *puts down his second basket and goes back in*]

CHORUS:
Let someone quickly bring a basket of wings;
and [*to* PEISETAERUS] do you again urge him on –

PEISETAERUS: By hitting him, like this [*gesture*]!

CHORUS: Because he's a very slow fellow, slow as a donkey.

PEISETAERUS: A miserable Manes, he is.

1310

1320

CHORUS:
　　But first of all you arrange   1330
　　these wings in order,
　　the musical wings together, and the prophetic wings,
　　and the sea-wings, and then make sure you intelligently
　　examine each individual when you wing him.
　　[*As* PEISETAERUS *is sorting out the wings,* MANES *comes
　　out with a third, even larger basket*]
PEISETAERUS: By the kestrels, I will not keep my hands off you
　　any longer, when I see you being so miserably slow! [*He
　　rushes at* MANES, *who evades his blows and runs back
　　inside*]
　　[*Enter a* YOUNG MAN, *singing*]
YOUNG MAN: O to be a high-flying eagle,
　　that I might soar high above the great unharvested
　　over the swell of the blue-grey sea!
PEISETAERUS: It looks as though that messenger will prove no   1340
　　liar. Here comes someone singing about eagles.
YOUNG MAN: Yahoo! There's nothing sweeter than flying!
⟨PEISETAERUS: You've come wanting wings, have you?⟩
YOUNG MAN: Yes, I'm bird-mad, I'm airborne, I want to live
　　with you, and I'm keen on your laws.
PEISETAERUS: What laws? The birds have many laws.
YOUNG MAN: All of them; but especially that among birds it's
　　considered creditable to throttle and peck your father.
PEISETAERUS: Yes, and indeed we consider any bird very manly
　　who has beaten up his father while still a chick.   1350
YOUNG MAN: That's just why I'm eager to migrate here, to
　　throttle my father and have the lot.
PEISETAERUS: Ah, but we birds have an ancient law written
　　on the Pillars of the Storks: 'When the father-stork has reared
　　all his young storks and made them ready to leave the nest,
　　then the young birds must in their turn maintain their father.'
YOUNG MAN: Then, by Zeus, I *have* profited by coming here,
　　if I'm actually even going to have to *feed* my father!
PEISETAERUS: No, not at all; because, my good fellow, since   1360
　　you've come here wishing us well, I'll wing you like an orphan

fowl. [*As he searches in one of the baskets*] And, my lad, I'll give you some rather good advice – the sort of thing I was taught myself when I was a boy. Don't you hit your father; just take this wing [*giving it to him*] and this spur in your other hand [*ditto*], imagine that this comb you've got is a cock's [*putting a crest on his head*], and do garrison duty, serve on expeditions, maintain yourself by earning pay, and let your father live. In fact, as you're a fighting type, fly off to the Thracian Coast and fight there.

1370 YOUNG MAN: By Dionysus, I think you're giving me good advice, and I'll follow it.

PEISETAERUS: You'll certainly be sensible to. [*Exit* YOUNG MAN]

[*Enter* CINESIAS, *singing and dancing on thin and unsteady legs*]

CINESIAS:
 Lo, I soar on light wings towards Olympus;
 I flit now to this path of song and now to that –

PEISETAERUS: This creature wants a whole load of wings!

CINESIAS: – fearless in mind and body, pursuing a new –

PEISETAERUS [*approaching him*]: We welcome Cinesias, the man of linden-bark. Why have you come here circling in circles with halting foot?

1380 CINESIAS: I want to become a bird – [*singing*]
 'a clear-voiced nightingale!'

PEISETAERUS: Stop singing. Just *tell* me what you're saying.

CINESIAS: I want to be given wings by you and then fly up aloft and procure from the clouds new air-whisked, snow-swept preludes.

PEISETAERUS: You mean one can get preludes from the *clouds*?

CINESIAS: Why, our whole art depends on them. The most
1390 brilliant of dithyrambs are misty, murky, black-rayed, wing-whisked. You'll soon know, when you hear some.

PEISETAERUS: Oh, no, I won't.

CINESIAS: Oh yes, by Heracles, you will! I'll go through all the airs for you. [*Singing and dancing*]
 'Likenesses of winged
 coursers of the sky,

of long-necked birds –'

PEISETAERUS [*trying to stop him*]: Whoa there!

CINESIAS [*taking no notice*]:

'O to leap my upward way

and travel together with the blasts of the wind –'

PEISETAERUS [*rummaging in one of the baskets*]: By Zeus, I am going to put a stop to these blasts of yours. [*He takes out a pair of wings and begins to chase the dancing* CINESIAS *around, flicking the wings at him like a lash*]

CINESIAS [*dodging hither and thither*]:

'– now going towards the way of the south,

now bringing myself closer to the north wind,

cleaving the harbourless furrows of the sky –'   1400

[*Stopping, out of breath; in an offended yet amused tone*] Really elegant, old man, this cleverness of yours, really clever!

PEISETAERUS: Why, don't you *enjoy* being 'wing-whisked'?

CINESIAS: Is this how you treat me, the trainer of cyclic choruses, whom the tribes are always fighting to have?

PEISETAERUS: Then would you like to stay with us and train here, for Leotrophides, a chorus of flying birds, a tribe of the Corncrakeites?

CINESIAS: It's plain you're making fun of me. But anyway I'm not going to stop, you can be sure of it, until I've got myself wings and run right through the airs. [*He dances off*]

[*Enter an* INFORMER. *He wears a patched and tattered cloak, and is singing softly to himself*]

INFORMER:

'Who are these birds, possessing nothing, with patterned   1410
   plumage?'

[*Louder*] O long-winged, many-hued swallow!

PEISETAERUS: This is no trivial nuisance we've stirred up. Here comes someone else this way singing to himself.

INFORMER:

O long-winged, many-hued, I say again!

PEISETAERUS: I think he's singing that ditty about his cloak; he looks as though he's in need of quite a lot of swallows.

INFORMER: Who is it who gives wings to people coming here?

PEISETAERUS: He's right here. But you should tell me what you need.

1420 INFORMER: Wings, wings I need! ask not a second time.

PEISETAERUS: You're not thinking of flying straight to Pellene, are you?

INFORMER: No, no; I'm a summons-server to the islanders, and an informer –

PEISETAERUS: Happy you, to have such a profession!

INFORMER: – and a lawsuit-hunter: and so I want to get wings and then sweep all the way round the allied states, serving summonses.

PEISETAERUS: Will you summons them any more skilfully with wings on your shoulders?

INFORMER: No, no; it's in order, for one thing, not to be bothered by pirates, and secondly so that I can come back again from those parts together with the cranes, having swallowed for ballast a large number of lawsuits.

1430 PEISETAERUS: You mean that's the job you do? Tell me – a strong young man like you – you denounce foreigners for a living?

INFORMER: What am I supposed to do? I never learnt how to dig.

PEISETAERUS: But surely there are other decent occupations, from which a big chap like you could make a living honestly, rather than cobbling up lawsuits.

INFORMER: My good sir, don't keep admonishing me – give me wings.

PEISETAERUS: I'm trying to do that now, don't you see, by my words.

INFORMER: And how, pray, can you give a man wings just by words?

PEISETAERUS: Why, don't you know, words can make everyone take wing.

INFORMER: Everyone?

1440 PEISETAERUS: Haven't you heard, in the barbers' shops, when the fathers of young men continually talk like this: 'It's terrible, the way Dieitrephes with his talk has winged my lad's ambition to be a chariot-driver'? And another says that his boy's mind has taken wing and gone a-flutter over tragedy.

INFORMER: So they're actually given wings by words?

PEISETAERUS: That's right. By words a man is uplifted and his mind is made to soar aloft. And in the same way *I* want to give wings to *your* mind by my good advice, and make you 1450 turn to a lawful occupation.

INFORMER: But I don't want to.

PEISETAERUS: Then what are you going to do?

INFORMER: I'll not disgrace my ancestry. Informing is my hereditary way of life. No, wing me with the light, swift wings of a hawk or a kestrel, so that I can summons the foreigners, then take proceedings here, then fly back there again.

PEISETAERUS: I understand. What you mean is this: in order that the foreigner will have a judgement against him here before he arrives.

INFORMER: You understand perfectly.

PEISETAERUS: And then *he's* on his way here by sea, while *you* fly back there to seize his property.   1460

INFORMER: You have it exactly. One has to be no different from a whipping-top.

PEISETAERUS: I understand your 'whipping-top'; and in fact, by Zeus [*rummaging in one of the baskets*], I have some splendid wings of just that kind – Corcyraean ones![52] [*He produces a double-thonged whip*]

INFORMER: Heaven help me, you've got a whip!

PEISETAERUS: No, a pair of wings – with which I'm going to make you act the whipping-top this very day! [*He begins to crack the whip at the informer*]

INFORMER [*trying to dodge the whip*]: Help, help!

PEISETAERUS: Wing it away from here, won't you? Drop off, damn and blast you! I'll give you some law-twisting villainy in a minute! [*The informer flees.* PEISETAERUS *turns to find that* XANTHIAS *and* MANES *have come out, perhaps attracted by the noise*] As for us, let's take the wings and go. [PEIS-ETAERUS *and the two* SLAVES *go inside, each carrying a basket*]

CHORUS:
1470   Many and unheard-of and marvellous
are the places we have overflown, and
strange the things we have seen.
There is an extraordinary tree
that grows far away
past Heartford, the Cleonymus,
useful for nothing, but all the same
huge and trem ... ulous.
In the spring it always
sprouts and produces denunciations,
1480   and in winter, contrariwise,
it sheds a foliage of shields.

There is also a country far away,
right next to the darkness, in
the lampless wilderness,
where men take lunch
with the Heroes, and live with them –
except in the evening:
at that time it ceased
to be safe to meet them.
1490   For if any mortal chanced to meet
the Hero Orestes by night,
he was left naked, after being stricken by him
all down his right side.

[Enter PROMETHEUS,[53] holding up his outer garment so as to muffle his head completely, and carrying a parasol, unopened, in his other hand]

PROMETHEUS [to himself]: Oh, dear, dear me! Zeus simply mustn't see me! [Aloud] Where is Peisetaerus?

[PEISETAERUS comes out, carrying a night-stool which presumably needs to be emptied. On seeing the muffled figure he stops abruptly]

PEISETAERUS: Hey, what is this? What's this mufflement?

PROMETHEUS: Can you see any of the gods there behind me?

PEISETAERUS: I certainly can't. But who are you?

PROMETHEUS [*not hearing him*]: What time of day might it be?

PEISETAERUS: What time? A little bit after midday. But *who are you?* 1500

PROMETHEUS [*still not hearing*]: Knocking-off time, or later?

PEISETAERUS [*almost shouting by now*]: Dammit, you're making me sick!

PROMETHEUS [*thinking he has been told the time*]: And what is Zeus doing? Is he clearing away the clouds, or gathering them together?

PEISETAERUS [*fortissimo*]: Blast you to blazes!

PROMETHEUS [*thinking he has been told it is cloudy*]: In that case, I'll uncover. [*He unmuffles himself*]

PEISETAERUS [*recognizing his distinctive garb*]: Our dear Prometheus!

PROMETHEUS: Stop, stop! don't shout!

PEISETAERUS: Why, what's the matter?

PROMETHEUS: Just be quiet and don't mention my name. You'll be the ruin of me, if Zeus sees me here. But so that I can tell you all the news from up above, take my parasol here and hold it over us, so that the gods up there won't see me.

PEISETAERUS [*as he takes the parasol and opens it*]: Wowee, 1510 that was a fine idea of yours – showed real forethought! Slip under here quickly now, and then speak with confidence. [PROMETHEUS *joins him under the parasol*]

PROMETHEUS: Listen now.

PEISETAERUS: Speak on; I'm listening.

PROMETHEUS: Zeus is *finished!*[54]

PEISETAERUS [*matter-of-factly*]: Oh? About when was he finished off?

PROMETHEUS: Right from the time that you colonized the air. You see, none of the human race sacrifices anything to the gods any longer, nor has any aroma from thigh-bones come up to us since that time, and without any sacrifices we're 1520 fasting like at the Thesmophoria.[55] And the barbarian gods are so hungry, they're shrieking like Illyrians and threatening to march from up-country against Zeus, unless he secures the opening of the ports so that sliced offals could be imported.

PEISETAERUS: You mean there are some other gods, barbarian ones, up-country from you?

PROMETHEUS: Of course there are Barbarian ones: that's where Execestides gets his ancestral patron from!

PEISETAERUS: And what name do these barbarian gods go by?

PROMETHEUS: What name? Triballians.⁵⁶

1530   PEISETAERUS: Ah, I see, so that's the origin of the swear-word 'bally'!

PROMETHEUS: Absolutely right. And I can tell you one thing for sure: there will be ambassadors coming here, to discuss a settlement, from Zeus and from the up-country Triballians. But don't you make peace, unless Zeus hands his sceptre back to the birds and also gives you Princess⁵⁷ to be your wife.

PEISETAERUS: Who's Princess?

PROMETHEUS: She's a most beautiful maiden, who is custodian of the thunderbolt of Zeus and of absolutely everything else –

1540   wisdom, law and order, good sense, dockyards, mudslinging, paymasters and three-obolses.

PEISETAERUS: You mean she looks after *everything* for him, does she?

PROMETHEUS: That's right: if you receive *her* from his hands, you've got everything. That's why I came here, in order to tell you this. I always have been friendly to human beings.

PEISETAERUS: Yes: thanks to you, alone of the gods, we can eat broiled sprats.⁵⁸

PROMETHEUS: And I hate all the gods, as you know.

PEISETAERUS: Yes, you always were one for the hatred of the gods.

PROMETHEUS: A downright Timon.⁵⁹ But now, so that I can

1550   go back again, let me have the parasol, so that even if Zeus does see me from up there, he'll think I'm an attendant to a basket-bearer.

PEISETAERUS [*giving him the parasol*]: Yes, and you can be stool-bearer as well – take this stool [*thrusting the night-stool into* PROMETHEUS' *other hand*].

[PROMETHEUS *leaves;* PEISETAERUS *goes inside*]

CHORUS:
  And near the Shadefeet there lies
  a lake where unwashed
  Socrates charms up men's souls.
  Thither it was that Peisander[60] came,
  asking to see the spirit
  which had deserted him while he still lived;
  for a sacrifice he had
  a camel-lamb, whose throat he cut,   1560
  just like Odysseus,[61] and then . . . made off;
  and then there came up to him from below,
  drawn by the jugulation of the camel,
  Chaerephon[62] the Bat.

  [*Enter* POSEIDON, HERACLES, *and a* TRIBALLIAN GOD]

POSEIDON: Here, presenting itself to the view, is the city of
  Cloudcuckooville, to which our embassy is directed. [*Turning, and noticing the* TRIBALLIAN's *dress*] Here, what are
  you trying to do? Is this how you drape yourself, from right
  to left? You'd better re-drape your cloak from left to right,
  like this. [*He shows the* TRIBALLIAN *how his own cloak is
  draped. The* TRIBALLIAN *tries to re-drape his, but gets in a
  tangle*] What now, you wretched fool? Are you made like
  Laespodias?[63] Oh, Democracy, where are you going to lead   1570
  us to one of these days, if the gods can actually vote *this*
  fellow into office? [*He proceeds to re-drape and adjust the*
  TRIBALLIAN's *cloak himself. Before he has finished, the*
  TRIBALLIAN *moves and spoils his work*] Will you keep still?
  [POSEIDON *tries to adjust the cloak again, but again the*
  TRIBALLIAN *moves*] Oh, go to blazes! You're far and away
  the most barbarous god I've ever seen! [*He tries again, and
  this time is satisfied with the result. He turns to* HERACLES]
  Well now, Heracles, what do we do?

HERACLES: You've already heard *my* opinion, which is that I
  want to throttle this man, whoever he is, who has blockaded
  the gods.

POSEIDON: But, my dear fellow, we've been chosen as
  ambassadors to discuss a settlement.

HERACLES: Then I'm twice as much resolved to throttle him.

[*A platform is rolled out of the central door, on which are* PEISETAERUS, *his two* SLAVES, *a table with food and kitchen utensils, and a brazier. Some birds are being prepared for roasting.* PEISETAERUS *is giving orders, which are rapidly carried out, to the two* SLAVES *alternately*]

1580 PEISETAERUS: Someone give me the cheese-grater. – Silphium,[64] please. – Pass me cheese, somebody. – Light the coals.

POSEIDON [*coming up to* PEISETAERUS, *followed by his colleagues*]: We three gods bid you greeting, sir.

PEISETAERUS [*not looking up*]: Look, I'm grating the silphium on.

HERACLES [*looking closely at the birds*]: Here, what sort of meat is this?

PEISETAERUS [*still not looking up*]: It's a number of birds who have been found guilty of attempting to rebel against the bird democracy.

HERACLES: And that's why you're grating silphium on them first, is it?

PEISETAERUS [*who now, having finished his grating, at last looks at his visitors*]: Oh, hullo, Heracles! What's up?

POSEIDON: We have come from the gods as ambassadors to discuss a termination of hostilities –

PEISETAERUS [*to one of his* SLAVES]: There's no oil in the flask. [*The* SLAVE *takes the flask away to be filled, returning with it unobtrusively during the following dialogue*]

1590 HERACLES: And bird-meat certainly should be glistening with the stuff.

POSEIDON [*continuing his speech*]: Since we for our part are gaining nothing by the war, and you for yours, if you were on friendly terms with us the gods, would now be having rainwater in your puddles and enjoying halcyon days the whole time. On all these matters we have come with full powers.

PEISETAERUS: Well, in the beginning we never initiated hostilities against you, and now we are willing, if you wish, to make a peace treaty – if, that is, you are prepared, even so

late, to do what is right. And what is right is the following: 1600
that Zeus should restore the sceptre to us, the birds, again.
And if we reach a settlement on these terms, I shall invite the
ambassadors to lunch.

HERACLES: That's good enough for me; I vote yes.

POSEIDON [*to* HERACLES]: What, you wretched fool? You're
an imbecile and a glutton, you are. Are you going to deprive
your father of his sovereignty?

PEISETAERUS: Is that what you say? Won't you gods actually
have *greater* power, if birds are in control down below? As
things are, mortals, hidden beneath the clouds, can swear
perjured oaths by you with bowed heads; but if you have the 1610
birds for allies, then, when a man swears 'by the Raven and
by Zeus', the raven will come by, swoop on the perjurer
before he's noticed, strike him in the eye and knock it out.

POSEIDON: By Poseidon, *that's* certainly a good idea!

HERACLES: I think so too. [*To the* TRIBALLIAN] What do you
say, eh?

TRIBALLIAN: Nabaisatreu.

HERACLES: You see? He approves as well.

PEISETAERUS: Now hear what a further great benefit we'll also
confer on you. If any man vows to sacrifice an animal to one
of the gods and then tries to slip out of it with a quibble, 1620
saying 'The gods are patient', and out of greed fails to pay
his vow, we'll dun him for that too.

POSEIDON: Tell me, how?

PEISETAERUS: When that man happens to be counting out
some little sum of money, or is sitting in the bath, a kite will
swoop down, snatch undetected the value of *two* sheep, and
carry it up to the god.

[*The three gods withdraw to confer among themselves*]

HERACLES: I again vote to hand over the sceptre to them.

POSEIDON: Ask the Triballian as well, then.

HERACLES [*raising his club*]: Hey, Triballian, do you want a
whopping?

TRIBALLIAN [*in evident terror*]: Yo basha hide wit steek?

HERACLES: He says I'm quite right.

POSEIDON: Well, if that's what you both think, then I agree. 1630

HERACLES [*eagerly leading his colleagues back to* PEISETA-
ERUS, *who has resumed preparing the meal*]: I say, we've
decided to do as you demand about the sceptre.

PEISETAERUS: Oh, yes, and there's something else that I've just
remembered. As regards Hera, I resign her to Zeus; but the
maiden Princess must be given to me as my wife.

POSEIDON: You have no desire for a settlement. [*To his colleagues*] Let us go back home. [*He turns to leave*]

PEISETAERUS: I couldn't care less. [*Calling into the stage-
house*] Cook! be sure you make the dressing sweet.

HERACLES [*taking* POSEIDON *by the arm*]: Poseidon, god bless
you, man, where are you rushing off to? Are we going to
fight a war for the sake of one woman?

1640 POSEIDON: Well, what *are* we to do?

HERACLES: What are we to do? Settle!

POSEIDON: What, you wretched fool? Don't you know he's
been taking you in the whole time? And you're harming
yourself, you know. If Zeus dies, after handing over his
sovereignty to these birds, you'll be a pauper; because you've
got all the property coming to you that Zeus leaves behind
at his death.

PEISETAERUS [*to* HERACLES]: Good grief, the way he's trying
to hoodwink you! Come over here to me, so I can tell you
something. [PEISETAERUS *and* HERACLES *converse apart*]

1650 Your uncle's trying to cheat you, you poor fool. According
to the law, you don't get the least little share of your father's
estate, because you're a bastard, you're not legitimate.

HERACLES: Me a bastard? What are you talking about?

PEISETAERUS: That's what you are, I tell you, because you're
the son of a foreign woman. Or how do you imagine that
Athena as a daughter could be the Heiress, if she had legitimate brothers?

HERACLES: Well, what if my father at his death leaves me his
property as bastard's portion?

PEISETAERUS: The law won't allow him to. Poseidon here,
who's raising your hopes now, will be the first to lay hold

1660 on your father's property, claiming that *he* is his legitimate
brother. Indeed, I'll actually quote you the law of Solon:

'A bastard shall not have the rights of a near kinsman, if there are legitimate children. Should there be no legitimate children, the next of kin shall share in the estate.'

HERACLES: And I, then, have no share at all in my father's property?

PEISETAERUS: No, indeed, absolutely not. And tell me, has your father yet introduced you to his phratry?[65]

HERACLES: Not me he hasn't. And actually I'd been wondering about that for a long time.   1670

PEISETAERUS [as HERACLES' *bewilderment shows signs of turning to anger*]: Then why stare open-mouthed at the sky with assault and battery in your eyes? If you side with us, I'll make you sovereign, and supply you with birds' milk.

HERACLES: For my part, I have thought all along that your claim as regards the girl is justified, and I am for handing her over to you.

PEISETAERUS [*to* POSEIDON]: And what do you say?

POSEIDON: I vote against.

PEISETAERUS: The whole thing depends on the Triballian. [*To the* TRIBALLIAN] What do you say?

TRIBALLIAN: Pitty tall gelly Pincess ah hand over to buds.

HERACLES: He says to hand her over.

POSEIDON: No, by Zeus, he does *not* say to hand her over;   1680
he's just twittering like the swallows.

HERACLES: So he's saying hand her over to the swallows!

POSEIDON [*to* HERACLES *and the* TRIBALLIAN]: You two settle it, then, and come to an agreement. That's your decision, so I won't say anything.

HERACLES [*to* PEISETAERUS]: We have decided to agree to all your demands. Now come yourself with us to heaven, so that there you can receive Princess and everything else.

PEISETAERUS [*pointing to the birds on the table, which he has by now got ready for cooking*]: Why, then, these birds have been cut up just at the right time for the wedding.

HERACLES: Do you want me, then, in the meantime, to stay   1690
here and roast this meat? *You* can go.

POSEIDON: Roast the meat? You're talking like a great big greedy-guts. Come with us, will you?

HERACLES [*reluctantly tearing himself away from the meat*]:
Oh, I would have been happily situated!

PEISETAERUS [*calling into the stage-house*]: Bring me out here
a bridegroom's robe, someone!

[*A robe is brought to* PEISETAERUS, *who then departs
with the three gods. The platform with the table, etc., is
withdrawn into the stage-house*]

CHORUS:
And found in Accusatia, near
the Clepsydra, is the villainous
race of Tongue-to-Belly Men,
who reap and sow
and gather vintage with their tongues –
and also figs;
1700   they are barbarian stock,
Gorgiases and Philips.
And it is because of these
philippic Tongue-to-Belly Men
that everywhere in Attica
the tongue is cut out by itself.

[*Enter* SECOND HERALD]

SECOND HERALD: O you who enjoy all good fortune, blessings
too great to express, O thrice-happy winged race of birds,
welcome your monarch to his opulent halls! For he
1710   approaches, shining as no brilliant star in gold-gleaming rush
has ever shone to behold, nor has the far-gleaming splendour
of the sun's rays ever so shone out as does he who comes,
bringing with him a wife of beauty unspeakable to describe,
and wielding the thunderbolt, the winged weapon of Zeus.
A nameless fragrance ascends to the depths of the sphere, a
beautiful spectacle, and the wreaths of incense-smoke are
wafted apart by the breezes. But here he is in person: now let
there be opened the holy, auspicious lips of the divine Muse!

[*As the* HERALD *retires,* PEISETAERUS *and* PRINCESS
enter, as bridegroom and bride, PEISETAERUS *holding the
thunderbolt of Zeus. The* CHORUS *make way for them and
then make a circle around them, singing*]

CHORUS:

    Arise, divide, deploy, make way!   1720
    fly round him who is blest with blest fortune.
    Oh, oh! her charm, her beauty!
    How enviable for this city the marriage you
     have made!

CHORUS-LEADER:

    Great, great is the good fortune that surrounds
    the race of birds
    thanks to this man; so now welcome
    with hymeneal chants and bridal songs
    our lord and his Princess.   1730

CHORUS:

    Once upon a time Olympian Hera
    and the Great One who ruled over the gods
    from his lofty throne
    were united by the Fates
    with such a wedding-song as this.

FIRST SEMICHORUS:

    Hymen O, Hymenaeus O!

SECOND SEMICHORUS:

    Hymen O, Hymenaeus O!

CHORUS:

    And blooming young Eros
    of the golden wings guided
    the tautened reins
    as groomsman at the wedding of Zeus   1740
    and the blessed Hera.

FIRST SEMICHORUS:

    Hymen O, Hymenaeus O!

SECOND SEMICHORUS:

    Hymen O, Hymenaeus O!

PEISETAERUS:

    Your chants delight me, your songs delight me;
    I rejoice in your words.

CHORUS-LEADER:

    Come now, glorify also

his earth-shaking thunders
and the fiery lightnings of Zeus
and the dreadful flashing thunderbolt.

CHORUS:

O mighty golden blaze of the lightning!
O immortal fiery bolt of Zeus!
1750   O thunders that rumble beneath the earth
and at the same time bring down the rain!
With you this man now shakes the earth;
he has gained power over all that Zeus possessed
and Princess too, who sat by Zeus's throne, is his.
Hymen O, Hymenaeus O!

CHORUS-LEADER:

Now follow the nuptial flight,
all you winged tribes
of my companions, to the courts of Zeus
and to the bridal bed.

PEISETAERUS [to PRINCESS]:

Stretch out your hand,
1760   blest one, take hold
of my wings, and dance with me;
I'll lift and bear you up.

[PEISETAERUS and PRINCESS lead the way out, dancing;
the CHORUS follow, singing as they go]

CHORUS:

Alalalai! Hail Paean!
Hurrah for your triumph,
O most exalted of gods!

Translated by Alan Sommerstein (1987)

MENANDER

THE GIRL FROM SAMOS

PREFACE

The Girl From Samos is not merely typical of Menander's comedies, it is typical of more than a *thousand* other New Comedies as well. It seemed as if the Athenian audience never tired of watching the same story with simply the names changed. Indeed, why they were so enamoured of the self-same rape/love story would be a good subject for a psychology thesis.

Demeas, the young man's stepfather, has had a long relationship with a lady he brought back from Samos sometime before. To say that the island is famous for its hookers will tell the whole story.

In the protracted absence of both their fathers, Moschion falls in love with Plangon, the neighbour's daughter, whom he has compromised in the dark corner of a party.

But what distinguishes this rape-in-the-dark scenario from the dozens of others where the bride is made pregnant is that here the two young people know each others' identities from the start. Moschion's only worry is that when his pragmatic father ultimately returns, he will disapprove of his desire to marry a woman whose own father is too poor even to provide a dowry.

Now here's the twist of this particular comedy: in the fullness of time, old Demeas' mistress, Chrysis, gives birth to a boy, who dies almost immediately. Soon after, Plangon makes young Moschion a parent as well. Since they fear the imminence of their older men's arrival, the generous Chrysis agrees to pretend that the youngsters' baby is her own. Thus when they arrive they merely think that old Demeas has been made a father, but he is ambivalent about this sudden parenthood being thrust upon him. As he sarcastically remarks to his son, he now has a mistress who's become a wife.

But he has some doubts that the baby was his in the first place and is now going to kick Chrysis out of the house. When Moschion protests he retorts:

DEMEAS: Why not? Do you expect me to bring up a bastard in my house, to humour someone else? That's not my line at all.

MOSCHION: For Heaven's sake! What's legitimacy or illegitimacy? We're all human, aren't we? . . . I don't think birth means anything. If you look at the thing properly, a good man's legitimate, a bad man's both a bastard and a slave. (134–41)

This is Menandrian humanism *avant la lettre* (the concept as well as the word was actually coined by the Romans). Although he was severe with his mistress/wife, he is overjoyed that his son is about to marry the very girl he has intended for him.

But as he is preparing for his son's wedding, he catches sight of Chrysis giving suck to the baby. He prizes the information from the annoying servant that the baby at his mistress's breast is the product of his stepson. He explodes, yet calms himself. It is not the lad's fault after all.

She's the one to blame for what's happened. She caught him, I imagine, when he'd had a spot too much to drink, when he wasn't quite in control of himself. Yes, that's obviously what happened. Strong wine and young blood can work a lot of mischief . . . (338–41)

But his strait-laced neighbour Nikeratos is shocked and furious at his future son-in-law's behaviour and upbraids him mythologically: 'O deed most dread! O Tereus, Oedipus, Thyestes! O all the incestuous loves of legend! You've put them all in the shade' (495–6). But the knot is quickly untied as Moschion explains that the baby is in fact his own. And the mother is Plangon.

And yet the father of the bride-to-be is quickly disabused. There follows a little bit of classical slapstick and even some lively stichomythia (sharp dialogue in alternate lines) as each grandparent attempts to snatch the infant from Chrysis.

NIKERATOS: Bring out my baby.
DEMEAS: That's a laugh. It's *mine*.
NIKERATOS: It is not.
DEMEAS: Yes, it is. (579)

Of course, this being a comedy, the tug of war with the baby ends nuptially.

But not before – and this occurs quite often in Menander – there are deep suspicions of incest, for example, Man, unaware, is about to marry his own daughter, etc., but is reprieved at the very last minute. And yet with a slight leap of the imagination we can see that, although, strictly speaking, Moschion is only a stepson, it does not diminish the temporary crisis in which the boy is accused of defiling his parents' bed. Indeed, this ending is not unlike Beaumarchais' *Marriage of Figaro* where the hero's mother, unwittingly, is about to be the bride.

All is saved at the usual time in such comedies – at the last minute. The ending is typically Menandrian. The air is thick with apologies, each contrite for mistrusting one another – especially young Moschion. And the most ashamed Nikeratos who ends the play with the blessing:

> In the face of witnesses, I give you, Moschion, this woman to be your wife, for the procreation of legitimate children. And as dowry I give her all my possessions when I die (which God forbid! May I live for ever). (725–8)

Of course he cannot live forever but the story they have first enacted will.

CHARACTERS

MOSCHION, *a young Athenian gentleman*
DEMEAS, *his adoptive father*
PARMENON, *their servant*
CHRYSIS, *a Samian girl, Demeas' mistress*
NIKERATOS, *Demeas' neighbour*
A COOK

Silent Characters

PLANGON, Nikeratos' daughter
Servants

[*The text of Acts I and II is badly mutilated, but from what does remain, and from the rest of the play, it is possible to make reasonable deductions about the content of the missing portions. The Prologue is spoken by Moschion, the junior lead. This play has no need of a divine Prologue, because Moschion can tell us all the necessary facts. Some ten or eleven lines are missing from the start of his speech: it is likely that in them he explained that he had been adopted by Demeas, an elderly bachelor.*]

ACT I

The scene is a street in Athens. There are two houses, that of DEMEAS *on the audience's left, that of* NIKERATOS *on the right. Between them is an altar and image of Apollo.*

MOSCHION [*addressing the audience*]: . . . Oh, what's the point of moaning? It hurts, because I *did* do wrong. Telling the story will be painful, I reckon, but it will make more sense to you if I explain in some detail what my father's like. Right from the time when I was a very small boy, I had everything I wanted; I remember it well, but I won't dwell on it now. He was kind to me when I was too young to appreciate it. I was treated just like every other boy of good family,[1] 'one of the crowd', as the saying goes, though I certainly wasn't born with a silver spoon in my mouth (we're all alone, so I can tell you that). I made my mark when I backed a dramatic production and gave generous contributions to charity. I had horses and hounds, too – at father's expense. I was a dashing officer in the Brigade, sufficiently in funds to give a bit of help to a friend in need. Thanks to my father, I was a civilized human being. And I gave him a civilized return: I behaved myself.

Then – I'll tell you all about us at one go, I've nothing else to do – then Father fell for a girl from Samos. Well, it could happen to anyone. He tried to keep it quiet, being a bit embarrassed. But I found out, for all his precautions, and I reckoned that if he didn't establish himself as the girl's protector, he'd have trouble with younger rivals for her favours. He felt a bit awkward about doing this (probably because of me), but I persuaded him to take her into the house.

[*Some twenty or so lines are missing here, in which Moschion probably explained that Chrysis was now in residence in Demeas' house, that she had been pregnant and under instructions from Demeas to get rid of the child,*

*that Demeas and his neighbour Nikeratos were abroad on
business, and that Nikeratos had a daughter, Plangon.*]

. . . Well, this girl's mother became friendly with Father's girl,
and she was often in their house, and they'd visit us, too.
One day, I came home from our farm, and happened to find
them all here in our house, with some other ladies, to celebrate the festival of Adonis.[2] The proceedings, as you can
imagine, were producing a good deal of fun, and I joined
them as a sort of spectator. In any case, the noise they were
making would be keeping me awake, for they were taking
their tray 'gardens' up to the roof, and dancing, and making
a real night of it, all over the place.

I hesitate to tell you the rest of the story. Perhaps I'm
ashamed, where shame is no help, but I'm still ashamed.
[*Pause*] The girl got pregnant. Now I've told you that, you
know what went before, too. I didn't deny that I was responsible, but went without being asked to the girl's mother, and
promised to marry her daughter as soon as my father came
home. I gave my word I would. The baby was born a few
days ago, and I formally acknowledged it as mine. Then, by
a lucky chance Chrysis – that's the girl from Samos – had her
baby too.

[*About twenty-five lines are missing, which must have
explained that Chrysis' baby had died, and that she had
taken Plangon's to nurse in its place. Moschion left the
stage, probably left, to the harbour, and Chrysis entered
from the house, possibly carrying the baby. Her opening
lines are lost – they may have been to or about the baby –
and then the text continues.*]

CHRYSIS: Here they come, hurrying home. I'll just wait and
hear what they're talking about.
[*Enter* MOSCHION *and* PARMENON, *left*]
MOSCHION: You actually *saw* my father with your own eyes,
Parmenon?
PARMENON: How often do I have to tell you? Yes, I did.

MOSCHION: And our neighbour, too?

PARMENON: Yes, they're both back.

MOSCHION: I'm very glad.

PARMENON: Now, you've got to brace yourself, and raise the question of your marriage right away.

MOSCHION: How can I? I've lost my nerve now that the crunch has come.

PARMENON: What do you mean?

MOSCHION: It's too embarrassing to face my father.

PARMENON [*his voice rising*]: And the girl you seduced, and her mother? What about *them*? Man, you're shaking like a leaf.

CHRYSIS [*coming forward*]: For goodness' sake, what's all the shouting about?

PARMENON: Oh, Chrysis is here, too. [*To* CHRYSIS] You really 70 want to know why I'm shouting? That's a laugh. I want the wedding *now*, I want this chap here to stop wailing at this door here. I want him to remember that he gave his word. Ceremonial offerings, garlands, pounding sesame for the wedding cake – that's what I want to be helping with. Don't you think I've got good reason to shout?

MOSCHION: I'll do everything that's required. No need to go *on* about it.

CHRYSIS: I'm sure you will.

MOSCHION: What about the baby? Do we let Chrysis here go on nursing it and saying it's her own?

CHRYSIS: Why ever not?

MOSCHION: Father will be furious.

CHRYSIS: He'll cool down again. For he's in love too, my dear, 80 desperately in love, just as much as you. And that brings even the angriest man to terms pretty fast. And I'd put up with anything, myself, before I'd let a wet-nurse bring up Baby here in some slum.

[*Some twenty-three lines are missing, during which Chrysis and Parmenon clearly went into the house, leaving Moschion soliloquizing on stage. Only fragments of the end of his speech remain.*]

90   MOSCHION: ... most miserable man in the world. I'd better
hang myself right away. A man conducting his own case
needs to win favour.³ I haven't enough experience of cases
like this. I'll go and practise in some quiet place. This is a
tricky case I've got on my hands. [*He goes off, right*]
     [*Enter* DEMEAS *and* NIKERATOS, *left, with luggage and
     servants*]
DEMEAS: You must notice the change of scene already, the
difference between here and that horrible place.
NIKERATOS: Oh, yes. Black Sea, thick old men, fish by the
boat-load, a life to make you sick: the city of Byzantium,
100 everything gall and wormwood. God! But here is pure benefit
for the poor.
DEMEAS: Dear Athens! I wish you all the blessings you deserve,
so that we who love our city may be prosperous and happy.
[*To servants*] Inside with the luggage, boys. You there, why
are you standing goggling at me like a paralytic? [*The servants take the luggage inside*]
NIKERATOS: What I found most extraordinary about that
place, Demeas, was that sometimes you couldn't see the sun
for weeks on end. It looked as if a thick fog was hiding it.
110 DEMEAS: Well, there was nothing very marvellous to see there,
so the natives get only the bare minimum of light.
NIKERATOS: How right you are.
DEMEAS: Well, let's leave that for others to worry about.
Apropos of the business we were discussing, what do you
mean to do?
NIKERATOS: You mean your son's marriage?
DEMEAS: Yes, of course.
NIKERATOS: I haven't changed my mind. Let's name a day and
get on with it. And good luck to it.
DEMEAS: That's your considered opinion?
NIKERATOS: It certainly is.
DEMEAS: Mine, too. And I got there first!
NIKERATOS: Call for me as soon as you come out.
DEMEAS: There are a few points ...

     [*About fourteen lines are missing from the end of the Act.*

*Demeas and Nikeratos obviously went into their respective
houses, and one of them must have indicated the arrival of
a band of revellers.*]

[FIRST CHORAL INTERLUDE]

ACT II

Enter MOSCHION, *right, and* DEMEAS, *from his house.
Neither sees the other*

[*The beginning of Moschion's speech is mutilated, but the
general sense is clear.*]

MOSCHION: Well, I haven't done any of the rehearsing I   120
intended. When I got outside the city on my own, I started
imagining the wedding service, planning the guest-list for the
reception, seeing myself escorting the ladies to the ritual bath,
cutting and handing round the wedding-cake, humming the
wedding-hymn – behaving like an utter fool. When I'd had
enough – help! Here's my father. He must have heard what
I was saying. Glad to see you, Father.

DEMEAS: Glad to see you, son.

MOSCHION: You look a bit – er – grim.

DEMEAS: I do. I thought I had a mistress, but I seem to have   130
acquired a wife.

MOSCHION: A wife? What do you mean? I don't understand.

DEMEAS: I seem to have become – quite without my knowledge
and consent – the father of a son. Well, she can take him and
get out of the house – to the Devil, for all I care.

MOSCHION: Oh, *no!*

DEMEAS: Why not? Do you expect me to bring up a bastard in
my house, to humour someone else? That's not my line at
all.

MOSCHION: For Heaven's sake! What's legitimacy or illegitimacy? We're all human, aren't we?

DEMEAS: You must be joking.

MOSCHION: By God I'm not, I'm perfectly serious. I don't think
140   birth means anything. If you look at the thing properly, a
       good man's legitimate, a bad man's both a bastard and a
       slave.

[*Some twenty lines are missing or mutilated, but it is clear
that in the course of them Moschion persuaded his father
to keep the child, and Demeas raised the question of his
son's marriage, and found him willing.*]

MOSCHION: I'm longing to get married ... and I want to be
       obedient, Father, not just to seem so.
DEMEAS: Good boy! ... If our neighbours here agree, you shall
150   marry her at once.
MOSCHION: I hope you'll ask no questions, but accept that I'm
       serious, and help me?
DEMEAS: Accept that you're serious? Ask no questions? I
       understand, Moschion. Now I'll run over to my neighbour
       here, and tell him to start getting ready for the wedding. All
       that you want from our household will be waiting for you.
MOSCHION: I'll go in now, sprinkle myself with holy water,
       pour a libation, put incense on the fire – and then I'll fetch
       the girl.
160   DEMEAS: No, not yet, until I'm sure we have her father's
       consent.
MOSCHION: He won't say no. But it wouldn't be the thing for
       me to go in with you, and get in the way of the preparations.
       [*He goes off left*]
DEMEAS: Coincidence must really be a divinity. She looks after
       many of the things we cannot see. I had no idea that Mos-
       chion had fallen in love!

[*About twenty-seven lines are missing, and the next
twenty-five are badly damaged. But enough survives to
make it clear that Nikeratos came out of his house, and
Demeas persuaded him that the wedding should take place
that day.*]

DEMEAS: Parmenon! Hey, Parmenon! [*Enter* PARMENON *from the house*] Go and get garlands, an animal for sacrifice, 190 sesame seeds for the cake. Buy up the market, and come back here.

PARMENON: You leave it to me, sir.

DEMEAS: And hurry up. Do it now. And bring a cook, too.

PARMENON: A cook too. After I've bought the rest?

DEMEAS: Yes.

PARMENON: I'll get some money and be off at the double. [*He goes into the house*]

DEMEAS: You not on your way to market yet, Nikeratos?

NIKERATOS: I must just go in and tell my wife to get the house ready. Then I'll be right on Parmenon's heels. [*He goes into his own house*]

PARMENON [*reappearing with a basket, and talking back over his shoulder*]: I haven't a clue what it's all about, except these are my orders, and I'm off to market *now*.

DEMEAS: Nikeratos will have a job persuading his wife, and 200 we mustn't waste time on explanations. [*Seeing* PARMENON] You still here? Run, man, run!

[*About ten lines are missing from the end of the Act, during which Parmenon obviously left for the market, right, Demeas went into his house, and the Chorus entered.*]

[SECOND CHORAL INTERLUDE]

ACT III

Enter DEMEAS, *from his house*

DEMEAS: In the midst of a fair voyage, a storm can suddenly appear from nowhere. Such a storm has often shattered and capsized those who a moment ago were running nicely before the wind. That's what's happened to me now. Five minutes 210 ago, I was organizing the wedding, attending to the religious obligations, with everything going according to plan. [*He moves down-stage and addresses the audience*] I'm coming

down-stage to you, now, as the victim of a knock-out blow.
It's incredible! Tell me if I'm sane or mad. Am I getting the
facts all wrong and bringing disaster on myself?

The minute I went in, full of enthusiasm to get the wedding
organized, I gave the servants a straightforward account of
everything, told them to make all the necessary preparations
– clean, bake, arrange the ritual basket.[4] Things were going
quite well, but the speed at which things were happening
naturally produced a certain amount of confusion. The baby
had been dumped out of the way on a couch, and it was
howling. The women servants were all shouting at once –
'Flour, please! Water, please! Oil, please! Charcoal, here!' I
was passing some of these, lending a hand, and I happened
to go into the pantry. I was inspecting and selecting more
supplies, and didn't come out immediately. Well, while I was
in there, a woman came downstairs into the room next to
the pantry – it's where the weaving's done, in fact, and you
have to go through it to go upstairs or into the pantry. This
woman was Moschion's old nurse, getting on now. She was
once my slave, but I set her free. She saw the baby crying and
no one taking a bit of notice of it. She didn't know I was
inside, but thought she could speak safely, so she went up to
the baby, with all the usual baby-talk like 'Who's a little
love, then?' and 'Precious treasure! Where's Mummy?' She
cuddled it, and walked it up and down, and when it stopped
crying, she murmured to herself, 'Dear me, it seems only
yesterday that I was cuddling and nursing Moschion, just
like this, and now that his son here has been born . . .'

[Four or five lines are lost or damaged.]

. . . Then a servant-girl came running in, and the Nurse
said, 'Give the baby his bath. What do you all think you're
doing? His father's wedding day, and you're neglecting the
little one.' The girl immediately hissed, 'Don't *shout*.
Master's at home.' 'No! Where is he?' 'In the pantry!' And
then, raising her voice, 'Mistress is asking for you, Nurse,'
and, quietly, 'Quick! He hasn't heard a word. We're in luck.'

The Nurse said, 'My tongue will be the death of me,' and off   260
she went, I don't know where.

I came walking out quite calmly just as I did here a moment
ago, as if I hadn't heard or understood a word. In the outer
room I saw my Samian, all by herself, with the baby in her
arms, breast-feeding it. So *she*'s obviously the baby's mother.
But the father, whether it's mine or – Ladies and Gentlemen,
I can't bring myself to say it or even to think it. I'm simply   270
telling you what I heard. I'm not angry – not yet. I know the
boy, of course I do, and he's always been a good boy, and
behaved very properly to me. But then again, when I remember that the woman was once Moschion's nurse, and that she
didn't know I could hear what she was saying; and when
I look at Chrysis, who adores the baby and has insisted
on keeping it against my wishes – well, I'm absolutely fit to
be tied.

Oh, good! Here's Parmenon back from the market. I must   280
let him take his party into the house.

[*Enter* PARMENON, *right, with provisions and* COOK]

PARMENON: For God's sake, Cook! I can't imagine why you
bother to carry knives around with you. You're quite capable
of slicing through everything with your tongue.

COOK [*loftily*]: You don't understand. You're not a professional.

PARMENON: No?

COOK: Not in my view, I assure you. I'm only asking about the
number of covers you mean to set, the number of ladies
coming, the time of the meal, whether I need an extra waiter,
if your dinner-service is big enough, if the kitchen's under   290
cover, if everything I need is available –

PARMENON: In case you haven't noticed, mate, you're making
a very fine mincemeat of me, a real professional job.

COOK: Go and boil your head.

PARMENON: The same to you, and make a right job of it.
Inside, all of you!

[COOK *and entourage go into* DEMEAS' *house*]

DEMEAS: Parmenon!

PARMENON: Someone want me?

DEMEAS: Yes, I do.

PARMENON: Oh, hello, sir.

DEMEAS: Deliver your basket, and come back here.

PARMENON: Sure. [*Swaggers into house*]

DEMEAS: I'm sure that no business like this would get past *him*.
300   He's got a finger in every pie. Ah, there's the door, he's
        coming out.

> [*Enter* PARMENON *from the house, speaking back over his
> shoulder*]

PARMENON: Chrysis, see that the cook gets everything he
        wants, and for God's sake keep the old crone away from the
        wine-bottles! [*To* DEMEAS] At your service, sir!

DEMEAS [*grimly*]: *My* service, indeed. Over here, you, away
        from the door. A bit farther.

PARMENON: There!

DEMEAS: Now you listen to me, Parmenon. I don't *want* to
        beat you, I really don't. I have my reasons.

PARMENON: Beat me? Whatever for?

DEMEAS: You're part of a conspiracy to keep something from
        me, so I've discovered.

310   PARMENON: *Me?* I swear by angels and archangels and all the
        hosts of heaven –

DEMEAS: Stop! No swearing. I'm not guessing. I *know*.

PARMENON: God strike me down –

DEMEAS: Look me straight in the face, man.

PARMENON: There. I'm looking.

DEMEAS: The baby – whose is it?

PARMENON: Well –

DEMEAS: Whose baby is it? I want an answer.

PARMENON: Chrysis'.

DEMEAS: And who's the father?

PARMENON: You are, according to her.

DEMEAS: That's done it. You're trying to cheat me.

PARMENON: Me, sir?

DEMEAS: I tell you, I know the whole story, every last detail.
        I've found out that it's *Moschion*'s child, that you're in the
        plot, and that Chrysis is nursing it now for his sake.

PARMENON: Who says?

DEMEAS: Everyone. Answer me – is this true?   320
PARMENON: Yes, sir, it's true, but we didn't want it to get out –
DEMEAS [*outraged*]: Not get *out*? [*Shouts*] Bring me a horse-
  whip, someone, to deal with this snake-in-the-grass.
PARMENON: Oh, please, NO.
DEMEAS: I'll *brand* you, so help me.
PARMENON: Brand *me*?
DEMEAS: This very minute.
PARMENON: I've had it. [*He runs off, right*]
DEMEAS: Hey, where are you going? I've a rod in pickle for
  you. Grab him, someone! [*Raising his hands to heaven*] O
  citadel of Cecrops' land, O vault of heaven on high, O – why
  the noisy imprecation, Demeas? Why all the shouting, you
  fool? Control yourself, stiffen the upper lip.

   It's not *Moschion* who's done you wrong. [*To the audience*] That may seem a remarkable statement, Ladies and
Gentlemen, but it's true. For if he'd done this from malice   330
aforethought, or in the grip of the passion of love, or from
dislike of me, he'd still be brazening it out and marshalling
his forces against me. As it is, he's cleared himself completely,
in my judgement, by his enthusiastic agreement to this
marriage, when it was proposed to him. It wasn't love, as I
thought then, that prompted his enthusiasm, but a desire to
get away somehow from the house, and from that Helen of
mine. *She*'s the one to blame for what's happened. She caught
him, I imagine, when he'd had a spot too much to drink,
when he wasn't quite in control of himself. Yes, that's obviously what happened. Strong wine and young blood can   340
work a lot of mischief, when a man finds at his side someone
who has used these things to set a trap for him. I *cannot*
believe that a boy who's always been well-behaved and con-
siderate to others could treat me like this: not if he's ten times
adopted and not my natural son. It's not his origins I care
about, it's his character. But that – creature – she's a trollop.
She's poison. She'll have to go.

   Now, Demeas, be a man. Forget how you've missed her,   350
stop loving her, cover up what's happened as far as you can
for your son's sake, and throw the fair Samian out on her

ear. The hell with her. You've got an excuse – she kept the
child. No need to give any other reason. Bite on the bullet,
stiff upper lip, honour of the family!

[*Enter* COOK *from the house*]

COOK: Is he here, by the front door? [*Shouts*] Hey, Parmenon!
Damn the fellow, he's run out on me, didn't lift a finger to
help me.

DEMEAS [*rushing into the house*]: Out of the way! Back, you!

360 COOK: Well! What's up? A maniac with a grey beard ran into
the house. What on earth's the matter? Oh, well, it's nothing
to do with me. I tell you, he's loopy, he must be. Well, he
was shouting his head off. A fine thing if he shatters all my
crockery that's been set out. Oh, there's the door. Damn and
blast Parmenon for bringing me here. I'll just step a bit out
of the way. [*He moves away as* DEMEAS *pushes* CHRYSIS
with the baby out of the house]

DEMEAS: Are you deaf? Get out!

CHRYSIS: But – where to?

DEMEAS: To hell. This minute.

CHRYSIS: Poor me.

370 DEMEAS: Yes, poor you. Very affecting, your tears. *I'll* stop
your game, I assure you.

CHRYSIS: What game?

DEMEAS [*remembering he wants to keep the scandal secret*]:
Never mind. You've got the child and the old crone. Now go
to hell.

CHRYSIS: Is it because I kept the baby?

DEMEAS: Yes, and because . . .

CHRYSIS: Because what?

DEMEAS: Just because of that.

COOK [*aside*]: Oh, that's what the trouble is. Now I see.

DEMEAS: You didn't know how to behave properly when you
were well off.

CHRYSIS: I don't understand.

DEMEAS: You came here to me, Chrysis, in a cotton frock – do
you understand *that*? – a simple cotton frock.

CHRYSIS: Well?

DEMEAS: I was everything to you then, when you were poor.

CHRYSIS: Aren't you now? 380

DEMEAS: Don't speak to me. You have all your belongings. I'll give you some servants too. Now, get out!

COOK [aside]: Here's a fine frenzy. I'd better go over. [Approaches] Look here, sir –

DEMEAS: Why are you shoving your oar in?

COOK: No need to bite my nose off.

DEMEAS [ignoring him]: Another girl will be happy with what I have to offer, Chrysis – yes, and give thanks to heaven for it.

COOK: What does he mean?

DEMEAS: You've got a son, you have all you want.

COOK [aside]: Not biting yet. [To DEMEAS] Still, sir –

DEMEAS: I'll smash your head in, fellow, if you say a word to me.

COOK: With some justice, too. There, I'm off inside now. [He goes into the house]

DEMEAS [to CHRYSIS]: A fine figure you make! Once you're 390 on the town, you'll very quickly find your true value. Other girls, Chrysis, not at all in your style, run off to dinner parties for a pound or two, and swallow strong drink until they die: or they starve, if they're not prepared to do this and do it smartly. You'll learn the hard way, like everyone else. And you'll realize what a stupid mistake you've made. [CHRYSIS moves towards him] Stay where you are! [He goes into the house]

CHRYSIS: What shall I do? What's to become of me?

[Enter NIKERATOS, right, with a sheep]

NIKERATOS: This sheep, once it's sacrificed, will satisfy the ritual demands of all the inhabitants of heaven. It's got blood, 400 an adequate gall-bladder, super bones and an enlarged spleen – all the things that the Olympians want. I'll chop up the skin, and send it to my friends as a tasty bit: it's all that'll be left for me. [Sees CHRYSIS] Heavens! What's this? Chrysis in tears in front of the house? Yes, it is. Whatever's the matter?

CHRYSIS: Your fine friend has thrown me out, that's all.

NIKERATOS: Heavens! Demeas?

CHRYSIS: Yes.

NIKERATOS: But why?

CHRYSIS: Because of the baby.

410 NIKERATOS: Yes, I did hear from my womenfolk that you'd kept a child and were nursing it. Sheer lunacy! But Demeas is an easy-going chap. He wasn't angry at first, was he? Only later on? Quite recently?

CHRYSIS: Yes. He'd told me to get the house ready for the wedding, and then, when I was up to my eyes in it, he burst in like a maniac, and he's locked me out of the house.

NIKERATOS: He's out of his mind. The Black Sea isn't a healthy place. You come along and see my wife. Cheer up. It'll be all 420 right. He'll come to his senses when he thinks over what he's doing. [*He escorts* CHRYSIS *into his house*]

[THIRD CHORAL INTERLUDE]

ACT IV

Enter NIKERATOS, *from his house, speaking back over his shoulder*

NIKERATOS: You'll be the death of me with your nagging, woman. I'm *on my way now* to tackle him. [*He shuts the door*] I'd have given a good deal – by God I would – for this not to have happened. Right in the middle of the wedding preparations, something very unlucky has happened. A woman, thrown out of house and home, has crossed our threshold with a child in her arms; there have been tears, and the women are all upset and disorganized. Demeas really is a clot. By God, I'll see that he pays for it.

[*Enter* MOSCHION, *left, not seeing* NIKERATOS]

MOSCHION: Will the sun *never* set? All I can say is, Night has forgotten her job. Will it be always afternoon? I'll go and 430 have a bath – my third. There's nothing else to do.

NIKERATOS: Glad to see you, Moschion.

MOSCHION [*eagerly*]: Are we starting the wedding now? Parmenon told me when I ran into him in the market just now. Can I fetch your daughter now?

NIKERATOS: You don't know what's been going on here!

MOSCHION: No, what?

NIKERATOS: You may well ask. Something very unpleasant indeed.

MOSCHION: Heavens, what is it? I've heard nothing.

NIKERATOS: My dear boy, your father has just thrown Chrysis out of the house.

MOSCHION: You can't mean it.

NIKERATOS: True, I assure you.

MOSCHION: But what for?

NIKERATOS: Because of the baby.

MOSCHION: Then where is she now?

NIKERATOS: In our house.

MOSCHION: What a terrible thing. Quite extraordinary.

NIKERATOS: You think so? Then ... [*They go on speaking quietly together*]

   [*Enter* DEMEAS *from his house, speaking back over his shoulder*]

DEMEAS: If I get my hands on a stick, I'll knock tears out of   440
you all right. Stop this nonsense! Get on and help the cook.
[*Sarcastically*] There's really something to cry about, I must
say; our house has lost a really valuable treasure. Her
behaviour makes that quite clear. [*He bows to the altar*]
Grant us, Lord, successfully to effect this marriage we are
about to celebrate. For [*turning to the audience*] celebrate it
I shall, Ladies and Gentlemen, and swallow my rage. [*He
turns back to the altar*] Guard me, O Lord, from self-betrayal,
and constrain me to sing the marriage-hymn. [*Gloomily*] I'll
not be in very good voice, in my present mood, but what of
it? Who cares what happens now?[5]   450

NIKERATOS: Go on, Moschion, you tackle him first.

MOSCHION: All right. [*He moves forward*] Father, why are
you behaving like this?

DEMEAS: Like what, Moschion?

MOSCHION: Need you ask? Why has Chrysis gone and left us?
Tell me that.

DEMEAS [*aside*]: Someone's organizing a diplomatic approach
to me. Oh, dear. [*To* MOSCHION] It's none of your business,

it's mine and mine alone. Such nonsense! [*Aside*] This is
dreadful. *He*'s part of the plot against me too.

MOSCHION: Beg your pardon?

DEMEAS [*aside*]: He must be: otherwise, why come and speak
for her? He should surely have been *pleased* at what's
happened.

MOSCHION: What do you imagine your friends will say when
they hear about this?

DEMEAS: I imagine my friends will – you leave my friends to
me, Moschion.

460   MOSCHION: I'd be failing in my duty if I let you do this.

DEMEAS: You'll try to stop me?

MOSCHION: Yes, I will.

DEMEAS: This beats all! This is more scandalous than the
previous scandals.

MOSCHION: It's never right to let anger rip.

NIKERATOS [*approaching*]: He's right, Demeas.

MOSCHION: Nikeratos, you go and tell Chrysis to come back
here at once.

DEMEAS: Let it be, Moschion, let it be. For the third time I tell
you, I know everything.

MOSCHION: Everything? What do you mean?

DEMEAS: Don't bandy words with me!

MOSCHION: But I've got to, Father.

DEMEAS: *Got* to? Am I not to be master in my own house?

MOSCHION: Then grant it to me as a favour.

DEMEAS: A favour? I suppose you're asking me to quit my
470   house and leave you two together? Let me get on with your
wedding arrangements. You will, if you've any sense.

MOSCHION: Well, of course I will. But I want Chrysis to be
one of the guests.

DEMEAS: You want *Chrysis* . . . ?

MOSCHION: I insist upon it – mainly for your sake.

DEMEAS [*aside*]: Now it's obvious. Now it's clear. I call
heaven to witness that Someone has joined my enemies and
is plotting against me. I'll burst a blood-vessel, I really
will.

MOSCHION: What are you talking about?

DEMEAS: You really want me to tell you?

MOSCHION: Of course I do.

DEMEAS [*moving away*]: Come here.

MOSCHION [*following*]: Tell me.

DEMEAS: Oh, I'll tell you. The child is yours. I know, I was told by Parmenon, who's in your confidence. So stop playing games with me.

MOSCHION: But – what harm is *Chrysis* doing you if the child is mine?

DEMEAS: Who is to blame, then? Tell me that.

MOSCHION: But – how is *she* at fault?

DEMEAS: I don't believe it! Have you two *no* conscience?   480

MOSCHION: What's all the shouting about?

DEMEAS: Shouting, is it, you scum? What a question. Listen: you take the blame on yourself, right? And you dare to look me in the face and ask this? Have you turned against me completely?

MOSCHION: Me? Against you? How?

DEMEAS: *How?* Need you ask?

MOSCHION: But, Father, what I did isn't such a terrible crime. I'm sure thousands of men have done it before.

DEMEAS: God in Heaven, what a nerve! In the face of this audience I ask you, who is the baby's mother? Tell Nikeratos, if you don't think it 'such a terrible crime'.

MOSCHION [*aside*]: It'll certainly turn into one, if I tell *him*.   490
He'll be furious when he finds out.

NIKERATOS [*suddenly joining in*]: You wicked monster! I'm beginning to have a suspicion of what's been going on. Absolutely outrageous!

MOSCHION [*misunderstanding*]: That's me done for now.

DEMEAS: Now do you see, Nikeratos?

NIKERATOS: I certainly do. [*In tragic vein*] O deed most dread! O Tereus, Oedipus, Thyestes![6] O all the incestuous loves of legend! You've put them all in the shade.

MOSCHION [*bewildered*]: Me?

NIKERATOS: How could you have the effrontery, the audacity, to behave like this? Demeas, now you should assume Amyntor's rage, and blind your son.[7]

500   DEMEAS [*to* MOSCHION]: It's your fault that he's got to know
         about this.
       NIKERATOS: Is nothing sacred? No one inviolate? And *you*'re
         the man to whom I'm to give my daughter in marriage? I'd
         rather – touch wood and *absit omen* – I'd rather marry her
         to our local Lothario. And we all know how unfortunate
         that would be.
       DEMEAS [*to* MOSCHION]: You did me great wrong, but I tried
         to keep it quiet.
       NIKERATOS: You're a coward and a slave, Demeas. If it were
         my bed he'd defiled, he'd certainly never again be abusing
         anyone else's. Nor would his partner. The trollop I'd be
         selling promptly next day. Simultaneously and publicly, I'd
510   disinherit my son. There wouldn't be an empty seat in
         barber's shop or public gardens – the whole world would be
         there from first light, talking about me and saying, 'Nikeratos
         is a *man*, prosecuting for murder, and quite right too.'
       MOSCHION: *Murder?* What murder?
       NIKERATOS: Murder's what I call it, when anyone acts against
         authority and behaves like this.
       MOSCHION: My throat's dry. I'm petrified with fright.
       NIKERATOS: And to crown it all, I've welcomed to my hearth
         and home the girl responsible for these horrors.
       DEMEAS: Throw her out, Nikeratos, do. Consider yourself
         wronged when I am, as a true friend should.
       NIKERATOS: I'll explode with rage at the sight of her. [*To*
         MOSCHION] You dare look me in the face, you barbarous
         savage? Out of my way! [*He rushes into his house*]
520   MOSCHION: Father, for God's sake, *listen.*
       DEMEAS: Not a word!
       MOSCHION: Not even if nothing you suspect is true? I'm just
         beginning to understand what's going on.
       DEMEAS: What do you mean, 'nothing'?
       MOSCHION: Chrysis isn't the mother of the baby she's nursing.
         She's doing me a favour by saying it's hers.
       DEMEAS: *What?*
       MOSCHION: It's true.
       DEMEAS: Why is she doing you this 'favour'?

MOSCHION: I don't want to tell you, but if you know the truth, I'll be cleared of the more serious charge, and admit to the minor one.

DEMEAS: You'll be the death of me, if you don't get on and tell me.

MOSCHION: The baby's mother is Nikeratos's daughter. I'm the father. I was trying to keep it from you.

DEMEAS: What are you saying?

MOSCHION: The simple truth.

DEMEAS: Be careful. No trying to pull wool over my eyes.   530

MOSCHION: You can check the facts. What good would it do me to lie?

DEMEAS: No good at all. There's the door – [NIKERATOS *staggers out of his house*]

NIKERATOS: O misery, misery me! What a sight I have seen! I'm rushing out in a frenzy, pierced to the heart with pain unlooked-for.

DEMEAS: What on earth is he going to tell us?

NIKERATOS: My daughter – my own daughter – I found her just now *breast-feeding the baby*.

DEMEAS [*to* MOSCHION]: Then your story's true.

MOSCHION: You listening, Father?

DEMEAS: You've done me no wrong, Moschion. But I've wronged you by suspecting what I did.

NIKERATOS: You're the man I want, Demeas.

MOSCHION: I'm off!

DEMEAS: Don't be afraid.

MOSCHION: It's death just to look at him. [*He runs off, left*]

DEMEAS: What on earth is wrong?

NIKERATOS: Breast-feeding the baby in the house – that's how   540
I've just found my daughter.

DEMEAS: Perhaps she was just pretending.

NIKERATOS: It was no pretence. When she saw me, she fainted.

DEMEAS: Perhaps she thought –

NIKERATOS: You'll be the death of me with your perhapses.

DEMEAS [*aside*]: This is my fault.

NIKERATOS: Beg your pardon?

DEMEAS: I find your story quite incredible.

NIKERATOS: I tell you, I *saw* it.

DEMEAS: You're drivelling.

NIKERATOS: It's not just a fairy-tale. But I'll go back and – [*He turns back towards the house*]

DEMEAS: Just a minute, my friend. I have an idea. [NIKERATOS *goes in*] He's gone. That's torn it. This is the end. Once he finds out the truth, he'll be in a real rage, bawling his head
550   off. He's a rough customer, insensitive, blunt as they come. To think that I – *I* – had such suspicions! I'm as good as a murderer, I deserve to die, I really do. [*Shouts are heard from* NIKERATOS' *house*] Heavens, what a noise. This is it. He's yelling for fire, threatening to burn the baby. I'll have to watch my grandson roasting. There's the door again. The man's a whirlwind, a positive tornado.

NIKERATOS [*rushing out*]: Demeas, Chrysis is plotting against me, and doing the most terrible things.

DEMEAS: Oh?

NIKERATOS: She's persuaded my wife and daughter to admit nothing, and she's grabbed the baby and refuses to
560   give it up. Don't be surprised if I kill her with my bare hands.

DEMEAS: *Her?* Your wife?

NIKERATOS: Yes, she's in the plot too.

DEMEAS: Don't do it, Nikeratos.

NIKERATOS: I just wanted to warn you. [*He rushes back in*]

DEMEAS: He's raving mad. Gone rushing back inside again. How shall we deal with this crisis? I don't ever remember being in such a mess. Best tell him frankly what has happened. God! There's the door *again*.

[*Enter* CHRYSIS, *running, from* NIKERATOS' *house, carrying the baby*]

CHRYSIS: Help! What'll I do? Where can I be safe? He'll take my baby.

DEMEAS: This way, Chrysis.

CHRYSIS: Who's that?

DEMEAS: Inside my house – run! [*She runs towards him, as* NIKERATOS *rushes out*]

NIKERATOS: Hey you! Where are you going?

DEMEAS: Lord, I'll be fighting a duel, I think, before the day's   570
over. [*He stands in* NIKERATOS' *way*] What do you want?
Who are you chasing?

NIKERATOS: Out of my way, Demeas. Just let me get my hands
on the baby, and the women'll talk.

DEMEAS: Never!

NIKERATOS: You'll fight me?

DEMEAS: I will. [*To* CHRYSIS] Quick! For God's sake, get
inside.

NIKERATOS: Then I'll fight *you*.

DEMEAS: Run, Chrysis, he's stronger than I am. [*She runs into*
DEMEAS' *house*]

NIKERATOS: You started this. I call witnesses to that.

DEMEAS: And *you*'re chasing a free woman, and trying to
hit her.

NIKERATOS: Blackmailer!

DEMEAS: Blackmailer yourself.

NIKERATOS: Bring out my baby.

DEMEAS: That's a laugh. It's *mine*.

NIKERATOS: It is not.

DEMEAS: Yes, it is.

NIKERATOS [*shouting*]: Good people all –

DEMEAS: Go on, bawl your head off.

NIKERATOS: I'll go and murder my wife. Nothing else for it.   580

DEMEAS: That's just as bad. I won't let you. Hey, stop! Where
are you going?

NIKERATOS: Don't you lay a finger on me.

DEMEAS: Control yourself.

NIKERATOS: You're doing me down, Demeas, that's quite clear.
You know all about it.

DEMEAS: Then ask your questions of me, and don't upset
your wife.

NIKERATOS: Your son's hocussed me, hasn't he?

DEMEAS: Rubbish. He'll still take the girl, it's not like that at
all. [*He takes* NIKERATOS' *arm*] Take a turn here with me.

NIKERATOS: Take a *turn*?

DEMEAS: Yes. Get a grip on yourself. Tell me, Nikeratos, have
you never heard actors in tragedies telling how Zeus once   590

turned into a stream of gold, flowed through a roof and seduced a girl who'd been locked up?[8]

NIKERATOS: So what?

DEMEAS: Perhaps we should be prepared for anything? Think! Does any part of your roof leak?

NIKERATOS: Most of it does. But what's that got to do with it?

DEMEAS: Sometimes Zeus is in a shower of gold, sometimes a shower of rain. Do you understand? This is *his* doing. How quickly we've found the solution!

NIKERATOS: You're having me on.

DEMEAS: Heavens, no! Wouldn't dream of it. You're surely just as good as Danaë's father. If Zeus honoured her, then perhaps your daughter –

NIKERATOS: Oh, dear, Moschion has made a cake of me.

600 DEMEAS: Don't worry, he'll marry her. But what happened was divinely inspired, you can be sure of that. I can name you thousands walking the streets of this city today, who are children of gods. And you think your case exceptional! To start with [*pointing*] there's Chairephon[9] – there he is – always dining out and never paying his share. Don't you think *he*'s divine?

NIKERATOS: I suppose so. There's no point in hair-splitting.

DEMEAS: Very wise, Nikeratos. Then there's Androcles[10] – so many years in this world, but he hops and skips his way into everything, a real busybody. His hair's black, but even if it were white, he wouldn't die, not even if someone were to cut his throat. He's divine, isn't he? But seriously, pray that this marriage turns out well. Burn your incense, make your offer-

610 ings. My son will come any minute to fetch his bride.

NIKERATOS: I suppose I must accept this.

DEMEAS: Wise man!

NIKERATOS: But if I'd caught him then –

DEMEAS: Let it be. Remember your blood-pressure. Go and get things ready in the house.

NIKERATOS: All right.

DEMEAS: And I'll do the same in here.

NIKERATOS: You do that.

DEMEAS: You're a smart chap. [NIKERATOS *goes in*] And thank

God I've discovered that my suspicions were quite un-
founded. [*He goes into his own house*]

[FOURTH CHORAL INTERLUDE]

ACT V

Enter MOSCHION, *left*

MOSCHION [*addressing the audience*]: Just now, when I was
cleared of the charge quite wrongly laid against me, I was
pleased, and thought myself quite lucky. But now that I've
had time to collect my wits and think over what happened,   620
I'm furious, absolutely livid, that my father could have
thought me capable of such behaviour. If it weren't for the
problem about the girl, if there weren't so many obstacles –
like my sworn word, my love for her, our long relationship
(things that leave me no freedom of choice) – he certainly
wouldn't make such a charge against me again, not to my
face. No, I'd have been off from the city, out of his way,
away to the Foreign Legion[11] to spend my life as a serving
soldier there. But no such heroics now, I won't do it, for *your*   630
sake, Plangon darling. It's impossible, forbidden by Love, the
master of my will.

   Still, that's no reason why I should ignore the insult, or
take it lying down. I'd like to scare him, even if it's only an
act, by *saying* that I'm off abroad. He'll be more careful in
future not to treat me so unfairly, if he sees me taking this
insult seriously. Ah, here's Parmenon. Just the man I want,   640
and just when I want him.

PARMENON [*entering right, and not seeing* MOSCHION]: God
Almighty! What a fool I've been, beneath contempt, really.
I'd done nothing wrong, but I panicked and ran away from
Master. What had I done to justify that? Let's look at the
case dispassionately and in detail:
   Item: Young master seduced a respectable girl: Parmenon's
      presumably not to blame for that!
   Item: She got pregnant: no fault of Parmenon's.

650   Item: The baby was brought to our house: Moschion
         brought him, not I.
         Item: One of our household said she was the mother:
         Parmenon had nothing to do with that. So why run
         away, you lily-livered ass? It's ludicrous.
         Item: Master threatened to brand me. Now you've got
         it. It makes not a scrap of difference whether that
         punishment is deserved or not, in either case it's not very
         pretty.
MOSCHION: Hey!
PARMENON: Good evening to you.
MOSCHION: Stop this nonsense, and go inside. Hurry up.
PARMENON: What for?
MOSCHION: Bring me a military cloak, and a sword.
PARMENON: A sword? For *you*?
660 MOSCHION: And do it now.
PARMENON: But what for?
MOSCHION: Go and do what I tell you, and keep quiet
         about it.
PARMENON: Why, what's up?
MOSCHION: If I get my hands on a whip –
PARMENON: No, no, I'm on my way.
MOSCHION: Then hurry up about it. [PARMENON *goes in*]
         Father'll come out now. Of course, he'll beg me to stay, and
         for some time he'll beg in vain. That's vital. Then, when I
         think fit, I'll let myself be persuaded. All that's needed is a
         bit of plausible acting – which, Heaven knows, I'm not very
         good at. Uh-uh. Here we go. That's the door, someone's
         coming out.
670 PARMENON [*entering from the house*]: You're quite out of date,
         I find, on what's going on here. Your information's inaccurate
         and your intelligence service poor. You're getting into a tizz
         and driving yourself to despair, *quite* unnecessarily.
MOSCHION: Where's the cloak and the sword?
PARMENON: You see, your wedding's under way. [*Raptly*]
         Wine a-mixing, incense a-burning, sacrifice ready, offerings
         alight with the Fire-god's flame!
MOSCHION: Parmenon, *where's the cloak and the sword?*

PARMENON: You're the one they're waiting for, for ages now. Why not fetch the bride right away? You're in luck, you've nothing to fear. Cheer up. [*In alarm, as* MOSCHION *advances*] What are you after?

MOSCHION [*slapping* PARMENON'*s face*]: Read me a lecture, would you, you outrageous oaf?

PARMENON: Oh, what are you doing, Moschion?

MOSCHION: Go inside this minute, and bring out what I told you to bring.

PARMENON: You've split my lip.

MOSCHION: Still talking back?

PARMENON: I'm going. A fine reward I've won, I must say.   680

MOSCHION: Get on with it.

PARMENON: They really are celebrating your wedding.

MOSCHION: The same old story still? Tell me something new. [PARMENON *goes in*] *Now* he'll come out. [*Pause*] Ladies and Gentlemen, suppose he doesn't beg me to stay, but loses his temper and lets me go? That's something I left out of my calculations just now. What do I do then? Perhaps he won't do it – but suppose he does? Anything's possible in this life. A fine fool I'll look if I have to do a U-turn.

[*Enter* PARMENON *from the house, with cloak and sword*]

PARMENON: There! Here's your cloak and sword. They're all yours.

MOSCHION: Give them here. [*Casually*] Anyone in the house see you?

PARMENON: No one.

MOSCHION: No one *at all?*

PARMENON: No.

MOSCHION: Oh, blast you!

PARMENON: On your way. You're talking twaddle.

DEMEAS [*entering from the house*]: Where is he then? Tell me   690
that. [*Sees* MOSCHION] Good heavens! What's this?

PARMENON [*to* MOSCHION]: Quick march! Now!

DEMEAS: What's the fancy dress for? What's wrong? Going on your travels, Moschion? Enlighten me.

PARMENON: As you see, he's already on the road and on the

march. And now I must say goodbye to the household too.
I'll do that now. [*He goes in*]

DEMEAS: Moschion, I love you for your anger, and I'm not
surprised[12] that you're hurt at being unfairly accused. But
consider the target for your bitter anger. I'm your *father*. I
took you when you were a little boy, and I brought you up.
700   If your journey through life has been a pleasant one, I'm the
man who made provision for it. So, it was your duty to put
up with anything I did, even if it hurt you, and to bear with
me as a good son should.

My charges against you were unjustified, I was wrong, I
made a mistake, I was out of my mind. All right. But ponder
this point. At the cost of hurting others, I still looked carefully
after your interests. I tried to keep my suspicion to myself,
and did not publish it for the entertainment of our enemies.
But now you want to make my mistake public, calling wit-
710   nesses to testify to my stupidity. That's not fair, Moschion.
Don't brood on the one day when I came a cropper, and
ignore all the others that went before.

There's a lot more I could say, but I'll let it go there.
You know very well that sons get no credit for reluctant
obedience. Give in gladly, that's the way to do it.

[*Enter* NIKERATOS *from his house, talking back over his
shoulder*]

NIKERATOS: Stop nagging me. Everything's *been* done – baths,
ritual, wedding ceremony, the lot. The bridegroom, if he
ever does come, can take his bride away. [*Sees the others*]
Heavens! What's going on here?

DEMEAS: I've no idea, I assure you.

NIKERATOS: Well, you *should* know. A soldier's cloak! I believe
he means to be off.

DEMEAS: That's what he says.

NIKERATOS: Oh, *does* he? Then he's got to be stopped. He's a
seducer, caught in the act, admitting his guilt. I'll arrest you
on the spot, boy.

MOSCHION [*drawing his sword*]: Yes, arrest me, do.

NIKERATOS: You never take me seriously. Put up your sword
at once.

DEMEAS: For heaven's sake, Moschion, put it up and don't   720
aggravate him.

MOSCHION [*sheathing sword*]: There! Let it go. Your entreaties
have succeeded, your appeals to me.

NIKERATOS: *Appeals?* You come here!

MOSCHION: You'll arrest me, perhaps?

DEMEAS: Stop this nonsense! Bring the bride out here.

NIKERATOS: You're sure?

DEMEAS: Quite sure. [NIKERATOS *goes into his house*]

MOSCHION: If you'd done this right away, Father, you
wouldn't have had to bother with your recent sermon.

NIKERATOS [*returning with his daughter*]: After you, dear.
[*Members of the two households assemble*] In the face of
witnesses, I give you, Moschion, this woman to be your wife,
for the procreation of legitimate children. And as dowry I
give her all my possessions when I die (which God forbid!
May I live for ever).

MOSCHION: I take her, to have, to hold and to cherish.

DEMEAS: All that remains is to fetch the ritual water. Chrysis,
send out the women, the water-carrier and the musician. And   730
someone bring us out a torch and garlands, so that we can
form a proper procession.

MOSCHION [*as these things are brought out*]: Here he comes.

DEMEAS: Moschion, put on your garland, and deck yourself
like a bridegroom.

MOSCHION: There!

DEMEAS [*to the audience*]: Pretty boys, young men, old men,
ladies and gentlemen, all together now – please clap loudly.
Dionysus[13] loves applause, and it shows you liked our play.
And may Victory, immortal patron of the finest festivals,
grant her perpetual favour to this company.

[*All leave, right, in procession*]

Translated by Norma Miller (1987)

PLAUTUS

THE BROTHERS MENAECHMUS

PREFACE

Plautus is known to have written only one comedy of errors. His Greek predecessors wrote so many (Menander at least four) that 'Miss Understanding' (*Agnoia*), a personification who speaks one of his prologues, has rightly been called the presiding deity of New Comedy. Plautus usually preferred wit to ignorance, shrewd deceptions to naive blunders. People in a comedy of errors are mere puppets; Plautus admired puppeteers, creative plotters, slaves like Palaestrio in *The Braggart Soldier* and Tranio in *The Haunted House*. Not to mention Pseudolus, the cleverest of them all.

The fine, if untypical, Plautine comedy *The Brothers Menaechmus* has enjoyed unceasing popularity over the ages. And not only in famous adaptations such as Shakespeare's *Comedy of Errors* and Rodgers and Hart's *Boys from Syracuse*. It has always been the most performed play of Plautus. Clearly, it has a very special appeal – both in its songs and snappy patter, and its atmosphere of carnival release from everyday rules. Moreover, it presents more simply than any comedy before or since the greatest of all wish-fulfilments: the surrogate self, the alter ego with no super-ego, the man who can get his pleasure free in every sense, because he is 'Jack in town and Ernest in the country'. Indeed, Plautus' twin-brother comedy might be aptly subtitled 'The Importance of Being Menaechmus'.

The two houses on stage represent the conflicting forces in the comedy. They are not unlike the statues of Artemis and Aphrodite which frame the setting of Euripides' *Hippolytus*. In both dramas the action takes place in a magnetic field between

poles of restraint and release. It is no coincidence that the house
of Menaechmus 1 stands at the exit nearer the forum. For the
local twin is bound by the business of everyday life, restrained
by legal, financial and social ties, especially by a wife who is
constantly 'at work'.

Across the stage, and nearer the harbour whence visitors
come, dwells a lady of pleasure aptly named Erotium. Throughout the play, Plautus associates the word *industria* ('work')
with Mrs Menaechmus (e.g. 123). To emphasize the contrast,
he constantly refers to Erotium as *voluptas* ('pleasure'). It
should be noted that his lawfully wedded spouse has no name
at all; Plautus merely calls her 'wife'. Shakespeare, in his adaptation, reverses this, making the courtesan the lady with no name.

But it is especially interesting to see why Menaechmus 1 needs
a twin in order 'to win', and since this is a comedy the hero
gets away with it all. The local married brother is the unwitting
victim of his twin's sudden appearance. Plautus gives him the
larger and more lyrical role (Shakespeare, on the other hand,
emphasizes the visiting twin). We first meet Menaechmus 1 in
the midst of a domestic battle, describing himself as a hardened
soldier in the war called marriage (127, 129). He craves rest
and recreation from this campaign. And this is, in fact, what
the play is all about. He takes several steps in the direction of
pleasure, that is, towards the other side of the stage, where
passion lives incarnate. He orders a banquet: the bill of fare
emphasizes various delicacies which were *forbidden* to the
Romans (209ff.). Plautus even concocts comic names for these
illegal dishes, to stress how much Menaechmus is savouring the
prospect of his breaking-of-the-rules banquet. And dessert will
be Erotium. The plans are elaborate, explicit and titillating.
Why, then, does Menaechmus 1 leave the stage and head for –
of all places – the forum, not to return till the party is over?

The very moment the local brother exits towards the business
district, his long-lost twin enters from the harbour. This boy
from Syracuse belongs to a great comic tradition: the lowly
stranger who arrives in town, is mistaken for someone else of
greater importance and receives the cardinal comic joys: food,
sex and money. This is a comedy of errors and it really starts

to gain momentum as the mistakes begin, when his twin brother arrives from nowhere, literally nowhere in the world, for Plautus' geography is cock-eyed to say the least. Xanthias in Aristophanes' *Frogs* is an earlier such type; a later one is Gogol's *Inspector General*, Klestakhov, the lowly government clerk who is mistaken for the Inspector-General. Like the Russian hero, Menaechmus II has come to town virtually penniless. As Messenio, his loyal slave, expresses it, 'We're travelling for summer – very, very light' (255). The sudden bounty seems too good to be true. But this hunter ultimately finds his prey – not before he enjoys a banquet of the senses being prepared for his brother. Certainly Erotium gives the visitor a lyrical welcome, in an aria which concludes: 'Since dinner's ready, come and dine, / As soon as suits you, come . . . recline' (367–8).

Some time later Menaechmus II emerges drunk and garlanded from Erotium's palace of pleasure. 'I've wined, I've dined, I've concubined, and robbed her blind – / No one but me will own this dress after today!' (473–7). He also receives some of Erotium's jewellery, which, like the dress, has been stolen by Menaechmus I from his wife. Two comic fantasies are here fulfilled. Not only does someone else pick up the tab for the banquet, but the whore ends up paying the customer for sex![1]

But what has kept our protagonist off-stage? He arrives, in fact, just in time to be too late, and though he sings elaborately of what has detained him, the cause may be summarized in a single word: business. While he was in the forum, a client stopped him and forced him to act as advocate in a complicated lawsuit. He sings of his frustration. He was obliged to do his (Roman) duty:

> So I just was delayed, forced to give legal aid, no evading
>   this client of mine who had found me.
> I wanted to do you know what – and with whom – but he
>   bound me and tied ropes around me. (585–9)

Menaechmus' punishment – for going to work on a day selected for play – is not yet complete. He is about to have an unpleasant encounter with his nameless wife, who will lock him out of his house, after which Erotium too will bolt her door. He is then *exclusissimus*, the most 'kicked-out' (698; see note 30) man in the world. To add diagnosis to other injuries, he is then pronounced insane by a psychiatrist *gloriosus*, a hilarious quack whose professional questions are not unlike those posed by 'Socrates' in Aristophanes' *Clouds*.

When one Menaechmus is at the acme of delight, the other is at the nadir of despair. The counterbalance is neatly crafted and helps to explain the meaning of the entire comedy. The local Menaechmus is married to a real harridan. Any sensible man would seek to avoid her even if he were not going to Erotium's pleasure-dome. His confrontation typifies Plautus' attitude towards wives in general. He is wont to scold her for her constantly intrusive behaviour. When he leaves the house in the morning their confrontation is typical:

> And if you act up once again, the way you've acted up today,
> I'll have you packed up – back to Daddy as a divorcée.
>
> . . .
>
> I don't have a wife, I have a customs office bureaucrat,
> For I must declare the things I've done, I'm doing, and all that!
>
> (116–18)

This image of the Roman wife is hardly appealing. But then it is characteristic of Plautus' attitude to women. Cleostrata, the shrill, strident and aggressive wife in the *Casina*, is another example. She is referred to literally as a bitch. His slave remarks sarcastically, 'you're a real hunter, master, because you spend all your time with a bitch.'[2]

The hero of *The Brothers* is a married man, a solid citizen of the town, who longs to go on a wild revel. In point of fact, somebody named Menaechmus does enjoy all the forbidden delights of which the hero dreams. But it is another Menaechmus, who, although a mirror image (1062), is still different in three vital aspects: he is unmarried, unattached and a non-citizen. In these three non-capacities, unmarried Menaechmus II can enjoy sex without 'sin', play without neglecting duty (he has no clients), and he can even eat whatever he wants – foreigners are exempt from local dietary restrictions. In brief, Menaechmus II is *free*.

He is also non-existent. He is the creature of someone's imagination – specifically, Menaechmus I's. The fantasy fulfilled is that of a workaday Roman, caught up in the forum, dreaming of getting away – from everything and with everything. *The Brothers Menaechmus* is Roman comedy par excellence, and demonstrates once again that even when he departs slightly from his usual comic domain, Plautus never loses sight of his public's desires. Here he has given them exactly what they and Menaechmus I have longed for: a Roman holiday.

NOTES

1. We recall the Braggart Soldier at the height of his *alazoneia*, drunk with joy at the prospect of being paid for his sexual attentions, 1059ff.
2. Plautus, *Casina* 319–20.

CHARACTERS

CHIEF ACTOR

PENICULUS, a parasite

MENAECHMUS I

MENAECHMUS II, his twin brother (born Sosicles)

MESSENIO, slave to Menaechmus II

EROTIUM, a lady of pleasure

CYLINDRUS, a cook in Erotium's employ

MAID, also in Erotium's employ

WIFE of Menaechmus

OLD MAN, father-in-law of Menaechmus

DOCTOR

The scene is a street in Epidamnus.[1] *There are two houses.*
On the right (from the audience's view) is MENAECHMUS'
house; on the left, EROTIUM's *house. The forum is off-stage*
to the audience's right. The harbour is off-stage to the
audience's left.

Enter the CHIEF ACTOR *to speak the prologue*

Now first and foremost, folks, I've this apostrophe:
May fortune favour all of you – and all of me.
I bring you Plautus. [*Pause*] Not in person, just his play.
So listen please, be friendly with your ears today.
Now here's the plot. Please listen with your whole attention
    span;
I'll tell it in the very fewest words I can.
[*A digression*] Now comic poets do this thing in every
    play:[2]
'It all takes place in Athens, folks,' is what they say.
So that way everything will seem *more Greek* to you.
But I reveal the real locations when I speak to you.   10
This story's Greekish, but to be exact,
It's not Athenish, it's Sicilyish, in fact.
[*Smiles*] That was a prelude to the prologue of the plot.
I now intend to pour a lot of plot for you.
Not just a cupful, fuller up, more like a pot.
Such is our storehouse, brimming full of plot!
[*Finally, to business*] There was at Syracuse a merchant old
    and worn
To whom a pair of baby boys – two twins – were born.
The babies' looks were so alike their nurse confessed
She couldn't tell to which of them she gave which breast.   20
Nor even could their own real mother tell between them.
I've learned about all this from someone who has seen
    them.
I haven't seen the boys, in case you want to know.
Their father, 'round the time the boys were seven or so,
Packed on a mighty ship much merchandise to sell –
The father also packed one of the twins as well.
They went to Tarentum to market, with each other,

And left the other brother back at home with mother.
A festival chanced to be on there when they docked there,

30 And piles of people for the festival had flocked there.
The little boy, lost in the crowd, wandered away.
An Epidamnian merchant, also there that day,
Made off with him to Epidamnus – there to stay.
The father, learning that he'd lost the lad,
Became depressed, in fact he grew so very sad
A few days later he was dead. It was that bad.

 When back to Syracuse this news was all dispatched,
The grandpa of the boys learned one was snatched,
And word of father's death at Tarentum then came.

40 The grandpa took the other twin and changed his name.
He so adored the other twin, who had been snatched,
He gave the brother still at home a name that matched:
Menaechmus. That had been the other brother's name.
It was the grandpa's name as well, the very same.[3]
In fact, it's not a name you quickly can forget,
Especially if you're one to whom he owes a debt.[4]
I warn you now, so later you won't be confused:
    [emphatically] for both of the twin brothers one same
        name is used.
    [Starts to cross the stage]
Metre by metre[5] to Epidamnus now I must wend,

50 So I can chart this map unto its perfect end.
If any of you wants some business handled there,
Speak up, be brave, and tell me of the whole affair.
But let him give me cash, so I can take good care.
If you don't offer cash, then you're a fool, forget it.
You do – [smiles] then you're a bigger fool, and you'll
    regret it.
I'll go back whence I came – still standing on this floor –
And finish up the story I began before:
    That Epidamnian who snatched the little lad,
He had no children; lots of cash was all he had.[6]

60 So he adopted him he snatched, became his dad.
And gave his son a dowried female for his bride.
And then – so he could make the boy his heir – he died.

By chance, out in the country in a rain severe,
He tried to cross a rapid stream – not far from here.
The rapid river rapt the kidnapper, who fell,
Caught in the current, heading hurriedly to hell.
The most fantastic riches thus came rolling in
To him who lives right in the house – the kidnapped
   twin.
   But *now*, from Syracuse where he had always been,
Today in Epidamnus will arrive the other twin,   70
With trusty slave, in search of long-lost brother-twin.
   This town is Epidamnus, while the play is on.
But when we play another play, its name will change
Just like the actors living here, whose roles can range
From pimp to papa, or to lover pale and wan,
To pauper, parasite, to king or prophet, on and on.
[And on and on and on . . .]⁷
   [*Enter the parasite* PENICULUS. *He speaks directly to the
   audience*]
PENICULUS:
By local boys I'm called Peniculus the sponge,
For at the table, I can wipe all platters clean.
[*A philosophical discourse*] The kind of men who bind their
   prisoners with chains,
Or clap the shackles on a slave that's run away,   80
Are acting very foolishly – in my own view.
If you compound the wretchedness of some poor wretch,
Why, all the more he'll long to flee and do some wrong.
For one way or another, he'll get off those chains.
The shackled men will wear the ring down with a file,
Or smash the lock. This kind of measure is a joke.
But if you wish to guard him so he won't run off,
You ought to chain the man with lots of food and drink.
Just bind the fellow's beak right to a well-stocked table,
Provide the guy with eatables and drinkables,   90
Whatever he would like to stuff himself with every day.
He'll never flee, though wanted for a murder charge.
You'll guard with ease by using chains that he can chew.
The nicest thing about these chains of nourishment –

The more you loosen them, the more they bind more
  tightly.
[*End of discourse*] I'm heading for Menaechmus; he's the
  man to whom
I've had myself condemned. I'm hoping that he'll chain me.
He doesn't merely feed men, he can breed men and
Indeed men are reborn through him. No doctor's better.
100 This is the sort of guy he is: the greatest eater,
His feasts are festivals.[8] He piles the table so,
And plants so many platters in the neatest piles
To reach the top, you have to stand up on your couch.
And yet we've had an intermission for some days
And tabled at my table, I've expended it.
I never eat or drink – except expensively.
But now my army of desserts has been deserting me.
I've got to have a talk with him. But wait – the door!
Behold, I see Menaechmus himself now coming out.
  [*Enter* MENAECHMUS, *still facing indoors, berating some-
  one. We will soon see that he is hiding a lady's dress under
  his usual garments*]
MENAECHMUS [*singing, in anger at his wife in the house*]:
110 If you weren't such a shrew, so uncontrolled, ungrateful
  too,[9]
Whatever thing your husband hated, you'd find hateful
  too.
And if you act up once again, the way you've acted up
  today,
I'll have you packed up – back to Daddy as a divorcée.
However often I try to go out you detain me, delay me,
  demand such details as
Where I'm going, what I'm doing, what's my business all
  about,
Deals I'm making, undertaking, what I did when I was out.
I don't have a wife, I have a customs office bureaucrat,
For I must declare the things I've done, I'm doing, and all
  that!
All the luxuries you've got have spoiled you rotten. I want
  to live for what I give:

Maids and aides, a pantry full, 120
Purple clothing, gold and wool:
You lack for nothing money buys.
So watch for trouble if you're wise;
A husband hates a wife who spies.
But so you won't have watched in vain, for all your
diligence and care,
I'll tell you: 'Wench to lunch today, lovely dinner off
somewhere.'

PENICULUS:

The man now thinks he hurts his wife; it's me he hurts:
By eating dinner somewhere else, he won't give me my just
desserts!

MENAECHMUS [*looks into house, satisfied, then turns to
audience with a big grin*]:

My word barrage has put the wife in full retreat. It's
victory!
Now where are all the married 'lovers'? Pin your medals
right on me.
Come honour me *en masse*. Look how I've battled with
such guts,
And look, this dress I stole inside – it soon will be my little
slut's. 130
I've shown the way: to fool a guard both hard and shrewd
takes aptitude.
Oh, what a shining piece of work! What brilliance, glitter,
glow and gloss!
I've robbed a rat – but lose at that, for my own gain is my
own loss!
[*Indicates the dress*] Well, here's the booty – there's my
foes, and to my ally – now it goes.

PENICULUS:

Hey, young man! Does any of that stolen booty go to
me?

MENAECHMUS:

Lost – I'm lost – and caught in crime!

PENICULUS:

Oh, no, you're found – and found in time.

MENAECHMUS:
   Who is that?
PENICULUS:
   It's me.
MENAECHMUS:
         Oh, *you* – my Lucky Charm, my Nick-of-Time!
Greetings. [*Rushes to him; they shake hands vigorously*]
PENICULUS:
   Greetings.
MENAECHMUS:
      Whatcha doing?
PENICULUS:
            Shaking hands with my good-luck charm.
MENAECHMUS:
   Say – you couldn't come more rightly right on time than
   you've just come.
PENICULUS:
140 That's my style: I know exactly how to pick the nick of
   time.
MENAECHMUS:
   Want to see a brilliant piece of work?
PENICULUS:
      What cook concocted it?
   Show me just a titbit and I'll know if someone bungled it.
MENAECHMUS:
   Tell me, have you ever seen those frescos painted on the
   wall –
   Ganymede snatched by the eagle, Venus . . . likewise . . .
   with Adonis?
PENICULUS:
   Yes, but what do those damn pictures have to do with me?
MENAECHMUS:
      Just look.
   [*He strikes a pose, showing off his dress*]
   Notice something similar?
PENICULUS:
      What kind of crazy dress is that?

MENAECHMUS [*very fey*]:
  Tell me that I'm so attractive.
PENICULUS:
    Tell me when we're going to eat.
MENAECHMUS:
  First you tell me –
PENICULUS:
    Fine, I'll tell you: you're attractive. So attractive.
MENAECHMUS:
  Don't you care to add a comment?
PENICULUS [*a breath*]:
    Also witty. Very witty.
MENAECHMUS:
  More!
PENICULUS:
    No more, by Hercules, until I know what's in it for
      me.
  Since you're warring with your wife, I must be wary and
    beware.
MENAECHMUS:
  Hidden from my wife we'll live it up and burn this day to
    ashes.
PENICULUS:
  Now you're really talking sense. How soon do I ignite the
    pyre?
  Look – the day's half dead already, right to near its belly
    button.
MENAECHMUS:
  You delay me by interrupting –
PENICULUS:
    Knock my eyeball through my ankle,
  Mangle me, Menaechmus, if I fail to heed a single word.
MENAECHMUS:
  Move – we're much too near my house.
    [*Tiptoes to centre-stage, motions to* PENICULUS]
PENICULUS [*follows* MENAECHMUS]:
    Okay.

150

MENAECHMUS [*moves more, motions*]:
     We're still too near.
PENICULUS [*follows*]:
       How's this?
MENAECHMUS:
  Bolder, let's go further from the bloody mountain lion's
  cave.
PENICULUS:

160 Pollux! You'd be perfect racing chariots – the way you
  act.
MENAECHMUS:
  Why?
PENICULUS:
     You're glancing back to see if *she's* there, riding
      after you.
MENAECHMUS:
  All right, speak your piece.
PENICULUS:
     My piece? Whatever piece you say is fine.
MENAECHMUS:
  How are you at smells? Can you conjecture from a simple
  sniff?
PENICULUS:
  Sir, my nose knows more than all the city prophets.[10]
MENAECHMUS:
  Here now, sniff this dress I hold. What do you smell? You
  shrink?
PENICULUS:
  When it comes to women's garments, prudence bids us
  smell the *top*.
  Way down there, the nose recoils at certain odours quite
  unwashable.[11]
MENAECHMUS:
  All right, smell up here, you're such a fussy one.
PENICULUS:
     All right, I sniff.
MENAECHMUS:
  Well? What do you smell? Well –

PENICULUS [*quickly*]:

> Grabbing, grubbing, rub-a-dub dubbing.[12]   170
> Hope I'm right.

MENAECHMUS:

> I hope so too . . .
> Now I'll take this dress to my beloved wench, Erotium,
> With the order to prepare a banquet for us both.

PENICULUS:

> Oh, good!

MENAECHMUS:

> Then we'll drink, we'll toast until tomorrow's morning star
> appears.

PENICULUS:

> Good, a perfect plan! May I proceed to pound the portals?

MENAECHMUS:

> Pound.
> No no – wait!

PENICULUS:

> Why wait? The flowing bowl's more than a mile
> away!

MENAECHMUS:

> Pound politely.

PENICULUS:

> Why? You think the door is made of pottery?

MENAECHMUS:

> Wait wait wait, by Hercules. She's coming out. Oh, see the
> sun!   180
> How the sun's eclipsed by all the blazing beauty from her
> body.

[*Grand entrance of* EROTIUM *from her house*]

EROTIUM [*to* MENAECHMUS]:

> Greetings, O my only soul!

PENICULUS:

> And me?

EROTIUM [*to* PENICULUS]:

> Not on my list at all.

PENICULUS:

> Such is life for us unlisted men – in every kind of war.

MENAECHMUS [*to* EROTIUM]:
  Darling, at your house today, prepare a little battleground.
EROTIUM:
  So I will.
MENAECHMUS:
      We'll hold a little drinking duel, [*indicating*
          PENICULUS] the two of us.
  Then the one who proves the better fighter with the flowing
      bowl,
  He's the one who'll get to join your company for night
      manoeuvres.
  [*Getting more enthusiastic*] Oh, my joy! My wife, my wife!
      When I see *you* – how I hate *her*!
EROTIUM [*sarcastically*]:
190   Meanwhile, since you hate your wife, you wear her
          clothing, is that it?
  What have you got on?
MENAECHMUS:
      It's just a dress addressed to you, sweet rose.
EROTIUM:
  You're on top, you outtop[13] all the other men who try for
      me.
PENICULUS [*aside*]:
  Sluts can talk so sweet, while they see something they can
      snatch from you.
  [*To* EROTIUM] If you really loved him, you'd have
      smooched his nose right off his face.
MENAECHMUS:
  Hold this now, Peniculus; religion bids me make redress.
PENICULUS:
  Fine, but while you've got a skirt on, why not pirouette a
      bit?
MENAECHMUS:
  Pirouette? By Hercules, you've lost your mind!
PENICULUS:
      Not more than you.
  Take it off – if you won't dance.

MENAECHMUS [*to* EROTIUM]:
  What risks I ran in stealing this!
  Hercules in labour number nine was not as brave as I,   200
  When he stole the girdle from that Amazon Hippolyta.[14]
  Take it, darling, since you do your duties with such
    diligence.[15]
EROTIUM:
  That's the spirit. Lovers ought to learn from you the way to
    love.
PENICULUS [*to the audience*]:
  Sure, that way to love's the perfect short cut to a
    bankruptcy.
MENAECHMUS:
  Just last year I bought my wife this dress. It cost two
    hundred drachmae.
PENICULUS [*to the audience*]:
  Well, there goes two hundred drachmae down the drain, by
    my accounts.
MENAECHMUS [*to* EROTIUM]:
  Want to know what I would like prepared?
EROTIUM:
    I know, and I'll prepare it.
MENAECHMUS:
  Please arrange a feast at your house; have it cooked for
    three of us.
  Also have some very special party foods bought in the
    forum:
  Glandiose, whole-hog and a descendant of the lardly ham.   210
  Or perhaps some pork chopettes, or anything along those
    lines.[16]
  Let whatever's served be *stewed*, to make me hungry as a
    hawk.
  Also hurry up.
EROTIUM:
    I will.
MENAECHMUS:
      Now we'll be heading to the forum.

We'll return at once and, while the dinner's cooking, we'll
  be drinking.
EROTIUM:
When you feel like it, come. It will be all prepared.
MENAECHMUS:
  And quickly too.
[*To* PENICULUS] Follow me –
PENICULUS:
  By Hercules, I'll follow you in every way.
No, I'd lose the gods' own gold before I lose your track
  today.
[MENAECHMUS *and* PENICULUS *exit towards the forum*]
EROTIUM:
Someone call inside and tell my cook Cylindrus to come
  out.
[CYLINDRUS *enters from* EROTIUM's *house*]
Take a basket and some money. Here are several coins for
  you.
CYLINDRUS:
Got 'em.
EROTIUM:
220   Do your shopping. See that there's enough for three of
        us,
Not a surplus or a deficit.
CYLINDRUS:
  What sort of guests, madam?
EROTIUM:
I, Menaechmus, and his parasite.
CYLINDRUS:
  That means I cook for *ten*:
By himself that parasite can eat for eight with greatest ease.
EROTIUM:
That's the list. The rest is up to you.
CYLINDRUS:
  Consider it as cooked already.
Set yourself at table.
EROTIUM:
  Come back quickly.

CYLINDRUS [*starting to trot off*]:
> I'm as good as back.

[*He exits. From the exit nearer the harbour enters the boy from Syracuse* – MENAECHMUS II – *accompanied by his slave* MESSENIO. *As chance* [*i.e. the playwright*] *would have it, the twin is also wearing the exact same outfit as his long-lost brother. Several sailor types carry their luggage*]

MENAECHMUS II:
> Oh, joy, no greater joy, my dear Messenio,
> Than for a sailor when he's on the deep to see
> Dry land.

MESSENIO:
> It's greater still, if I may speak my mind,
> To see and then arrive at some dry land that's *home*.
> But tell me, please[17] – why have we come to Epidamnus?   230
> Why have we circled every island like the sea?

MENAECHMUS II [*pointedly, melodramatically*]:
> We are in search of my beloved long-lost twin.

MESSENIO:
> But will there ever be a limit to this searching?
> It's six entire years since we began this job.
> Through Istria, Iberia, Illyria,
> The Adriatic, up and down, exotic Greece,[18]
> And all Italian towns. Wherever sea went, *we* went!
> I frankly think if you were searching for a needle,
> You would have found it long ago, if it existed.
> We seek and search among the living for a dead man.   240
> We would have found him long ago if he were living.

MENAECHMUS II:
> But therefore I search on till I can prove the fact;
> If someone says he knows for sure my brother's dead,
> I'll stop my search and never try an instant further.
> But otherwise, I'll never quit while I'm alive,
> For I alone can feel how much he means to me.

MESSENIO:
> You seek a pin in haystacks. Let's go home –
> Unless we're doing this to write a travel book.

MENAECHMUS II [*losing his temper*]:
  Obey your orders, eat what's served you, keep from
    mischief!
  And don't annoy me. Do things *my* way.
MESSENIO:
250   Yessir, yessir.
  I get the word. The word is simple: I'm a slave.
  Concise communication, couldn't be much clearer.
  [*A chastened pause, then back to harping at his master*]
  But still and all, I just can't keep from saying this:
  Menaechmus, when I inspect our purse, it seems
  We're travelling for summer – very, very light.
  By Hercules, unless you go home right away,
  While you search on still finding *no* kin . . . you'll be
    'bro-kin'.[19]
  Now here's the race of men you'll find in Epidamnus:
  The greatest libertines, the greatest drinkers too,
260 The most bamboozlers and charming flatterers
  Live in this city. And as for wanton women, well –
  Nowhere in the world, I'm told, are they more dazzling.
  Because of this, they call the city Epidamnus,
  For no one leaves unscathed, 'undamaged',[20] as it were.
MENAECHMUS II:
  Oh, I'll have to watch for that. Give me the purse.
MESSENIO:
  What for?
MENAECHMUS II:
  Because your words make me afraid of you.
MESSENIO:
  Of me?
MENAECHMUS II:
  That you might cause . . . Epidamnation for me.
  You love the ladies quite a lot, Messenio.
  And I'm a temperamental man, extremely wild.
270 If I can hold the cash, it's best for both of us.
  Then you can do no wrong, and I can't yell at you.
MESSENIO [*giving the purse*]:
  Take it, sir, and guard it; you'll be doing me a favour.

[*Re-enter cook* CYLINDRUS, *his basket full of goodies*]

CYLINDRUS:

I've shopped quite well, and just the sort of things I like.
I know I'll serve a lovely dinner to the diners.
But look – I see Menaechmus. Now my back is dead![21]
The dinner guests are strolling right outside our door
Before I even finish shopping. Well, I'll speak.
    [*Going up to* MENAECHMUS II]
Menaechmus, sir . . .

MENAECHMUS II:

God love you – God knows who you are.

CYLINDRUS [*thinks it's a joke*]:

Who am I? Did you really say you don't know me?

MENAECHMUS II:

By Hercules, I don't.

CYLINDRUS:

Where are the other guests?   280

MENAECHMUS II:

What kind of other guests?

CYLINDRUS:

Your parasite, that is.

MENAECHMUS II:

My parasite? [*To* MESSENIO] The man is simply raving
    mad.

MESSENIO:

I *told* you there were great bamboozlers in this town.

MENAECHMUS II [*to* CYLINDRUS, *playing it cool*]:

Which parasite of mine do you intend, young man?

CYLINDRUS:

The Sponge.

MENAECHMUS II [*jocular, points to luggage*]:

Indeed, my sponge is here inside my bag.

CYLINDRUS:

Menaechmus, you've arrived too early for the dinner.
Look, I've just returned from shopping.

MENAECHMUS II:

Please, young man,
What kind of prices do you pay for sacred pigs,[22]

290   The sacrificial kind?
CYLINDRUS:
          Not much.
MENAECHMUS II:
          Then take this coin,
And sacrifice to purify your mind at my expense.
Because I'm quite convinced you're absolutely raving mad
To bother me, an unknown man who doesn't know you.
CYLINDRUS:
You don't recall my name? Cylindrus, sir, Cylindrus!
MENAECHMUS II:
Cylindrical or Cubical, just go away.
Not only don't I know you, I don't *want* to know you.
CYLINDRUS:
Your name's Menaechmus, sir, correct?
MENAECHMUS II:
          As far as *I* know.
You're sane enough to call me by my rightful name.
But tell me how you know me.
CYLINDRUS:
          How I know you? . . . *Sir* –
300   [*Discreetly, but pointedly*] You have a mistress . . . she
          owns me . . . Erotium?
MENAECHMUS II:
By Hercules, I haven't – and I don't know you.
CYLINDRUS:
You don't know me, a man who many countless times
Refilled your bowl when you were at our house?
MESSENIO:
          Bad luck!
I haven't got a single thing to break the fellow's skull with.
[*To* CYLINDRUS] Refilled the bowl? The bowl of one who
          till this day
Had never been in Epidamnus?
CYLINDRUS [*to* MENAECHMUS II]:
          You deny it?
MENAECHMUS II:
By Hercules, I do.

CYLINDRUS [*points across stage*]:
 And I suppose that house
Is not your house?
MENAECHMUS II:
 God damn the people living there!
CYLINDRUS [*to audience*]:
 Why, *he's* the raving lunatic – he cursed himself! 310
Menaechmus –
MENAECHMUS II:
 Yes, what is it?
CYLINDRUS:
   Do take my advice,
And use that coin you promised me a while ago,
And since, by Hercules, you're certainly not sane,
I mean, Menaechmus, since you just now cursed
  yourself –
Go sacrifice that sacred pig to cure yourself.
MENAECHMUS II:
 By Hercules, you talk a lot – and you annoy me.
CYLINDRUS [*embarrassed, to audience*]:
 He acts this way a lot with me – he jokes around.
He can be very funny if his wife is gone.
[*To* MENAECHMUS] But now, what do you say?
MENAECHMUS II:
 To what?
CYLINDRUS [*showing basket*]:
   Is this enough?
I think I've shopped for three of you. Do I need more 320
For you, your parasite, your girl?
MENAECHMUS II:
 What girls? What girls?
What parasites are you discussing?
MESSENIO [*to* CYLINDRUS]:
 And what madness
Has caused you to be such a nuisance?
CYLINDRUS [*to* MESSENIO]:
 What do *you* want now?
I don't know you. I'm chatting with a man I know.

MESSENIO [*to* CYLINDRUS]:
  By Pollux, it's for sure you're not exactly sane.
CYLINDRUS [*abandons the discussion*]:
  Well then, I guess I'll stew these up. No more delay.
  Now don't you wander off too far from here.
  [*Bowing to* MENAECHMUS] Your humble servant.
MENAECHMUS II [*half aside*]:
    If you *were*, I'd crucify you!
CYLINDRUS:
  Oh, take a cross yourself – cross over and come in –
330   Whilst I apply Vulcanic arts to all the party's parts.[23]
  I'll go inside and tell Erotium you're here.
  Then she'll convince you you'll be comfier inside.
    [*Exit*]
MENAECHMUS II [*stage whisper to* MESSENIO]:
  Well – has he gone?
MESSENIO:
    He has.
MENAECHMUS II:
      Those weren't lies you told.
  There's truth in every word of yours.
MESSENIO [*his shrewd conclusion*]:
      Here's what I think:
  I think the woman living here's some sort of slut.
  That's what I gathered from that maniac who left.
MENAECHMUS II:
  And yet I wonder how that fellow knew my name.
MESSENIO:
  Well, I don't wonder. Wanton women have this way:
340   They send their servants or their maids to port
  To see if some new foreign ship's arrived in port.
  To ask around, 'Where are they from? What are their
    names?'
  Right afterward, they fasten on you hard and fast.
  They tease you, then they squeeze you dry and send you
    home.
  Right now, I'd say a pirate ship is in *this* port
  And I would say we'd better both beware of it.

MENAECHMUS II:
 By Hercules, you warn me well.
MESSENIO:
     I'll know I have
 If you stay well aware and *show* I've warned you well.
MENAECHMUS II:
 Be quiet for a minute now; the door just creaked.
 Let's see who comes out now.
MESSENIO:
     I'll put the luggage down.
 [*To the sailors*] Me hearties, if you please, please guard this
     stuff for us.   350
 [EROTIUM *appears, in a romantic mood, singing*]
EROTIUM:
 Open my doors, let my welcome be wide,
 Then hurry and scurry – get ready inside.
 See that the incense is burning, the couches have covers.
 Alluring decor is exciting for lovers.
 Lovers love loveliness, we don't complain; their loss is
     our gain.
 But the cook says someone was out here – [*looks*] I see!
 It's that man of great worth – who's worth so much to
     me.
 I ought to greet him richly – as he well deserves to be.
 Now I'll go near, and let him know I'm here.   360
 [*To* MENAECHMUS] My darling-darling, it's a mite amazing
 To see you standing out-of-doors by open doors.
 You know full well how very much my house is yours.
 All you ordered we're supplied with,
 All your wishes are complied with.
 So why stay here, why delay here? Come inside with . . .
     me.
 Since dinner's ready, come and dine,
 As soon as suits you, come . . . recline.
 [*To say the very least,* MENAECHMUS II *is stunned. After
 a slight pause, he regains his powers of speech*]
MENAECHMUS II [*to* MESSENIO]:
 Who's this woman talking to?

EROTIUM:
>   To you.
MENAECHMUS II:
>   To me?
370   What have we – ?
EROTIUM:
>   By Pollux, you're the only one of all my lovers
>   Venus wants me to arouse to greatness. You deserve it, too.
>   For, by Castor, thanks to all your gifts, I've flourished like a
>   flower.
MENAECHMUS II [aside to MESSENIO]:
>   She is surely very mad or very drunk, Messenio.
>   Speaking to a total stranger like myself so ... sociably.
MESSENIO:
>   Didn't I predict all this? Why, these are only falling leaves.
>   Wait three days and I predict the trees themselves will drop
>   on you.
>   Wanton women are this way, whenever they can sniff some
>   silver.
>   Anyway, I'll speak to her. [To EROTIUM] Hey, woman –
>   there.
EROTIUM [with hauteur]:
>   Yes, can I help you?
MESSENIO:
>   Tell me where you know this man from.
EROTIUM:
>   Where? Where he knows me for years.
380 Epidamnus.
MESSENIO:
>   Epidamnus, where he's never set a foot,
>   Never been until today?
EROTIUM [laughing]:
>   Aha – you're making jokes with me.
>   Dear Menaechmus, come inside, you'll see that things ...
>   will pick up right.
MENAECHMUS II [to MESSENIO]:
>   Pollux, look, the creature called me by my rightful name as
>   well.

How I wonder what it's all about.

MESSENIO:

The perfume from your purse.

That's the answer.

MENAECHMUS II:

And, by Pollux, you did warn me rightfully.

[*Gives purse back to* MESSENIO]

Take it then. I'll find out if she loves my person or my
purse.

EROTIUM:

Let's go in, let's dine.

MENAECHMUS II [*declining*]:

That's very nice of you. Thanks just the same.

EROTIUM:

Why on earth did you command a dinner just a while
ago?

MENAECHMUS II:

I commanded dinner?

EROTIUM:

Yes. For you, and for your parasite.

MENAECHMUS II:

What the devil parasite? [*Aside*] This woman's certainly
insane.   390

EROTIUM:

Your old sponge, Peniculus.

MENAECHMUS II:

A sponge – to clean your shoes, perhaps?

EROTIUM:

No, of course – the one that came along with you a while
ago.

When you brought the dress you'd stolen from your wife to
give to me.

MENAECHMUS II:

Are you sane? I gave a dress I'd stolen from my wife to
you?

[*To* MESSENIO] Like some kind of horse this woman's fast
asleep still standing up.

EROTIUM:

> Do you get some pleasure making fun of me, denying
>   things,
> Things completely true?

MENAECHMUS II:

> What do you claim I've done that I deny?

EROTIUM:

> Robbed your wife and gave the dress to me.

MENAECHMUS II:

> *That* I'll deny again!
> Never have I had or do I have a wife, and never have I
> Ever set a single foot inside that door, since I was born.
> I had dinner on my ship, then disembarked and met you –

EROTIUM:

> Oooh!
> Pity me – what shall I do? What ship is this?

MENAECHMUS II:

> A wooden one,
> Much repaired, re-sailed, re-beamed, re-hammered and
>   re-nailed and such.
> Never did a navy have so numerous a nail supply.

EROTIUM:

> Please, my sweet, let's stop the jokes and go inside together
>   . . . mmmm?

MENAECHMUS II:

> Woman, you want someone else. I mean . . . I'm sure you
>   don't want me.

EROTIUM:

> Don't I know you well, Menaechmus, know your father's
>   name was Moschus?
> You were born, or so they say, in Syracuse, in Sicily,
> Where Agathocles was king, and then in turn, King
>   Phintia,[24]
> Thirdly, King Liparo, after whom King Hiero got the
>   crown.
> Now it's still King Hiero.

MENAECHMUS II [*to* MESSENIO]:

> Say, that's not inaccurate.

400

410

MESSENIO:
        By Jove –
If she's not from Syracuse, how does she know the facts so
    well?
MENAECHMUS II [*getting excited*]:
Hercules, I shouldn't keep refusing her.
MESSENIO:
        Oh, don't you dare!
Go inside that door and you're a goner, sir.
MENAECHMUS II:
        Now you shut up!
Things are going well. Whatever she suggests – I'll just
    agree.
Why not get a little . . . hospitality? [*To* EROTIUM] Dear
    lady, please –
I was impolite a while ago. I was a bit afraid that   420
[*indicating* MESSENIO] He might go and tell my wife . . .
    about the dress . . . about the dinner.
Now, when you would like, we'll go inside.
EROTIUM:
        But where's the parasite?
MENAECHMUS II:
I don't give a damn. Why should we wait for him? Now if
    he comes,
Don't let him inside at all.
EROTIUM:
        By Castor, I'll be happy not to.
Yet [*playfully*] there's something I would like from
    you.
MENAECHMUS II:
        Your wish is my command.
EROTIUM:
Bring the dress you gave me to the Phrygian embroiderer.
Have him redesign it, add some other frills I'd like him to.
MENAECHMUS II:
Hercules, a good idea. Because of all the decoration,
When my wife observes you in the street, she won't know
    what you're wearing.

EROTIUM:

430   Therefore take it with you when you leave.

MENAECHMUS II:

Of course, of course, of course.

EROTIUM:

Let's go in.

MENAECHMUS II:

I'll follow you. [*Indicates* MESSENIO]
I want a little chat with him.
[*Exit* EROTIUM]
Hey, Messenio, come here!

MESSENIO:

What's up?

MENAECHMUS II:

Just hop to my command.

MESSENIO:

Can I help?

MENAECHMUS II:

You can. [*Apologetically*] I know you'll criticize –

MESSENIO:

Then all the worse.

MENAECHMUS II:

Booty's in my hands. A fine beginning. You continue, fast –
Take these fellows [*indicating sailors*] back to our lodging
    tavern, quicker than a wink,
Then be sure you come to pick me up before the sun goes
    down.

MESSENIO [*protesting*]:

Master, you don't know about these sluts –

MENAECHMUS II:

Be quiet! Just obey.
If I do a stupid thing, then I'll be hurting, not yourself.

440   Here's a woman stupid and unwitting, from what I've just
    seen.
Here's some booty we can keep.

MESSENIO:

I'm lost. [*Looks*] Oh, has he gone? He's lost!
Now a mighty pirate ship is towing off a shipwrecked skiff.

I'm the fool as well. I tried to argue down the man who
  owns me.
But he bought me only as a sounding board, not to sound
  off.
Follow me, you men [*to the sailors*], so I can come on time
  – as I've been ordered.
  [*They exit. Stage empty for a moment* [*musical interlude?*].
  Enter PENICULUS – *all upset*]
PENICULUS:
More than thirty years I'm on this earth and during all that
  time
Never till today have I done such a damned and dopey
  deed!
Here I had immersed my whole attention in a public
  meeting.
While I stood there gaping, that Menaechmus simply stole
  away,
Went off to his mistress, I suppose, and didn't want me
  there.   450
Curse the man who was the first to manufacture public
  meetings,
All designed to busy men already busy with their business.
They should choose the men who have no occupation for
  these things,
Who, if absent when they're called, would face fantastic
  fines – and fast.
Why, there's simply gobs of men who only eat just once a
  day,
Who have nothing else to do; they don't invite, they're not
  invited.
Make *these* people spend their time at public meetings and
  assemblies.
If this were the case today, I'd not have lost my lovely
  feast.   460
Sure as I'm alive, that man had really wished to feed me
  well.
Anyhow, I'll go. The thought of scraps left over lights my
  soul.

But – what's this? Menaechmus with a garland, coming
   from the house?
Party's over, I'm arriving just in time to be too late!
First, I'll spy how he behaves and then I'll go accost the
   man.
   [MENAECHMUS II *wobbles happily out of* EROTIUM's
   *house, wearing a garland, and carrying the dress earlier
   delivered by his brother*]

MENAECHMUS II [*to* EROTIUM]:
Now, now, relax, you'll get this dress today for sure,
Returned on time, with lovely new embroidery.
I'll make the old dress vanish – it just won't be seen.

PENICULUS [*indignant, to the audience*]:
He'll decorate the dress now that the dinner's done,
470   The wine's been drunk, the parasite left in the cold.
No, Hercules, I'm not myself, if not revenged,
If I don't curse him out in style. Just watch me now.

MENAECHMUS II [*drunk with joy – and a few other things*]:
By all the gods, what man in just a single day
Received more pleasures, though expecting none at all:
I've wined, I've dined, I've concubined, and robbed her
   blind –
No one but me will own this dress after today!

PENICULUS:
I just can't bear to hide and hear him prate like this.
Smug and satisfied, he prates about *my* party.

MENAECHMUS II:
480   She says I gave her this – and tells me that I stole it.
I stole it from *my wife*! [*Confidentially*] I knew the girl was
   wrong,
Yet I pretended there was some affair between us two.
Whatever she proposed, I simply said, 'Yes, yes,
Exactly, what you say.' What need of many words?
I've never had more fun at less expense to me.

PENICULUS:
Now I'll accost the man, and make an awful fuss.

MENAECHMUS II:
Now who's this fellow coming toward me?

PENICULUS [*in a fury*]:
    Well, speak up!
You lighter than a feather, dirty, rotten person,
You evil man, you tricky, worthless individual!
What did I ever do to you that you'd destroy me?   490
You stole away from me, when we were in the forum;
You dealt a death blow to the dinner in my absence!
How could you dare? Why, I deserved an equal part!

MENAECHMUS II:
    Young man, please indicate precisely what you want from
      me.
And why you're cursing someone you don't know at all.
Your dressing-down of me deserves a beating-up!

PENICULUS:
    By Pollux, you're the one who beat me out, just now.

MENAECHMUS II:
    Now please, young man, do introduce yourself at least.

PENICULUS:
    And now insult to injury! You don't know *me*?

MENAECHMUS II:
    By Pollux, no, I don't, as far as I can tell.   500
I've never seen you, never met you. Whoever you are –
At least behave, and don't be such a nuisance to me.

PENICULUS:
    Wake up, Menaechmus!

MENAECHMUS II:
        I'm awake – it seems to me.

PENICULUS:
    And you don't recognize me?

MENAECHMUS II:
        Why should I deny it?

PENICULUS:
    Don't recognize your parasite?

MENAECHMUS II:
        My dear young man,
It seems to me your brain is not so very sane.

PENICULUS:
    Just answer this: did you not steal that dress today?

It was your wife's. You gave it to Erotium.

MENAECHMUS II:
By Hercules, I have no wife. Erotium?
510   I gave her nothing, didn't steal this dress. You're mad.

PENICULUS [*to audience*]:
Total disaster! [*To* MENAECHMUS II] But I saw you wear
    that dress
And, wearing it, I saw you leave your house.

MENAECHMUS II:
    Drop dead!
You think all men are fags because *you* are?
You claim I actually put on a woman's dress!

PENICULUS:
By Hercules, I do.

MENAECHMUS II:
    Oh, go where you belong!
Get purified or something, raving lunatic!

PENICULUS:
By Pollux, all the begging in the world won't keep me
From telling every single detail to your wife.
520   Then all these present insults will rebound on you.
You've gobbled up my dinner – and I'll be revenged!
    [*He storms into* MENAECHMUS' *house*]

MENAECHMUS II:
What's going on? Everyone I run across
Makes fun of me . . . but why? Oh, wait, the door just
    creaked.
    [*Enter* EROTIUM'S MAID, *a sexy little thing. She carries a
    bracelet*]

MAID:
Menaechmus, your Erotium would love a favour –
Please, while you're at it, take this to the goldsmith for
    her
And have him add about an extra . . . ounce . . . of gold,
So that the bracelet is remodelled, shining new.

MENAECHMUS II [*ironically*]:
I'm happy to take care of both these things for her,
And any other thing that she'd like taken care of.

MAID:

> You recognize the bracelet?

MENAECHMUS II:

> Uh – I know it's gold.   530

MAID:

> This very bracelet long ago was once your wife's,
> And secretly you snatched it from her jewel box.

MENAECHMUS II:

> By Hercules, I never did.

MAID:

> You don't recall?
> Return the bracelet, if you don't remember.

MENAECHMUS II:

> Wait!
> I'm starting to remember. Why, of course I gave it.
> Now where are those two armlets that I gave as well?

MAID:

> You never did.

MENAECHMUS II:

> Of course, by Pollux – this was all.

MAID:

> Will you take care of things?

MENAECHMUS II [*ironically*]:

> I said I'd take good care.
> I'll see that dress and bracelet are both carried back
>   together.

MAID [*the total coquette*]:

> And, dear Menaechmus, how about a gift for me?   540
> Let's say four drachmae's worth of jingly earrings?
> Then when you visit us, I'll really welcome you.

MENAECHMUS II:

> Of course. Give me the gold, I'll pay the labour costs.

MAID:

> Advance it for me, afterwards I'll pay you back.

MENAECHMUS II:

> No, you advance it, afterwards I'll double it.

MAID:

> I haven't got it.

MENAECHMUS II:
> If you ever get it – give it.

MAID [*frustrated, she bows*]:
> I'm at your service.
>   [*Exit*]

MENAECHMUS II:
> I'll take care of all of this
> As soon as possible, at any cost – I'll sell them.
550 Now has she gone? She's gone and closed the door behind
>   her.
> The gods have fully fostered me and favoured me
>   unfailingly!
> But why do I delay? Now is the perfect chance,
> The perfect time to flee this prostitutish place.
> Now rush, Menaechmus, lift your foot and lift the pace!
> I'll take this garland off, and toss it to the left,
> So anyone who follows me will think I'm thataway.
> I'll go at once and find my slave, if possible,
> And tell him everything the gods have given me today.[25]
>   [*Exit. From* MENAECHMUS' *house enter* PENICULUS *and*
>   MENAECHMUS' WIFE]

WIFE [*melodramatic, a big sufferer*]:
> Must I keep suffering this mischief in my marriage?
560 Where husband sneaks and steals whatever's in the house
> And takes it to his mistress?

PENICULUS:
> Can't you quiet down?
> You'll catch him in the act, if you just follow me.
> He's drunk and garlanded – at the embroiderer's,
> Conveying that same dress he stole from you today.
> Look – there's the garland. Do I tell you lies or truth?
> He's gone in that direction; you can follow clues.
> But wait – what perfect luck – he's come back right now!
> Without the dress.

WIFE:
> What should I do? How should I act with him?

PENICULUS:
    The very same as always: make him miserable.
    But let's step over here – and spread a net for him.   570
      [*Enter* MENAECHMUS I]
MENAECHMUS [*singing*]:
    We have this tradition, we have this tradition,[26]
    An irksome tradition, and yet it's the best
    Who love this tradition much more than the rest.
    They want lots of clients, all want lots of clients.
    Who cares if they're honest or not – are they rich?
    Who cares if they're honest, we'll take them with zest –
      If they're rich.

    If he's poor but he's honest – who cares for him?
    He's dishonest but rich? Then we all say our prayers for
      him.
    So it happens that lawless, corrupting destroyers   580
      Have overworked lawyers.
    Denying what's done and delivered, this grasping and
      fraudulent sort
    Though their fortunes arise from exorbitant lies
      They're all anxious to step into court.[27]
    When the day comes, it's hell for their lawyer as well,
    For we have to defend things unjust and unpretty
    To jury, to judge, or judicial committee.

    So I just was delayed, forced to give legal aid, no evading
      this client of mine who had found me.
    I wanted to do you know what – and with whom – but he
      bound me and tied ropes around me.
    Facing the judges just now, I had countless despicable deeds
      to defend.   590
    Twisting torts with contortions of massive proportions,
    I pleaded and pleaded right down to the end.
    But just when an out-of-court settlement seemed to be
      sealed – *my client appealed!*
    I never had seen someone more clearly caught in the act:

For each of his crimes there were three who could speak to
the fact!

By all the heavens, cursed be he
Who just destroyed this day for me.
And curse me too, a fool today,
For ever heading forum's way.
The greatest day of all – destroyed.
The feast prepared, but not enjoyed.
The wench was waiting too, indeed.
The very moment I was freed
I left the forum with great speed.
She's angry now, I'm sure of it.
The dress I gave will help a bit,

Taken from my wife today . . . a token for Erotium.
[*A pause.* MENAECHMUS *catches his breath, still not noticing his* WIFE *or the* PARASITE, *who now speaks*]

PENICULUS:
Well, what say you to that?
WIFE:
          That I've married a rat.
PENICULUS:
                    Have you heard quite enough to complain to him?
WIFE:
Quite enough.
MENAECHMUS:
          Now I'll go where the pleasures will flow.
PENICULUS:
          No, remain. Let's be flowing some *pain* to him.
WIFE:
You'll be paying off at quite a rate for this!
PENICULUS [*to wife*]:
          Good, good attack!
WIFE:
Do you have the nerve to think you'd get away with secret
smuggling?

600

MENAECHMUS:
   What's the matter, Wife?
WIFE:
      You're asking me?
MENAECHMUS [*indicating* PENICULUS]:
      Should I ask him instead?
WIFE:
   Don't turn on the charm.
PENICULUS:
      That's it!
MENAECHMUS:
      But tell me what I've done to you.
   Why are you so angry?
WIFE:
      You should know.
PENICULUS:
      He knows – and can't disguise it.
MENAECHMUS:
   What's the matter?
WIFE:
      Just a dress.
MENAECHMUS:
      A dress?
WIFE:
         A dress.
PENICULUS [*to* MENAECHMUS]:
         Aha, you're scared.
MENAECHMUS:
   What could I be scared of?
PENICULUS:
      Of a dress – and of a dressing-down.   610
   You'll be sorry for that secret feast. [*To* WIFE] Go on,
   attack again!
MENAECHMUS:
   You be quiet.
PENICULUS:
      No, I won't. He's nodding to me not to speak.

MENAECHMUS:
  Hercules, I've never nodded to you, never winked at
    you!
PENICULUS:
  Nothing could be bolder: he denies it while he's doing it!
MENAECHMUS:
  By Jove and all the gods I swear – is that enough for you,
    dear Wife? –
  Never did I nod to him.
PENICULUS [*sarcastically*]:
      Oh, she believes you. Now go back!
MENAECHMUS:
  Go back to what?
PENICULUS:
      Go back to the embroiderer's – and get the dress!!
MENAECHMUS:
  Get what dress?
PENICULUS:
      I won't explain, since he forgets his own . . . affairs.
WIFE:
  What a woeful wife I am.
MENAECHMUS [*playing very naive*]:
      Woeful wife? Do tell me why?
620   Has a servant misbehaved, or has a maid talked back to
        you?
  Tell me, dear, we'll punish misbehavers.
WIFE:
      Oh, is *that* a joke.
MENAECHMUS:
  You're so angry. I don't like to see you angry.
WIFE:
      That's a joke!
MENAECHMUS:
  Someone from the household staff has angered you.
WIFE:
      Another joke!
MENAECHMUS:
  Well, of course, it isn't me.

WIFE:
>   Aha! At last he's stopped the jokes!

MENAECHMUS:
Certainly I haven't misbehaved.

WIFE:
>   He's making jokes again!

MENAECHMUS:
Tell me, dear, what's ailing you?

PENICULUS:
>   He's giving you a lovely line.

MENAECHMUS:
Why do you annoy me? Did I talk to you?
[*Throws a punch at* PENICULUS]

WIFE [*to* MENAECHMUS]:
>   Don't raise your hand!

PENICULUS [*to* WIFE]:
Let him have it! [*To* MENAECHMUS] Now go eat your little
>   feast while I'm not there.
Go get drunk, put on a garland, stand outside, and mock
>   me now!

MENAECHMUS:
Pollux! I've not eaten any feast today – or been in there.   630

PENICULUS:
You deny it?

MENAECHMUS:
>   I deny it all.

PENICULUS:
>   No man could be more brazen.
Didn't I just see you here, all garlanded, a while ago?
Standing here and shouting that my brain was not exactly
>   sane?
And you didn't know me – you were just a stranger here in
>   town!

MENAECHMUS:
I've been absolutely absent, since the second we set out.

PENICULUS:
I know you. You didn't think that I could get revenge on
>   you.

All has been recounted to your wife.

MENAECHMUS:
> What 'all'?

PENICULUS:
> Oh, I don't know.
> Ask her for yourself.

MENAECHMUS:
> Dear Wife, what fables has this man been telling?
> What's the matter? Why are you so silent? Tell me.

WIFE:
> You're pretending,[28]

640
> Asking what you know.

MENAECHMUS:
> Why do I ask, then?

PENICULUS:
> What an evil man!
> How he fakes. But you can't hide it, now the whole affair is
> out.
> Everything's been publicized by me.

MENAECHMUS:
> But *what*?

WIFE:
> Have you no shame?
> Can't you tell the truth yourself? Attend me and please pay
> attention:
> I will now inform you what he told, and why I'm angry at
> you.
> There's a dress been snatched from me.

MENAECHMUS:
> There's a dress been snatched from me?

PENICULUS:
> Not from *you*, from *her*. [*To* WIFE] The evil man resorts to
> every dodge.
> [*To* MENAECHMUS] If the dress were snatched from you, it
> *really* would be lost to us.

MENAECHMUS:
> You're not anything to me. [*To* WIFE] Go on, my dear.

WIFE:
> A dress is gone.

MENAECHMUS:
> Oh – who snatched it?

WIFE:
> Pollux; who'd know better than the man himself?

MENAECHMUS:
> Who is this?

WIFE:
> His name's Menaechmus.

MENAECHMUS:
> Pollux, what an evil deed!   650
> What Menaechmus could it be?

WIFE:
> Yourself.

MENAECHMUS:
> Myself?

WIFE:
> Yourself.

MENAECHMUS:
> Who says?

WIFE:
> *I* do.

PENICULUS:
> I do, too. And then you gave it to Erotium.

MENAECHMUS:
> *I* did?

WIFE:
> You, you, you!

PENICULUS:
> Say, would you like an owl for a pet –
> Just to parrot 'you you you'? The both of us are all worn
>   out.

MENAECHMUS:
> By Jove and all the gods, I swear – is that enough for you,
>   dear Wife? –
> No, I didn't give it to her.[29]

PENICULUS:
   No, we know *we* tell the truth.
MENAECHMUS [*backing down*]:
   Well . . . that is to say . . . I didn't *give* the dress. I loaned it
   to her.
WIFE:
   Oh, by Castor, do I give your tunics or your clothes away –
   Even as a loan? A woman can give women's clothes away.
660   Men can give their own. *Now will you get that dress back
   home to me?*
MENAECHMUS [*cowed*]:
   Yes, I'll . . . get it back.
WIFE:
      I'd say you'd better get it back, or else.
   Only with that dress in hand will you re-enter your own
   house.
   Now I'm going in.
PENICULUS [*to* WIFE]:
      But what of me – what thanks for all my help?
WIFE [*sweetly bitchy*]:
   I'll be glad to help you out – when someone steals a dress
   from you.
PENICULUS:
   That'll never happen. I don't own a single thing to steal.
   Wife and husband – curse you both. I'll hurry to the forum
   now.
   I can very clearly see I've been expelled from this whole
   house.
   [*He storms off*]
MENAECHMUS:
   Hah – my wife thinks that she hurts me, when she shuts the
   door on me.
   But, as far as entering, I've got another, better place.
670   [*To* WIFE's *door*] You don't like me. I'll live through it
   since Erotium here does.
   She won't close me out, she'll close me tightly in her arms,
   she will.

I'll go beg the wench to give me back the dress I just now
    gave,
Promising another, better one. [*Knocks*] Is there a doorman
    here?
Open up! And someone ask Erotium to step outside.
    [EROTIUM *steps outside her house*]

EROTIUM:
Who has asked for me?

MENAECHMUS:
    A man who loves you more than his own self.

EROTIUM:
Dear Menaechmus, why stand here outside? Come in.

MENAECHMUS:
    Wait just a minute.
Can you guess what brings me here?

EROTIUM:
    I know – you'd like some . . . joy with me.

MENAECHMUS:
Well . . . indeed, by Pollux. But – that dress I gave to you
    just now.
Please return it, since my wife's discovered all in full detail.
I'll replace it with a dress that's twice the price, and as you
    like it.   680

EROTIUM:
But I gave it to you for embroidery a moment back,
With a bracelet you would bring the goldsmith for
    remodelling.

MENAECHMUS:
What – you gave me dress and bracelet? No, you'll find that
    isn't true.
No – I first gave *you* the dress, then went directly to the
    forum.
Now's the very second I've returned.

EROTIUM:
    Aha – I see what's up.
Just because I put them in your hands – you're out to
    swindle me.

MENAECHMUS:

Swindle you? By Pollux, no! Why, didn't I just tell you
why?

Everything's discovered by my wife!

EROTIUM [*exasperated*]:

I didn't ask you for it.

No, you brought it to me of your own free will – and as a
gift.

690   Now you want the dress right back. Well, have it, take it,
wear it!

You can wear it, or your wife – or lock it in your money
box.

But from this day on you'll never set a foot inside my
house.

After all my loyal service, suddenly you find me hateful,

So you'll only have me now by laying cash right on the line.

Find yourself some other girl to cheat the way you've
cheated me!

MENAECHMUS:

Hercules, the woman's angry! Hey – please wait, please
listen to me –

[EROTIUM *exits, slamming her door*]

Please come back! Please stay – oh, won't you do this
favour for me?

Well, she's gone – and closed the door. I'm universally
kicked out.[30]

Neither wife nor mistress will believe a single thing I say.

700   What to do? I'd better go consult some friends on what
they think.

[*Exit* MENAECHMUS. *A slight pause* [*musical interlude?*].
Then enter MENAECHMUS II *from the opposite side of the
stage. He still carries the dress*]

MENAECHMUS II:

I was a fool a while ago to give that purse

With all that cash to someone like Messenio.

I'm sure by now the fellow's 'oozing' in some dive.

[WIFE *enters from her house*]

WIFE:
    I'll stand on watch to see how soon my husband comes.
    Why, here he is – I'm saved! He's bringing back the dress.
MENAECHMUS II:
    I wonder where Messenio has wandered to . . .
WIFE:
    I'll go and greet the man with words that he deserves.
    [To MENAECHMUS II] Tell me – are you not ashamed to
        show your face,
    Atrocious man – and with that dress?
MENAECHMUS II:
                I beg your pardon,
    What seems to be the trouble, madam?
WIFE:
                Shame on you!   710
    You dare to mutter, dare to speak a word to me?
MENAECHMUS II:
    Whatever have I done that would forbid my talking?
WIFE:
    You're asking me? Oh, shameless, brazen, wicked man!
MENAECHMUS II [with quiet sarcasm]:
    Madam, do you have any notion why the Greeks
    Referred to Hecuba as . . . female dog?[31]
WIFE:
    I don't.
MENAECHMUS II:
    Because she acted just the way you're acting now.
    She barked and cursed at everyone who came in sight,
    And thus the people rightly called her . . . female dog.
WIFE:
    I simply can't endure all this disgracefulness –
    I'd even rather live my life . . . a divorcée   720
    Than bear the brunt of this disgracefulness of yours.
MENAECHMUS II:
    What's it to me if you can't stand your married life –
    Or ask for a divorce? Is it a custom here
    To babble to all foreigners who come to town?

WIFE:

'To babble'? I won't stand for that. I won't! I won't!
I'll die a divorcée before I'd live with you.

MENAECHMUS II:

As far as I'm concerned you can divorce yourself,
And stay a divorcée till Jupiter resigns his throne.

WIFE:

Look – you denied you stole that dress a while ago,
730   And now you wave it at me. Aren't you ashamed?

MENAECHMUS II:

By Hercules, you are a wild and wicked woman!
You dare to claim this dress I hold was stolen from you?
Another woman gave it to me for . . . repairs.

WIFE:

By Castor – no, I'd better have my father come,
So I can tell him all of your disgracefulness.
[*Calls in to one of her slaves*] Oh, Decio – go find my
    father, bring him here.
And tell my father the entire situation.
[*To* MENAECHMUS II] I'll now expose all your
    disgracefulness.

MENAECHMUS II:

        You're sick!
All what disgracefulness?

WIFE:

        A dress – and golden bracelet.
740   You rob your legal wife at home and then you go
Bestow it on your mistress. Do I 'babble' truth?

MENAECHMUS II:

Dear Madam, can you tell me please what I might drink
To make your bitchy boorishness more bearable?
I've not the slightest notion who you think I am.
I know you like I know the father-in-law of Hercules!³²

WIFE:

You may mock me, by Pollux, but you can't mock *him*.
My father's coming. [*To* MENAECHMUS II] Look who's
    coming, look who's coming;
You do know *him*.

MENAECHMUS II [*ironically*]:
  Of course, a friend of Agamemnon.[33]
  I first met him the day I first met you – *today*.
WIFE:
  You claim that you don't know me, or my father?   750
MENAECHMUS II:
  And how about your grandpa – I don't know him either.
WIFE:
  By Castor, you just never change, *you never change!*
  [*Enter the* OLD MAN, MENAECHMUS' *father-in-law, groaning and wheezing*]
OLD MAN [*to the audience, in halting song*]:
  Oh, my old age, my old age, I lack what I need,
  I'm stepping unlively, unfast is my speed,
  But it isn't so easy, I tell you, not easy indeed.
  For I've lost all my quickness, old age is a sickness.
  My body's a big heavy trunk, I've no strength.
  Oh oh, old age is bad – no more vigour remains.
  Oh, when old age arrives, it brings plenty of pains.
  I could mention them all but I won't talk at length.   760
  But deep in my heart is this worry:
  My daughter has sent for me now in a hurry.
  She won't say what it is,
  What it is I've not heard.
  She just asked me to come, not explaining a word.

  And yet I've a pretty good notion at that:
  That her husband and she are involved in a spat.
  Well, that's how it is always with big-dowry wives,[34]
  They're fierce to their husbands, they order their lives.
  But then sometimes the man is ... let's say ... not so
    pure.
  There's limits to what a good wife can endure.
  And, by Pollux, a daughter won't send for her dad.   770
  Unless there's some cause, and her husband's been bad.
  Well, anyway I can find out since my daughter is here.
  Her husband looks angry. Just what I suspected, it's
    clear.

        [*The song ends. A brief pause*]
        I'll address her.
WIFE:
           I'll go meet him. Many greetings, Father dear.
OLD MAN:
        Same to you. I only hope I've come when all is fine and
           dandy.
        Why are you so gloomy, why does he stand off there,
           looking angry?
        Has there been some little skirmishing between the two of
           you?
        Tell me who's at fault, be brief. No lengthy arguments at
           length.
WIFE:
780   *I've* done nothing wrong, dear Father, you can be assured
           of that.
        But I simply can't go on and live with him in any way.
        Consequently – take me home.
OLD MAN:
           What's wrong?
WIFE:
           I'm made a total fool of.
OLD MAN:
        How and who?
WIFE:
           By him, the man you signed and sealed to me as
               husband.
OLD MAN:
        Oh, I see, disputing, eh? And yet I've told you countless
           times
        Both of you beware, don't either one approach me with
           complaints.
WIFE:
        How can I beware, when he's as bad as this?
OLD MAN:
           You're asking me?
WIFE:
        Tell me.

OLD MAN:
> Oh, the countless times I've preached on duty to your
>   husband:
Don't check what he's doing, where he's going, what his
    business is.[35]

WIFE:
But he loves a fancy woman right next door.

OLD MAN:
> He's very wise!   790
Thanks to all your diligence, I promise you, he'll love her
    more.

WIFE:
But he also boozes there.

OLD MAN:
> You think you'll make him booze the less,
If he wants to, anywhere he wants? Why must you be so
    rash?
Might as well go veto his inviting visitors to dine,
Say he can't have guests at home. What do you women
    want from husbands?
Servitude? Why, next you'll want him to do chores around
    the house!
Next you'll order him to sit down with the maids and card
    the wool!

WIFE:
Father dear, I called you to support my cause, not help my
    husband.
You're a lawyer prosecuting your own client.

OLD MAN:
> If *he's* wrong,
I'll attack him ten times harder than I'm now attacking you.   800
Look, you're quite well dressed, well jewelled and well
    supplied with food and maids.
Being well off, woman, why, be wise, leave well enough
    alone.

WIFE:
But he filches all the jewels and all the dresses from the
    house.

Stealing on the sly, he then bestows the stuff on fancy
women.

OLD MAN:

Oh, he's wrong if he does that, but if he doesn't, then
you're wrong,

Blaming blameless men.

WIFE:

He has a dress this very moment, Father,

And a bracelet he's brought from her because I've found
him out.

OLD MAN:

Well, I'll get the facts, I'll go accost the man, and speak to
him.

[*He puffs over to* MENAECHMUS II]

Say, Menaechmus, tell me why you're muttering. I'll
understand.

810   Why are you so gloomy? Why is she so angry over
there?

MENAECHMUS II:

Whatever your name is, old man, and whoever you are, I
swear by Jove supreme,

Calling all the gods to witness –

OLD MAN:

Witness for what, about what in the world?

MENAECHMUS II:

Never ever did I hurt this woman now accusing me of

Having sneaked into her house and filched this dress.

WIFE:

He's telling lies!

MENAECHMUS II:

If I've ever set a single foot inside that house of hers,

Anxiously I long to be the very saddest man on earth.

OLD MAN:

No, you can't be sane too long for that, to claim you've not
set foot

In the house you live in. Why, you're the very *maddest* man
on earth!

MENAECHMUS II:
   What was that, old man? You claim I live right here and in
   this house?   820
OLD MAN:
   You deny it?
MENAECHMUS II:
   I deny it.
OLD MAN:
            Your denial isn't true.
   That's unless you moved away last night. Daughter, come
   over here.
   [*Father and daughter walk aside;* OLD MAN *whispers con-*
   fidentially]
   Tell me – did you move away from here last night?
WIFE:
            Where to? What for?
OLD MAN:
   I don't know, by Pollux.
WIFE:
            He's just mocking you – or don't you get it?
OLD MAN:
   That's enough, Menaechmus, no more joking, now let's
   tend to business.
MENAECHMUS II:
   Tell me, sir, what business do you have with me? Just who
   are you?
   What have I to do with you or – [*points to* WIFE] that one,
   who is such a bother?
WIFE:
   Look – his eyes are getting green, a greenish colour's now
   appearing
   From his temples and his forehead. Look, his eyes are
   flickering!   830
MENAECHMUS II [*aside, to the audience*]:
   Nothing could be better. Since they both declare that I'm
   raving mad
   I'll pretend I am insane, and scare them both away from me.

[MENAECHMUS *begins to 'go berserk'*]

WIFE:

What a gaping mouth, wide open. Tell me what to do, dear
Father.

OLD MAN:

Over here, dear Daughter, get as far as possible from him.

MENAECHMUS II [*caught up in his own act, 'hearing' divine
words*]:

Bacchus! Yo-ho, Bacchus, in what forest do you bid me
hunt?

Yes, I hear you, but I can't escape from where I am just
now:

On my left I'm guarded by a very rabid female dog.

Right behind her is a goat who reeks of garlic, and this goat
has

Countless times accused a blameless citizen with perjury.[36]

OLD MAN [*enraged*]:

You you you, I'll –

MENAECHMUS II [*'hearing'*]:

840   What, Apollo? Now your oracle commands me:

Take some hotly blazing torches, set this woman's eyes on
fire.

WIFE:

Father, Father – what a threat! He wants to set my eyes on
fire!

MENAECHMUS II [*aside, to audience*]:

They both say I'm crazy; I know they're the really crazy
ones!

OLD MAN:

Daughter –

WIFE:

        Yes?

OLD MAN:

                Suppose I go, and send some servants here at
                        once.

Let them come and take him off, and tie him up with ropes
at home.

Now – before he makes a bigger hurricane!

MENAECHMUS II:

    I'm caught!

I'll be taken off unless I find myself a plan right now.

[*'Hearing oracle', aloud*] Yes, Apollo, 'Do not spare thy
    fists in punching in her face?

That's unless she hurries out of sight and quickly goes to
    hell!'

Yes, Apollo, I'll obey you.

OLD MAN:

    Run, dear Daughter – quickly home!   850

Otherwise, he'll pound you.

WIFE:

    While I run, please keep an eye on him.

See he doesn't get away. [*A final groan*] What wifely woe to
    hear such things!

[*Exit*]

MENAECHMUS II:

Hah, not bad, I got *her* off. And now I'll get *this* – poisoned
    person,

White-beard, palsied wreck. Tithonus was a youth
    compared to him.[37]

[*To 'Apollo'*] What's my orders? Beat the fellow limb from
    limb and bone from bone?

Use the very stick he carries for the job?

OLD MAN:

    I'll punish you –

If you try to touch me, if you try to get much closer to me!

MENAECHMUS II [*to 'Apollo'*]:

Yes, I'll do thy bidding: take a double axe and this old
    fogey,

Chop his innards into little pieces, till I reach the bone?

OLD MAN [*panicked*]:

Goodness, now's the time for me to be on guard and very
    wary.   860

I'm afraid he'll carry out his threats and cause some harm
    to me.

MENAECHMUS II [*to 'Apollo' again*]:
  Dear Apollo, you command so much. I now must hitch up
    horses,
  Wild, ferocious horses, and then mount up in my chariot,
  Then to trample on this lion – creaking, stinking, toothless
    lion?
  Now I'm in the chariot, I've got the reins, I've got the whip.
  Up up up, ye steeds, now let us see the sound of horses'
    hoofbeats.[38]
  Quickly curve your course with splendid speed and swifty
    swoop of steps.

OLD MAN:
  Threatening me with hitched-up horses?

MENAECHMUS II:
        Yea, Apollo, once again,
  Now you bid me charge and overwhelm the man who's
    standing here.
870 [*Fakes Homeric divine intervention*] But what's this? Who
    takes me by the hair and hauls me from the car?[39]
  Look, Apollo, someone's changing your command as spoke
    to me!

OLD MAN:
  By Hercules, he's sick, he's very sick. Ye gods!
  And just a while ago, the man was very sane,
  But suddenly this awful sickness fell on him.
  I'll go and get a doctor – fast as possible.
    [*Exit at a senile sprint*]

MENAECHMUS II:
  Well, have they disappeared from sight, the two of them,
  Who forced a normal, healthy man to act insane?
  I shouldn't wait to reach my ship while things are safe.
880 [*To the audience*] But, everybody, please – if that old man
    returns,
  Don't tell him, please, which street I took to get away.
    [*He dashes off-stage, towards the harbour. Enter* OLD
    MAN,[40] *tired, annoyed, complaining*]

OLD MAN:
  My limbs just ache from sitting and my eyes from looking,

While waiting for that doctor to leave office hours.
At last, unwillingly, he left his patients. What a bore!
He claims he'd set Asclepius' broken leg,
And then Apollo's broken arm. I wonder if
The man I bring's a doctor or a carpenter!
But here he's strutting now. [*Calling off*] Why can't you
    hurry up?
    [*Enter* DOCTOR, *the superprofessional*]

DOCTOR [*right to the point*]:
As for illness does he have? Speak up, old man.
Is he depressed, or is he frantic?[41] Give the facts.   890
Or is he in a coma? Has he liquid dropsy?

OLD MAN:
But that's precisely why I've brought you – to tell *me* –
And make him well again.

DOCTOR:
        Of course. A snap.
He shall be well again. You have my word on that.

OLD MAN:
I want him to be cared for with the greatest care.

DOCTOR:
I'll sigh a thousand sighs, I'll take great pains with him.
For you – I'll care for him with all the greatest care.
But here's the man himself; let's see how he behaves.
    [*They step aside to eavesdrop. From the forum side enter*
    MENAECHMUS, *addressing himself in soliloquy*]

MENAECHMUS:
Pollux, what a day for me: perverted and inverted too.
Everything I plotted to be private's now completely public.   900
My own parasite has filled me full of fearful accusations!
My Ulysses, causing so much trouble for his royal patron![42]
If I live, I'll skin him live. I'll cut off all his livelihood.
What a foolish thing to say. What I call his is really mine.
My own food and fancy living nurtured him. I'll starve him
    now.
And my slut has been disgraceful. Typical of slutitude.
All I did was ask her to return the dress to give my wife.
She pretends she gave it to me. Pollux, I'm in awful shape!

OLD MAN [*to* DOCTOR]:
Did you hear his words?

DOCTOR [*nods*]:
Admits his 'awful shape'.

OLD MAN:
Go up to him.

DOCTOR [*aloud*]:
910   Greetings, dear Menaechmus. Do you realize that your
cloak has slipped?
Don't you know how dangerous that sort of thing is for
your health?

MENAECHMUS:
Why not hang yourself?

OLD MAN [*whispers to* DOCTOR]:
You notice anything?

DOCTOR:
Of course I do!
This condition couldn't be relieved with tons of hellebore.[43]
[*To* MENAECHMUS, *again*] Tell me now, Menaechmus.

MENAECHMUS:
Tell what?

DOCTOR:
Just answer what I ask.
Do you drink white wine or red?

MENAECHMUS:
And why don't you go straight to hell?

DOCTOR:
Hercules, I notice teeny traces of insanity.

MENAECHMUS:
Why not ask
Do I favour purple bread, or pink or maybe even mauve?
Do I eat the gills of birds, the wings of fishes – ?

OLD MAN:
Oh, good grief!
920   Listen to his ravings, you can hear the words. Why wait at
all?
Give the man some remedy before the madness takes him
fully.

DOCTOR:

Wait – I have more questions.

OLD MAN:

But you're killing him with all this blab!

DOCTOR [*to* MENAECHMUS]:

Tell me this about your eyes: at times do they get glazed at
all?

MENAECHMUS:

What? You think you're talking to a lobster, do you, rotten
man!

DOCTOR [*unfazed*]:

Tell me, have you ever noticed your intestines making
noise?

MENAECHMUS:

When I've eaten well, they're silent; when I'm hungry, they
make noise.

DOCTOR:

Pollux, that's a pretty healthy answer he just gave to me.
[*To* MENAECHMUS] Do you sleep right through till dawn,
sleep easily when you're in bed?

MENAECHMUS:

I sleep through if all the debts I owe are paid. But listen
you, you   930
Question-asker, you be damned by Jupiter and all the gods!

DOCTOR:

Now I know the man's insane, those final words are proof.
[*To* OLD MAN]
Take care!

OLD MAN:

He speaks like a Nestor now,[44] compared to just a while
ago.
Just a while ago he called his wife a rabid female dog.

MENAECHMUS:

I said that?

OLD MAN:

You're mad, I say.

MENAECHMUS:

I'm mad?

OLD MAN:

               And do you know what else? You

Also threatened that you'd trample over me with teams of
   horses!

940   Yes, I saw you do it. Yes, and I insist you did it, too.

MENAECHMUS [to OLD MAN]:

You, of course, have snatched the sacred crown of Jove,
   that's what I know.

Afterwards, they tossed you into prison for this awful
   crime.

When they let you out, while you were manacled, they beat
   you up.

Then you killed your father. Then you sold your mother as
   a slave.

Have you heard enough to know I'm sane enough to curse
   you back?

OLD MAN:

Doctor, please be quick and do whatever must be done for
   him.

Don't you see the man's insane?

DOCTOR:

       I think the wisest thing for you's to

Have the man delivered to my office.

OLD MAN:

       Do you think?

DOCTOR:

          Of course.

There I'll treat him pursuant to diagnosis.

OLD MAN:

       As you say.

DOCTOR [to MENAECHMUS]:

950   Yes, I'll have you drinking hellebore for twenty days or so.

MENAECHMUS:

Then I'll have you beaten hanging upside down for thirty
   days.

DOCTOR [to OLD MAN]:

Go and call for men who can deliver him.

OLD MAN:
>How many men?

DOCTOR:
From the way he's acting, I'd say four, none less could do the job.

OLD MAN [*exiting*]:
They'll be here. You watch him, Doctor.

DOCTOR [*anxious to retreat*]:
>No, I think I'd best go home.
Preparations are in order for the case. You get the slaves. Have them carry him to me.

OLD MAN:
>I will.

DOCTOR:
>>I'm going now.

OLD MAN:
>>Goodbye.

MENAECHMUS:
Doctor's gone, father-in-law's gone. I'm now alone. By Jupiter! –
What does all this mean? Why do these men insist that I'm insane?
Really, I have not been sick a single day since I've been born.
Nor am I insane, nor have I punched or fought with anyone.
Healthy, I see healthy people, only talk with folks I know.
Maybe those who wrongly say I'm mad are really mad themselves.
What should I do now? My wife won't let me home, as I would like.
[*Pointing to* EROTIUM*'s house*] No one will admit me there.
All's well[45] – well out of hand, that is.
Here I'm stuck. At least by night – I think – they'll let me in my house.
[MENAECHMUS *sits dejectedly in front of his house, all wrapped up in his troubles. From the other side of the*

960

stage, enter MESSENIO *singing about How to Succeed in Slavery*]

MESSENIO:

If you should seek the proof of whether someone's slave is
   good,
See, does he guard his master's interest, serve right to the
   letter
When Master is away – the way he should
If Master were at hand – or even better.
For if the slave is worthy, and he's well brought up,
970   He'll care to keep his shoulders empty – not to fill his cup.
His master will reward him. Let the worthless slave be told
The lowly, lazy louts get whips and chains,
And millstones, great starvation, freezing cold.
The price for all their misbehaviours: pains.
I therefore fully fear this fate and very gladly
Remain determined to be good – so I won't turn out badly.
I'd so much rather be bawled out than sprawled out on a
   pillory,
I'd so much rather eat what's cooked than have some work
   cooked up for me.
980   So I follow Master's orders, never argue or protest.
Let the others do it their way; I obey; for me, that's
   best[46] ...
But I haven't much to fear; the time is near for something
   nice.[47]
My master will reward his slave for 'thinking with his back'
   – and thinking twice.

[*Enter* OLD MAN, *leading four burly servants*]

OLD MAN:

990   Now, by all the gods and men, I bid you all obey my
   orders.
Be most careful so you'll follow what I've ordered and will
   order.
Have that man picked up aloft, and carried to the doctor's
   office.
That's unless you're not a bit concerned about *your* back
   and limbs.

Every man beware. Don't pay attention to his threats of
   violence.
But why just stand? Why hesitate? It's time to lift the man
   aloft!
[*Not very brave himself*] And I'll head for the doctor's
   office. I'll be there when you arrive.
MENAECHMUS [*notices the charging mob*]:
   I'm dead! What's this? I wonder why these men are rushing
      swiftly toward me?
   Hey, men, what do you want? What are you after? Why
      surround me now?
   [*They snatch up* MENAECHMUS]
   Where are you snatching me and taking me? Won't
      someone help me, please?
   O citizens of Epidamnus, rescue me! [*To slaves*] Please let
      me go!   1000
MESSENIO:
   By the immortal gods, what am I seeing with my very eyes?
   Some unknown men are lifting Master in the air.
      Outrageously!
MENAECHMUS:
   Won't someone dare to help?
MESSENIO:
      Me, me! I'll dare to help with derring-do!
   O citizens of Epidamnus, what a dirty deed to Master!
   Do peaceful towns allow a free-born tourist to be seized in
      daylight?
   [*To slaves*] You let him go!
MENAECHMUS [*to* MESSENIO]:
      Whoever you may be, please help me out!
   Don't allow this awful outrage to be perpetrated on me.
MESSENIO:
   Why, of course I'll help, and hustle hurriedly to your
      defence.
   Never would I let you down. I'd rather let myself down
      first.   1010
   [*To* MENAECHMUS] Grab that fellow's eye – the one who's
      got you by the shoulder now.

I can plough the other guys and plant a row of fists in them.
[*To slaves*] Hercules, you'll lose an awful lot by taking him.
Let go!
[*A wild mêlée ensues*]
MENAECHMUS [*while fighting, to* MESSENIO]:
Hey, I've got his eye.
MESSENIO:
          Then make the socket in his head appear!
Evil people! People snatchers! Bunch of pirates!
SLAVES [*together*]:
          Woe is us!
Hercules! No – please!
MESSENIO:
          Let go!
MENAECHMUS:
               What sort of handiwork is this?
Face a festival of fists.
MESSENIO:
          Go on, be gone, and go to hell!
[*Kicking the slowest slave*] You take that as your reward for
     being last to get away.
[*They are all gone.* MESSENIO *takes a deep breath of satis-
     faction*]
Well, I've really made my mark – on every face I've faced
     today.
1020   Pollux, Master, didn't I come just in time to bring you aid!
MENAECHMUS:
Whoever you are, young man, I hope the gods will always
     bring you blessings.
If it hadn't been for you, I'd not have lived to see the
     sunset.
MESSENIO:
If that's true, by Pollux, then do right by me and free me,
     Master.
MENAECHMUS:
Free you? I?
MESSENIO:
          Of course. Because I saved you, Master.

MENAECHMUS:
            Listen here, you're
Wand'ring from the truth –
MESSENIO:
        I wander?
MENAECHMUS:
            Yes, I swear by Father Jove
I am not your master.
MESSENIO [*stunned*]:
        Why proclaim such things?
MENAECHMUS:
            But it's no lie.
Never did a slave of mine serve me as well as you just
    did.
MESSENIO:
    If you're so insistent and deny I'm yours, then I'll go free.
MENAECHMUS:
    Hercules, as far as I'm concerned, be free. Go where you'd
        like.
MESSENIO:
    Am I really authorized?
MENAECHMUS:
            If I've authority for you.   1030
MESSENIO [*dialogue with himself*]:
    'Greetings, patron.' – 'Ah, Messenio, the fact that you're
        now free
    Makes me very glad.' – 'Well, I believe that's true.' [*To*
        MENAECHMUS] But, patron dear,
    You can have authority no less than when I was a slave.
    I'll be glad to live with you, and when you go, go home
        with you.
MENAECHMUS [*doesn't want some strange person in his
        house*]:
    Not at all, no thank you.
MESSENIO [*jubilant*]:
            Now I'll get our baggage at the inn –
    And, of course, the purse with all our money's sealed up in
        the trunk

With our travel cash. I'll bring it to you.

MENAECHMUS [*eyes lighting up at this*]:
    Yes! Go quickly, quickly!

MESSENIO:
    I'll return it just exactly as you gave it to me. Wait right
    here.
    [MESSENIO *dashes off towards the harbour*]

MENAECHMUS [*soliloquizing*]:
    What unworldly wonders have occurred today in wondrous
    ways:

1040   People claim I'm not the man I am and keep me from their
    houses.
    Then this fellow said he was my slave – and that I set him
    free!
    Then he says he'll go and bring a wallet full of money to
    me.
    If he does, I'll tell him he can go quite freely where he'd
    like –
    That's so when he's sane again he won't demand the money
    back.
    [*Musing more*] Father-in-law and doctor said I was insane.
    How very strange.
    All this business seems to me like nothing other than a
    dream.
    Now I'll go and see this harlot, though she's in a huff with
    me.
    Maybe I'll convince her to return the dress, which I'll take
    home.
    [*He enters* EROTIUM's *house. Enter* MENAECHMUS II *and*
    MESSENIO]

MENAECHMUS II [*angry with* MESSENIO]:
1050   Effrontery in front of me! You dare to claim we've seen
    each other
    Since I gave you orders that we'd meet back here?

MESSENIO:
    But didn't I just
    Snatch and rescue you from those four men who carried
    you aloft

Right before this house? You called on all the gods and men
    for aid.
I came running, snatched you from them, though with fists
    they fought me back.
For this service, since I saved your life, you made a free
    man of me.
[*Ruefully*] Now just when I said I'd get the cash and
    baggage, you sped up and
Ran ahead to meet me, and deny you've done the things
    you've done.

MENAECHMUS II:
Free? I said you could go free?

MESSENIO:
    For sure.

MENAECHMUS II:
        Now look, for *super*-sure
I would rather make *myself* a slave than ever set you free.
    [MENAECHMUS I *is pushed by* EROTIUM *out of her house*]

MENAECHMUS I:
If you would like to swear by your two eyes, go right
    ahead, but still   1060
You'll never prove that I absconded with your dress and
    bracelet – [*door slams*] hussy!

MESSENIO [*suddenly seeing double*]:
By the gods, what do I see?

MENAECHMUS II:
    What do you see?

MESSENIO:
        Why – your reflection!

MENAECHMUS II:
What?

MESSENIO:
    Your very image just as like yourself as it could be.

MENAECHMUS II:
Pollux – he's not unlike me . . . I notice . . . similarities.

MENAECHMUS I [*to* MESSENIO]:
Hey, young man, hello! You saved my life – whoever you
    may be.

MESSENIO:
> You, young man, if you don't mind, would you please tell
> me your name?

MENAECHMUS I:
> Nothing you could ask would be too much since you have
> helped me so.
> My name is Menaechmus.

MENAECHMUS II:
> Oh, by Pollux, so is mine as well!

MENAECHMUS I:
> Syracuse-Sicilian –

MENAECHMUS II:
> That's my city, that's my country too!

MENAECHMUS I:
1070   What is this I hear?

MENAECHMUS II:
> Just what is true.

MESSENIO [to MENAECHMUS II]:
> I know you – *you're* my master!
> [*To audience*] I belong to this man though I thought that I
> belonged to that man.
> [*To* MENAECHMUS I, *the wrong man*] Please excuse me, sir,
> if I unknowingly spoke foolishly.
> For a moment I imagined he was you – and gave him
> trouble.

MENAECHMUS II:
> Madness, nothing but! [*To* MESSENIO] Don't you recall
> that we were both together,
> Both of us got off the ship today?

MESSENIO [*thinking, realizing*]:
> That's right. You're very right.
> *You're* my master. [*To* MENAECHMUS I] Find another
> slave, farewell. [*To* MENAECHMUS II] And you,
> hello!
> [*Pointing to* MENAECHMUS II] Him, I say, this man's
> Menaechmus.

MENAECHMUS I:
> So am I!

MENAECHMUS II:
> What joke is this?
You're Menaechmus?
MENAECHMUS I:
> That I say I am. My father's name was Moschus.
MENAECHMUS II:
You're the son of my own father?
MENAECHMUS I:
> No, the son of *my* own father.
I'm not anxious to appropriate your father or to steal him
   from you.   1080
MESSENIO:
Gods in heaven, grant me now that hope unhoped-for I
   suspect.
For, unless my mind has failed me, these two men are both
   twin brothers.
Each man claims the selfsame fatherland and father for his
   own.
I'll call Master over. O Menaechmus!
MENAECHMUS I *and* II [*together*]:
> Yes?
MESSENIO:
> Not both of you.
Which of you two travelled with me on the ship?
MENAECHMUS I:
> It wasn't me.
MENAECHMUS II:
Me it was.
MESSENIO:
> Then you I want. Step over here [*motioning*].
MENAECHMUS II [*following* MESSENIO *to a corner*]:
> I've stepped. What's up?
MESSENIO:
That man there is either one great faker or your lost twin
   brother.
Never have I seen two men more similar than you two
   men:
Water isn't more like water, milk's not more alike to milk

1090   Than that man is like to you. And what's more he named
         your father.
      And your fatherland. It's best to go and question him still
         further.

MENAECHMUS II:
      Hercules, you do advise me well. I'm very grateful to you.
      Please work on, by Hercules. I'll make you free if you
         discover
      That man is my brother.

MESSENIO:
         Oh, I hope so.

MENAECHMUS II:
         And I hope so too.

MESSENIO [to MENAECHMUS I]:
      Sir, I do believe you've just asserted that you're named
         Menaechmus.

MENAECHMUS I:
      That is so.

MESSENIO:
         Well, his name is Menaechmus, too. You also said
      You were born in Sicily at Syracuse. Well, so was he.
      Moschus was your father, so you said. That was *his* father,
         too.
      Both of you can do yourselves a favour – and help me as
         well.[48]

MENAECHMUS I:
1100   Anything you ask me I'll comply with, I'm so grateful to
         you.
      Treat me just as if I were your purchased slave – although
         I'm free.

MESSENIO:
      It's my hope to prove you are each other's brothers, twins
         in fact,
      Born of the selfsame mother, selfsame father, on the
         selfsame day.

MENAECHMUS I:
      Wonder-laden words. Oh, would you could make all your
         words come true.

MESSENIO:
> Well, I can. But, both of you, just give replies to what I ask
> you.

MENAECHMUS I:
> Ask away. I'll answer. I won't hide a single thing I know.

MESSENIO:
> Is your name Menaechmus?

MENAECHMUS I:
>> Absolutely.

MESSENIO [to MENAECHMUS II]:
>> Is it yours as well?

MENAECHMUS II:
> Yes.

MESSENIO:
>> You said your father's name was Moschus.

MENAECHMUS I:
>> Yes.

MENAECHMUS II:
>>> The same for me.

MESSENIO:
> And you're Syracusan?

MENAECHMUS I:
>> Surely.

MESSENIO [to MENAECHMUS II]:
>>> You?

MENAECHMUS II:
>>> You *know* I am, of course.

MESSENIO:
> Well, so far the signs are good. Now turn your minds to
> further questions.   1110
> [To MENAECHMUS I] What's the final memory you carry
> from your native land?

MENAECHMUS I [reminiscing]:
> With my father . . . visiting Tarentum for the fair. Then
> after that . . .
> Wandering among the people, far from Father . . . Being
> snatched —

MENAECHMUS II [*bursting with joy*]:
Jupiter above, now help me –!

MESSENIO [*officiously*]:
What's the shouting? You shut up.
[*Turning back to* MENAECHMUS I] Snatched from father
and from fatherland, about how old were you?

MENAECHMUS I:
Seven or so. My baby teeth had barely started to fall out.
After that, I never saw my father.

MESSENIO:
No? Well, tell me this:
At the time how many children did he have?

MENAECHMUS I:
I think just two.

MESSENIO:
Which were you, the older or the younger?

MENAECHMUS I:
Neither, we were equal.

MESSENIO:
1120   Do explain.

MENAECHMUS I:
We were both twins.

MENAECHMUS II [*ecstatic*]:
Oh – all the gods are with me now!

MESSENIO [*sternly, to* MENAECHMUS II]:
Interrupt and I'll be quiet.

MENAECHMUS II [*obedient*]:
I'll be quiet.

MESSENIO [*to* MENAECHMUS I]:
Tell me this:
Did you both have just one name?

MENAECHMUS I:
Oh, not at all. My name is mine,
As it is today – Menaechmus. Brother's name was
Sosicles.

MENAECHMUS II [*mad with joy*]:
Yes, I recognize the signs. I can't keep from embracing
you!

Brother, dear twin brother, greetings! I am he – I'm
 Sosicles!

MENAECHMUS I:

How is it you afterward received the name Menaechmus,
 then?

MENAECHMUS II:

When we got the news that you had wandered off away
 from Father
And that you were kidnapped by an unknown man, and
 Father died,
Grandpa changed my name. The name you used to have he
 gave to me.

MENAECHMUS I:

Yes, I do believe it's as you say. [*Goes to embrace him,
 suddenly stops*] But tell me this.

MENAECHMUS II:

Just ask.   1130

MENAECHMUS I:

What was Mother's name?

MENAECHMUS II:

Why, Teuximarcha.

MENAECHMUS I:

That's correct, it fits.
Unexpectedly I greet you, see you after so much time!

MENAECHMUS II:

Brother, now I find you after so much suffering and toil,
Searching for you, now you're found, and I'm so very, very
 glad.
[*They embrace*]

MESSENIO [*to* MENAECHMUS II]:

That's the reason why the slut could call you by your
 rightful name,
Thinking you were he, I think, when she invited you to
 dinner.

MENAECHMUS I:

Yes, by Pollux, I had ordered dinner for myself today,
Hidden from my wife – from whom I filched a dress a while
 ago – and

Gave it to her. [*Indicates* EROTIUM's *house*]

MENAECHMUS II:
>   Could you mean this dress I'm holding, Brother dear?

MENAECHMUS I:
1140   That's the one. How did you get it?

MENAECHMUS II:
>   Well, the slut led me to dinner.
>   There she claimed I gave it to her. *Wonderfully* have I just
>   dined,
>   Wined as well as concubined, of dress and gold I robbed
>   her blind.

MENAECHMUS I:
>   Oh, by Pollux, I rejoice if you had fun because of me!
>   When she asked you in to dinner, she believed that you
>   were me.

MESSENIO [*impatient for himself*]:
>   Is there any reason to delay the freedom that you promised?

MENAECHMUS I:
>   Brother, what he asks is very fair and fine. Please do it for
>   me.

MENAECHMUS II [*to* MESSENIO, *the formula*]:
>   'Be thou free.'

MENAECHMUS I:
>   The fact you're free now makes me glad, Messenio.

MESSENIO [*broadly hinting for some cash reward*]:
1150   Actually, I need more facts, *supporting* facts to keep me
>   free.

MENAECHMUS II [*ignoring* MESSENIO, *to his brother*]:
>   Since our dreams have come about exactly as we wished,
>   dear Brother,
>   Let us both return to our homeland.

MENAECHMUS I:
>   Brother, as you wish.
>   I can hold an auction and sell off whatever I have here.
>   Meanwhile, let's go in.

MENAECHMUS II:
>   That's fine.

MESSENIO [*to* MENAECHMUS I]:
> May I request a favour of you?

MENAECHMUS I:
What?

MESSENIO:
> Please make me do the auctioneering.

MENAECHMUS I:
> Done.

MESSENIO:
> > All right. Then please inform me:
> When should I announce the auction for?

MENAECHMUS I:
> Let's say – a week from now.
> [*The brothers go into* MENAECHMUS' *house, leaving* MESSENIO *alone on stage*]

MESSENIO [*announcing*]:
In the morning in a week from now we'll have
Menaechmus' auction.
Slaves and goods, his farm and city house, his everything
will go.
Name your prices, if you've got the cash in hand, it all will
go.
Yes, and if there's any bidder for the thing – his wife will
go.   1160
Maybe the entire auction will enrich us – who can tell?
For the moment, dear spectators, clap with vigour. Fare ye
well!

Translated by Erich Segal (1996)

TERENCE

THE EUNUCH

PREFACE

We know that the *Eunuch* was Terence's most successful play
– but some readers are hard pressed to understand why. It was
raunchy and bawdy, but it was not as 'vulgar and useless', or
still worse, 'abjectly Plautine' as one scholar complained. What
is important is that it thrilled the Roman audience. Let us think
positively and enumerate its virtues.

To begin with, it has a full-blown Terentian double plot
featuring complementary love affairs. Young Phaedria is enamoured of a courtesan Thais. His brother Chaerea is smitten
by a young slave girl offered to Thais as a present by Phaedria's
rival Thraso, a blustering soldier. The piquant aspect of this
second plot involves a masquerade that will become a familiar
element in later comedy, but is presented here perhaps for the
first time.

Love-struck at the sight of the maiden Pamphila, Chaerea is
so desperate to meet her that he disguises himself as a eunuch
(very useful for guarding the harem) and changes places with
the exotic gift (Eunuch) his brother is giving the courtesan. The
results are predictable. Thought to be harmless, he is put in
charge of watching the young girl – and at the first opportunity
rapes her.

This brutal stratagem provided the raw material for such
later plays as Wycherley's masterpiece *The Country Wife*
(1675), where Horner the protagonist pretends he is impotent
and therefore gains access to any woman he wants. It is hardly
the tenderest of themes, even before the substitution of Restor-
ation cynicism for Terentian sentimentality. The audience could
no doubt guess the outcome of the young girl's violation. For

there is no rape in all of ancient comedy that is not set straight at the end by a lawful marriage. The 'forced seduction' of Pamphila will be righted by the revelation that she is in reality freeborn and therefore marriageable. This is accomplished when her ancient nurse is sent for and recognizes 'all the clues' which reveal the heroine to be the long-lost sister of a rich and noble lad named Chremes. Thus much for the younger brother, we may even call this a conventional ending. But the experience of his older brother is a bit more problematic.

From another play Terence has grafted the farcical figure of a braggart soldier, Thraso, who is silly, vain and rich. His name survives in the English adjective 'thrasonic', attesting to his memorable effect on audiences. His side-kick Gnatho ('Mr Gobbler') is both a vainglorious and a grovelling, professional parasite. The toady fancies himself a philosopher, but this is merely a sideline to his professional appetite. These characters appear to be barely integrated into Terence's comedy. We might say they are presented, for lack of a better term, as comic relief. Indeed, this may be part of the point, given that they have some of the best scenes, but Thraso and Gnatho also develop the play's theme and make its conclusion possible.

The more unusual aspect of *The Eunuch* is the older brother's campaign to win the favours of the good-natured prostitute, Thais. The family praises her generous actions whereby, as Chaerea exclaims, their household is 'Just one big happy family' (1038). Negotiating on behalf of his military master, Gnatho, the parasite, proposes an unusual deal: the young hero, Phaedria, could *share* the favours of Thais with his military master (who is relatively harmless), in exchange for which the soldier will foot all the bills. Phaedria agrees and all three of them live happily ever after.

This *ménage à trois* was scandalous in the Rome of Cato the Elder. Could this piquant arrangement alone explain the crowd's demand for an immediate encore? Is it not the ideal reward for a comic hero – sex with neither strings nor price-tag attached? For this Terence received the unprecedented reward of eight thousand sesterces, the largest sum ever paid to a Roman comic playwright.

And yet it was for other reasons that Terence became a 'classic', a paradigm for comic authors forever after. And paradoxically, it was his most problematic play that best demonstrated the essence of his achievement.

CHARACTERS

PHAEDRIA, *a young Athenian, elder son of Demea*
PARMENO, *slave to Demea*
THAIS, *a professional woman*
GNATHO, *a diner-out*
CHAEREA, *younger son of Demea*
THRASO, *a military man*
PYTHIAS, *chief maid to Thais*
DORIAS, *maid to Thais*
CHREMES, *a young country gentleman*
ANTIPHO, *friend to Chaerea*
DORUS, *a eunuch*
SANGA, *cook to Thraso*
SOPHRONA, *an elderly nurse*
DEMEA,[1] *an elderly Athenian, father of Phaedria and Chaerea*

Silent Characters

PAMPHILA, *a virgin*
Her maid
An Ethiopian girl slave
WOMEN *of Thais' household*
SIMALIO ⎫
DONAX ⎬ *household slaves to Thraso*
SYRISCUS ⎭

The Scene is Athens.

PROLOGUE

Conceivably, playwrights exist who strive to supply
Maximum pleasure and minimum pain to people
Of taste. If so, our author declares himself their team-mate.
Conceivably, someone exists[2] who may deduce
That he is the object, in these remarks, of a harsh
Attack. If so, let's have this someone make
Another deduction: *These* words are defensive; the first,
Offensive attack was his.
    After all, a man
Who phrases straight translations in such a tortured
Fashion that the best Greek plays are turned to Latin
Flops; a man who recently managed to murder
Menander's *Ghost*; a man whose *Contested Treasure*[3]   10
(A gem of a play) contains a lawsuit in which
Defendant argues his right to the gold *before*
Plaintiff has brought that right into question – well, such
A man should scarcely presume that he is immune
To critics, or that he's silenced all fire from this quarter.
Fair warning: He really ought to give up war.
His shortcomings fill a long list; I'm glad to forget them –
But I'll publish them all unless he desists from this ceaseless
Sniping. Take today's play – Menander's *Eunuch*.   20
The authorities came, rehearsals began . . . and so
Did he:
    'A pirate did this, not a playwright.
  But he can't fool me. He lifted the leech and the major
  Straight from that antique farce by Naevius and Plautus,
  The Yes-Man.'
    If our author slipped, it was ignorance, void
Of any intent to steal. Here, judge for yourselves:
Menander wrote the original *Yes-Man*, containing   30
A leech (the title role) and a blowhard soldier.

Terence admits that he borrowed both from the Greek
For the cast of his *Eunuch*, but flatly denies any knowledge
Of their previous Latinization.
     If he's still enjoined from employing
This pair by virtue of their prior use ... why, then,
All Comedy must be illegal: Running slaves,
Benevolent ladies, malevolent whores, the changeling
Routine, the stock deception of master by servant,
40   And love ... and hate ... and jealousy ... come down to
    it,
There's nothing to say that hasn't been said before.
Therefore, please be fair. Face facts, and excuse
This new generation for doing once what the old did ...
Over,
     And over,
        And over,
            – I now request
Your silence. Turn your minds to *The Eunuch*'s meaning.

A street in Athens,[4] *on which front two houses: stage
right, that of* DEMEA; *stage left, that of* THAIS. *The latter
possesses an upper window which is, at the moment (and
for most of the play), shuttered. In addition to the
housedoors, there are also two wing exits: stage right, to
the harbour and the country (and hence to the farms of*
DEMEA *and* CHREMES, *as well as to* ANTIPHO's *house);
stage left, to downtown Athens (and hence to* THRASO's
house).

ACT I

Scene 1

PHAEDRIA *and* PARMENO *enter from* DEMEA'*s house*

PHAEDRIA:

... So what do I do *now?* She takes the trouble
To ask me over; do I go? Or make a resolution
To give up paying whores for nothing but insults?
Locks me out ... summons me back ...
    Well, no.
She can go down on her knees; I'm not coming back.

PARMENO:

The perfect approach. Has honour, quality ... *but*   50
It needs ability. Once you start, you've got
To stay with it. Let *her* request a parley. Peace
On *your* terms. Don't weaken. Don't make the first move.
   If you do,
You might as well wear a sign: I LOVE YOU. CAN'T
   LIVE
WITHOUT YOU. And *that* is it, goodbye, you're dead.
   You lose
The war, and she knows it; she'll be one up for life.
Look, boss, you've got some time; give this some concerted
Thought: A state without reason or rules can*not*
Be ruled by reason. You're in that state – in Love,
A mixture of messy, uncivilized drives: Hurt,
Jealousy, Hatred, Forgiveness, Conflict ... the Peace   60
Again ... for a while. No mind can reduce this mess
To any controllable order; you're better off
To spend your effort devising a plan to go mad on.
As for your current private dialogue, this blend
Of pronouns and wounded pride – 'Me to her
While she's with him? I used to be hers; now *he's* it.
I know; I'll die, and then she'll appreciate me' –
Just words. If she can manage to rub her eyes
And squeeze out a dribble of bogus moisture, their fire

Is quenched . . . and you'll be guilty because she says so,
70   And submit to torture because *you* say so.

PHAEDRIA:
        It isn't
Fair. I see it all now: She's a bitch
And I'm a wretch. It makes my gorge rise, and yet
The rest of me burns with love. With wisdom and
        forethought,
All faculties working, fully alive . . . I'm dying
And don't know how to stop.

PARMENO:
        I do. You're held
For ransom; buy your way out. As cheap as you can,
Of course, but hang the expense. Pay what you have to;
Don't worry about it.

PHAEDRIA:
        You think I should?

PARMENO:
        You know
You should. Love itself brings troubles enough;
Brace yourself and bear them – but don't go borrowing
More.
        – Oh-oh. Here comes the blight on the family
80   Farm. She gleans the profits before we can reap.

Scene 2

THAIS *enters from her house. She does not see* PHAEDRIA
and PARMENO

THAIS:
    I'm worried sick about Phaedria. He's mad at me.
    When I sent him away from the house yesterday, I'm afraid
    He got the wrong impression.

PHAEDRIA:
        I'm shaking, Parmeno.
    One look at her and I turn to gooseflesh.

PARMENO:
        Be brave.

[*Pushing* PHAEDRIA *towards* THAIS]
Move up close to the fire. You'll thaw soon enough –
And more than enough.

THAIS:

Who's this? Why, Phaedria, darling!
Have you been waiting out here – standing in the street?
Why didn't you come right in?

PARMENO [*aside*]:

She threw him out,
Of course – but why bring that up?

THAIS:

Now, what's your reason?

PHAEDRIA [*clenched teeth*]:

Because your door's never shut to me. Because
I'm always first in your affections.

THAIS:

Let's forget that.   90

PHAEDRIA:

Forget? Oh, Thais, why is our love so lopsided?
Why is our affair so unfair? Can't we adjust it –
Either you suffer the way I suffer . . . or else
I learn not to give a damn whatever you do?

THAIS:

Phaedria, darling, please don't torture yourself.
I adore you. I swear that I didn't do what I did
Because I prefer someone else. It was just – circumstances.
I had to do it.

PARMENO:

Happens all the time.
So much in love she had to lock you out.

THAIS:

Is that the way you're playing it, Parmeno? My, my.
[*To* PHAEDRIA] First, let me tell you why I had you come
    here.

PHAEDRIA:

Please do.

THAIS [*pointing to* PARMENO]:

But what about *him?* Is he discreet?   100

Can he keep a secret?

PARMENO:
    Nobody better. My tact,
However, has strings attached: I seal my lips
On principle. For truth, no trouble, my mouth stays shut.
But fibs, falsehoods, fabrications . . . right away, I shatter;
I'm a mass of cracks; I leak the secrets everywhere.
So, if you want integrity, tell the truth.

THAIS:
My mother was born on Samos, but lived at Rhodes.

PARMENO:
That secret I can keep.

THAIS:
    While we were there,
A businessman gave her a present – a little girl
Who'd been kidnapped from Attica.

PHAEDRIA:
    From here? A citizen?

THAIS:
I think she is; we couldn't be sure. She could only
Tell us her parents' names, but not her country,
Or any other clues. Too tiny. Her buyer
Had one more report: The pirates who'd sold her to him
Said that they stole her from Sunium.
    From the moment she got her,
Mother trained her thoroughly, and brought her up
Like her very own daughter. In fact, most people thought
That she was my sister. But then the gentleman who kept me
Moved to Athens, and I came along. He was my only
Protector; he left me everything I own.

PARMENO:
    Two lies;
Two leaks.

THAIS:
    How so?

PARMENO:
    First, you weren't content
With one lone keeper; second, he wasn't your only

Source of funds. Phaedria's made considerable
Contributions.

THAIS:
  I agree; but do let me get to the point.
  Later, I began an affair with a military man,
  But he was transferred to Caria. Right after that
  I met you, Phaedria. Since then, you know how close
  You've been to me. I have no secrets from you.

PARMENO:
Parmeno can't keep that one.

THAIS:
  Do you really doubt me?
  Please pay attention.
  Mother died at Rhodes   130
  Just recently. Her brother, who tends, where money's
     concerned,
  To greed, took one look at the girl and saw
  Her beauty and musical talent as potential profit.
  He listed her right on the spot and sold her at auction.
  By great good luck, the buyer was my former lover –
  The military man. In complete and utter ignorance
  Of all this business, he bought her for me as a present.
  But now that he's back in Athens, darling, and knows
  About us – about you and me – he works overtime
  At inventing excuses to keep her.
  According to him,
  It's a matter of trust: If he were completely certain
  That I'd prefer him to you, if he weren't afraid
  That I'd take the girl and drop him, he'd be quite happy   140
  To hand her over. But he has his doubts.
  Or so
  He says. I have my suspicions. I think he's fallen
  For her himself.

PHAEDRIA:
  Anything further than falling?

THAIS:
  Not yet. I asked her. But anyway, Phaedria poopsie,
  I've got to wangle her out of his sweaty paws,

And fast. I have a whole raft of reasons.
　　First,
She *is* my sister, so to speak.
　　Then second,
I want to be the one who brings her back safe
To her family's bosom. I'm on my own in Athens;
I don't have powerful friends or family here.
But by that act of altruism, I can win
Myself an entry, some backing, and all through a labour
Of love. A labour that you can facilitate, Phaedria.

150　　Be a dear and help me, please, by letting
The Major head the cast with me for the next
Few days? [*A pause*]
　　No answer at all?

PHAEDRIA:
　　Of all the unblushing
Tripe! How do I answer behaviour like that?

PARMENO:
Three cheers for our side, boss. It took long enough,
But she got your goat. Today you are a man.

PHAEDRIA:
As if I didn't know what you're aiming at.
'Little girl kidnapped from Attica . . . Mother
Brought her up like her very own . . . my sister,
So to speak . . . I've got to wangle her away . . .
Bring her back to her family's bosom . . .'
　　This whole damned
Prologue was programmed to arrive at the same old point:
He's a guest, and *I'm* dismissed!
　　And why?

160　　There's only one reason: You love him more than me;
You're afraid this imported talent will purloin your military
Paragon – she'll steal your Major!

THAIS:
　　I'm afraid of *that*?

PHAEDRIA:
What other possible worries could you have?
Gifts, for instance? Is he your only donor?

Has my openhandedness ever been closed for repairs?
You told me you were mad for an African maid –
Remember? All my business went by the board
While I went shopping. You told me you wanted a eunuch,
Because only queens have eunuchs.
      Well, yesterday
I found both items. Twenty *minae* I paid
For the set. Rebuffed as I was, did I forget?
Not me. And what's my reward for such service? A snub!   170

THAIS:
Such language, darling.
      But look: I'm honestly
Anxious to work her loose from him, and I really
Believe that this is far and away the best,
The only plan . . . but no. Forget it. Sooner
Than lose your love, I'll do whatever you say.

PHAEDRIA:
I wish you meant that. I wish those words were real.
'Sooner than lose your love . . .' If I could believe
You were telling the truth, no torture would be too much.

PARMENO [*aside*]:
He's wobbling. Worsted by a word. So quickly, too.

THAIS:
That hurts me, dear. Of course I'm telling the truth.
Did you ever hint for anything, even in fun,
That you didn't get from me? But all I want   180
From you is two little days, and I can't get those.

PHAEDRIA:
Well, if it's only two days . . . But don't let two
Turn into twenty.

THAIS:
      I swear it. No more than two.
Two or . . .

PHAEDRIA:
      Two or nothing.

THAIS:
         Two. At most.
You've set the conditions. Now grant me my request.

PHAEDRIA:
  Absolutely. Milady's will must be fulfilled.
THAIS:
  Is it any wonder that I love you? You're such a help!
PHAEDRIA:
  I'll go to the country and waste away for the next
  Two days. It's settled. Thais must be humoured.
  – Parmeno, see that that pair's delivered.
PARMENO:
    Assuredly.
    [*He exits into* DEMEA's *house*]
PHAEDRIA:
  Until we meet again, in two days' time,
190 Thais, farewell.
THAIS:
    Goodbye, Phaedria dearest. [*A pause*]
  Will that be all?
PHAEDRIA:
    Just this. One last request:
  When you're with your Major, be without him.
  Fill your days and nights with loving *me*:
  Miss me, crave me, want me, ache and yearn for me,
  Think me, dream me, hope for bliss with me –
  To sum up, be my soul. As I am yours.
    [*He exits into* DEMEA's *house*]
THAIS:
  Oh, dear. He doesn't seem to trust me much.
  Basically, I'm afraid, he rates me the same
  As other girls. I'm not. My conscience is clear.
  I know I haven't told any lies; I know
200 That I love Phaedria more than anyone else.
  Whatever I've done in this business, I've done to save
  My sister. And now I think (and I certainly hope)
  That I've discovered her brother. He's a young man
  Of the highest background. Comes of excellent family.
  He made an appointment to see me at home today;
  I'll go inside and wait there till he comes.
    [*She exits into her house*]

ACT II

Scene 1

PHAEDRIA *and* PARMENO *enter from* DEMEA's *house.*
PARMENO *stands by the door as* PHAEDRIA *starts reluctantly off right*

PHAEDRIA:
You've got my directions. Have those two delivered.

PARMENO:
Right.
[*He turns to enter the house.* PHAEDRIA *turns back*]

PHAEDRIA:
And don't bungle.
[PARMENO *stops and turns back to him*]

PARMENO:
All right.
[*He turns back to the door.* PHAEDRIA *starts off right, quickly turns back*]

PHAEDRIA:
And don't dawdle.

PARMENO [*as before*]:
All right.
[*He turns back to the door.* PHAEDRIA *starts; turns back again*]

PHAEDRIA:
Are those instructions sufficient?

PARMENO [*giving up any attempt at re-entry*]:
All this asking. You'd think   210
The job was a hard one. Throwing your money away, that's
   easy.
I wish you could make it as simply.

PHAEDRIA:
I'm throwing myself away, too,
And I'm worth more to me than money. Don't be so stingy.

PARMENO:
You're the boss. I'll see it's done.

That's all, I hope.

PHAEDRIA:
Gift-wrap the present in pretty words. Please do your best.
[*He starts off, then stops*]
And do your best at warding the enemy off.

PARMENO:
Okay, but
I knew that already. No orders needed.

PHAEDRIA:
And, as for me,
I'm going to the country.
What's more, I'm going to stay in the country.
[*He starts off*]

PARMENO:
I heartily approve.
[*He turns to the door.* PHAEDRIA *stops*]

PHAEDRIA:
Hold on.

PARMENO [*turning back*]:
You called?

PHAEDRIA:
Do you think I can do it?
Resist returning – stay holed up – holed out to the bitter
End?

PARMENO:
Well, frankly, no. You'll return tonight, if not before –
Chased back by lack of sleep.

PHAEDRIA:
I'll work in the fields till I drop.
I'll sleep in spite of myself.

PARMENO:
You'll be a very fagged
Insomniac.

PHAEDRIA:
Beat it. You're no help.
I must Take Steps
To stiffen up my willpower. I'm flabby, that's it, flabby.
But *I can do it*. Come right down to it, I can do

Without that girl, if duty demands, for as much as three
days.
PARMENO:
Three whole days? That's eternity. Don't make extravagant
claims.
PHAEDRIA:
My resolve is fixed.
[*He stalks off right*]
PARMENO:
    Pathological, god preserve us. A morbid
Infection, love. Induces complete dissolution of character.
There goes a boy once famous for standards, scruples, and
brains.
[*Looking off left*]
Somebody's coming. Who is it?
    Oh-oh. If it isn't Gnatho
The sponger, moocher-in-chief to Thais's Major. He's
bringing
A virgin with him – Thais' present. She's gorgeous, too.
Worse luck. And here I am to present one ramshackle
eunuch.
What a revolting contrast. This girl's more stunning than
Thais.
[*He moves to* THAIS' *house, and takes up a position before
her door*]

230

Scene 2

GNATHO *enters left, followed by* PAMPHILA *and the maid
who attends her. Not perceiving* PARMENO, *he stops his
procession and addresses the audience*
GNATHO:
I shall never cease my amazement at the qualitative abyss
That yawns between man and man – the positive gulf that
partitions
Sage from clod.
    This reflection was brought by a chance encounter
Just now as I was en route. Fell in with a fellow whose birth

And status exactly parallel mine: A goodish background,
But gourmandized away the ancestral estates. A sight.
He'd let himself go rather sadly: Seedy, sick, shabby.
White at the temples, out at the heels. A mess.
    'What means
This sad masquerade?' I asked.
    'I'm broke. I've lost all I had,'
He replied. 'I'm reduced to this. My friends, both casual
    and close,
Have left me flat.'
    The contrast with me was too much. I couldn't
Conceal my contempt.
    'You colossal ass,' was the way I put it,
240   'Have you deliberately lost your hope as well? Did your
    brains go
The way of your fortune? We had the same origins, you
    and I,
But just take a look at me – my colour, clothing,
    condition –
The picture of creature comfort. All possessions are mine,
Though I own nothing. My assets may be absolutely nil,
But I never suffer a shortage.'
    'I'm no good at that,' he countered.
'I can't stand beatings; I won't be a butt.'
    'Tut,' I riposted.
'Do you really believe that's how it's done? You're utterly
    off.
I admit the profession proceeded by such outmoded
    methods
A century or so ago, but now we've changed all that.
There's a new system of swindling these days; a style, I
    might add,
That I pioneered. Attend:
    There exists a subspecies of humans
Who lust to be first in all things, and aren't.
    These are my game.
I dog their footsteps, ever ready to furnish laughter –
But not as a butt: *I* laugh at *them* . . . and show, of course,

My amazed amusement at their wit. Their least remark
   evokes   250
My praise; if they contradict it, well, I praise that, too.
I yea their yeas and nay their nays ... in sum, I obey
A self-imposed command to reflect their smallest
   expression.
And such is the current procedure.
    It simply brims with profit.'
PARMENO [*aside*]:
Talented fellow. Transforms idiots straight into madmen.
GNATHO:
This exchange endured until we attained the market, where
An absolute mass of small tradesmen rose in joy and ran
To greet me. Dealers in candy, pastry, meat, and fish,
Sausage-stuffers and herring-hawkers – to whom I, flush
Or insolvent, have always been a constant source of profit.
They flooded me with welcomes, effusions of love,
   invitations to dinners.
Such an expression of status, such ease at winning a living
Was simply too much for my hapless companion's hunger
   to behold.   260
He beseeched me, then and there, to take him on as a pupil.
I told him to follow and observe.
    I'm rather thinking of founding
A professional school of sponging. Named after me, of
   course –
Just like the philosophers:
    Plato, Platonists.
       Gnatho, Gnathonists.
It has a ring.
PARMENO [*aside*]:
    And that's what comes of free time and free meals.
GNATHO:
To work: Presentation of girl to Thais, invitation of Thais
To lunch. [*Aside*] – But who's this slouching in front of
   Thais's door?
Parmeno. The competition's slave. To judge from his
   gloom, the game

Is ours. I swear they're frozen out. My course is clear:
A little innocent fun at this clown's expense.

PARMENO [*aside*]:
> How like them.

This gift, and they think they've taken a permanent lease on
> Thais.

GNATHO:

270 Felicitous greetings from Gnatho to his most adored
> acquaintance,

Parmeno. How do things stand with us, eh?

PARMENO:
> Still.

GNATHO:
> I see.

Nothing here that upsets you, I trust?

PARMENO:
> Just you.

GNATHO:
> Indeed.

But nothing else?

PARMENO:
> Why should you ask?

GNATHO:
> You appear so sour.

PARMENO:
> Oh. Nothing. [*He makes an effort at smiling*]

GNATHO:
> Spare me. [*He indicates* PAMPHILA]
> What's your impression of this little item,

Fresh from the market?

PARMENO:
> Not absolutely disgusting.

GNATHO [*aside*]:
> Got him

Spitted and sizzling.

PARMENO [*aside*]:
> But as it happens, our friend's all wet.

GNATHO:
    It's a present for Thais. Imagine her gratitude.
PARMENO:
        You mean to imply
We've gotten the gate? Well, that's the way of the world.
    Now in,
    Now out.
GNATHO:
        Parmeno, I am about to make *you* a present:
Six months of total vacation, an end to this jack-in-the-box
Existence, these ceaseless sleepless nights. No more scurry,
No more worry. Now, how does such generosity strike
    you?
PARMENO:
    Goody.
GNATHO:
        Merely the way I treat my friends.
PARMENO:
            Well, great.
GNATHO:
    I mustn't detain you. You were doubtless on your way
        somewhere?   280
PARMENO:
    Nowhere.
GNATHO:
        Then be a good fellow and do me a smallish service:
Gain me admittance to Thais's presence.
PARMENO [*moving out of the way*]:
        But go right in.
You're bringing the girl; the door is open to you. For now.
GNATHO [*as he enters* THAIS' *house with* PAMPHILA *and her
    maid*]:
    No messages, I imagine?
PARMENO [*to the closed door*]:
    Just you wait for two days.
Your luck's in now; you can open the door in my face with
    your little

Finger – but when I'm done, you'll have to kick it black
And blue to find out nobody's home.

GNATHO [*emerging alone*]:
    Ah, steadfast Parmeno.
Still at your post? Have you been left behind on watch
To intercept secret messages between my Major and Thais?
[*He exits left*]

PARMENO:
Witty as hell. Just what you'd expect from the Major's pet.
[*Looking off right*]
– Well, look at this. Here comes the old man's younger son.
290 Why'd he leave the Piraeus, I wonder? This is his day
For guard duty there.⁵ Something's up, depend on that . . .
He's running fast enough. Seems to be searching for
    something.

Scene 3

    CHAEREA *enters right, at a run, stops, and looks around.*
    He does not see PARMENO

CHAEREA:
Oh, damn! Disappeared!
    That girl – she's lost!
        And me – I'm lost!
Because I lost the girl!
    Now what?
        Where do I look?
Where should I hunt? Who can I ask? Which way do I go?
I don't have the slightest idea.
    At least, there's one bit of hope:
No matter where she is, they can't keep her hidden for
    long –
Good god, what gorgeous, raving beauty!
    From this day forward,
I'm crossing the rest of the female sex right off my list.
Those garden-variety pretties turn my stomach.

PARMENO [*aside*]:
    And here

We have the other brother. His topic is also Love.
Please shed a tear for their father: This one's a potential
  madman.
Once *he* gets started, you can file away the other affair   300
Under *Fun & Games*.

CHAEREA:
        Oh gods, please damn that doddering clod
For holding me up. And while you're at it, please damn me
For stopping, for giving a good goddamn about him.
        – Oh, look,
It's Parmeno.
        Hi.

PARMENO:
                What's the trouble? And why the hurry?
And where've you been?

CHAEREA:
        I'm damned if I know where I've been
Or where I'm going. I don't even know who I am.

PARMENO:
        Pardon
My asking, but why?

CHAEREA:
        I'm in love.

PARMENO:
                Uh-*huh!*

CHAEREA:
                        Oh, Parmeno, now's
The time for you to show me how much of a man you are.
Remember your promise. You made it a thousand times:
  'Chaerea,
Just you find something to love,' you'd say, 'and then I'll
  make
You realize just how useful I am.' That's what you'd tell
  me,
All those times when you were locked up in your little
  room,
And I'd raid Dad's private pantry, and sneak down to bring
  you food . . .   310

PARMENO:
  Stop it, stupid!

CHAEREA:
      Well, this is it – so please let me see
Those promises.
      Or take it as a challenge that's really worth
Your effort. This girl – she's not like your other girls. Their
  mothers
Make them sag their shoulders and strap their breasts to
  look skinny.
If one's a little bit pretty, up goes a chorus of 'Heavyweight'
And slap she's put on a diet. Natural charm receives
The Treatment; it shrinks to a beanstalk.
      For most girls, that's the road
To Love.

PARMENO:
      But yours?

CHAEREA:
        A new departure in beauty.

PARMENO:
            Of course.

CHAEREA:
  Complexion, real; figure, not flabby but firm and plump
And juicy.

PARMENO:
      Age?

CHAEREA:
        Her age? Sixteen.

PARMENO:
          Bursting into bloom.

CHAEREA:
You've got to get her for me. Beg, borrow, or steal her . . .
The means don't matter, just so long as she's mine.

PARMENO:
      Now, wait –
Whose *is* she?

CHAEREA:
      I don't have the slightest idea.

320

PARMENO:
          So where's she from?
CHAEREA:
    Ditto to that.
PARMENO:
          So where's she staying?
CHAEREA:
              Not even that.
PARMENO:
    So where'd you see her?
CHAEREA:
        Back there.
PARMENO:
        So how'd you manage to lose her?
CHAEREA:
    Exactly. That's what I got so mad at myself about
    Just now. I don't think there's another man alive
    Whose good luck's so damn bad.
PARMENO:
        And what went wrong?
CHAEREA:
              My life.
PARMENO:
    What happened?
CHAEREA:
          I'll tell you what happened. That crony of Dad's – a
            cousin
    Or something; about the same age – Archidemides. Know
        him?
PARMENO:
    Oh boy.
CHAEREA:
    Guess who I met while I was trailing this girl?
PARMENO:
        That's pretty
    Distressing.
CHAEREA:
        Distressing, hell. Reserve 'distressing' for trifles.

Parmeno, this was disaster.
            I can freely swear
That I hadn't seen him once in six, no, seven months
Before that moment, a moment when I had every motive
To miss him.
            Does something up there hate me?

PARMENO:
            It looks that way.

CHAEREA:
    This old galoot was a good distance off, but he ran right
        up,
    Bent double, loose-lipped, wobbly, and whinnying all the
        way:
    'Whoa there! Whoa! I've got to talk to you, Chaerea!' So
    I stopped. 'You know what I wanted you for?'
            'Tell me.'
                    'My case
    Comes up tomorrow.'
            'So what?'
                    'So be a good boy and remind
340 Your daddy to get to court early and give my plea some
        support.'
    To get this out, it took him an hour.
            Would there be anything
    Else, I asked.
            'That's all,' he says.
                    And away I go.
    I look back after the girl, and find she's just that minute
    Turned up this way, into our street.

PARMENO [aside]:
            I won't be surprised if he means
    Thais's recent present.

CHAEREA:
            But when I got here, she was gone.

PARMENO:
    Point of information: Anyone with her?

CHAEREA:
            Oh, yes. A flunky

Of sorts, and a maid.
PARMENO:
  That's her.
    We can all go home.
  Give up. The funeral's over.
CHAEREA:
  I don't understand what you mean.
PARMENO:
 I do. This business of yours.
CHAEREA:
  You know her, you mean, or you saw her?
 Which?
PARMENO:
  I saw her. I know her. I can even tell where they took
   her.   350
CHAEREA:
 Parmeno – buddy – you know her? And you can tell me
  where
 She is?
PARMENO:
  They took her to Thais the whore. She went as a gift.
CHAEREA:
 What man has money enough to make a present like that?
PARMENO:
 Major Thraso, Phaedria's rival.
CHAEREA:
  You're casting my brother
 In a pretty tough part.
PARMENO:
  Tougher than you think. Just wait till you see
 The present *he's* got to match her.
CHAEREA:
  What in the world could it be?
PARMENO:
 A eunuch.
CHAEREA:
  Oh no. You couldn't mean that nauseating thing
 He bought yesterday, that antique freak?

PARMENO:
    The very same.
CHAEREA:
  With a gift like that she'll bounce him out of the house.
    I didn't
Know Thais was living next door to us.
PARMENO:
    She just moved in.
CHAEREA:
360 Damn. Just think, I've never met her. Tell me, is she
As pretty as everyone says?
PARMENO:
    Easily.
CHAEREA:
      Nothing compared
To my girl, of course?
PARMENO:
    A different type.
CHAEREA:
      Oh, god, I implore you,
Parmeno, get her for me!
PARMENO:
    All right, all right, I'll help you.
Undivided attention.
    [*He starts for* DEMEA's *house*]
    That all?
CHAEREA:
      Where are you going?
PARMENO:
        Home.
I have to deliver those slaves to Thais. Your brother's
orders.
CHAEREA:
  Delivered, inside this house! Oh, for the luck of that
    eunuch!
PARMENO [*returning*]:
  How so?

CHAEREA:

> Well, *think*: Within these walls, he'll have, as his
>> constant
> Companion in slavery, that vision of total beauty. He'll see
>> her,
> Talk to her, share the same house with her. Sometimes he'll
>> eat
> The very food she eats. Or even sleep beside her.

PARMENO [*offhand*]:

You could have that luck right now.

CHAEREA:

> I could? But how?
> Well, Parmeno, *how*?

PARMENO:

> Trade clothes with our eunuch.

CHAEREA:

>> Trade clothes?
> Then what?   370

PARMENO:

> Then I'd deliver you instead of him . . .

CHAEREA:

>> I see.

PARMENO:

And say that you were the eunuch.

CHAEREA:

> Got you.

PARMENO:

>> You could enjoy
> These bits of bliss you've been talking about: This eating
>> together
> And sharing the house. This touching, playing, sleeping
>> beside her.
> None of the women in here has any idea who you are.
> And one thing more: You're a pretty boy, and just the right
>> age;
> You'd easily pass for a eunuch. A casual inspection, of
>> course.

CHAEREA:
    Beautiful! I've never seen such advising!
    [*Grabbing* PARMENO's *arm and setting off for* DEMEA's
    house]
380   Well, let's go.
Into the house this minute. Wrap me up and send me.
Special delivery. Quick!
PARMENO:
    What do you think you're doing?
I'm only fooling.
CHAEREA:
    Baloney.
PARMENO:
        Dammit, what have I done
To myself?
    Now, quit this pushing. You'll knock me over.
        I tell you,
Stop!
CHAEREA:
    Let's go.
PARMENO:
      You mean it?
CHAEREA:
        I do.
PARMENO:
          It may be too hot
To handle.
CHAEREA:
    I can handle it. Please, just let me try.
PARMENO:
But I'm the one who'll have to take the rap.
CHAEREA:
    No, no.
PARMENO:
We are committing a crime.
CHAEREA:
    A crime?
        Parmeno, this

Is a whorehouse. It shelters tools of torture who take our
    youth
And fling it away, who torment us in every possible fashion.
Place me inside to pay them back, to victimize them
As they do us – is *this* a crime?
        Would it be more just
To play their game and dupe my Dad? That would be
    condemned,
And rightly so, if the world found out; but what we're
    doing
Can only bring us applause, and shouts of 'Serves 'em
    Right.'

PARMENO:
So what's to reply?
        If you mean business, I'll do it, but afterward,
Don't throw the blame on me.

CHAEREA:
        I won't.

PARMENO:
            Then this is an order?

CHAEREA:
No, no order . . . it's a command, an ultimatum. I
Shall never shirk a moral obligation.

PARMENO:
        God save us all.   390
        [*They exit into* DEMEA's *house*]

ACT III

Scene 1

    THRASO *and* GNATHO *enter left*

THRASO:
Really? Heartfelt thanks to me from Thais?

GNATHO:
In thousands.

THRASO:
        Thrilled, you say?

GNATHO:
              And not so much
    By gift as by giver. Yourself. She's riding in triumph.
PARMENO [*peering out of* DEMEA's *house*]:
    I'd better see if the coast is clear before
    I make delivery.
        [*Seeing* THRASO *and* GNATHO]
            Lo, the conq'ring hero.
        [*He watches unnoticed from the doorway*]
THRASO:
    Naturally endowed that way, you know. A sort
    Of innate grace enhancing all my actions.
GNATHO:
    Oh, yes. I've been quite struck by it.
THRASO:
            Likewise the King.
    My smallest service, he greeted with effusive thanks.
    Less to others, of course.
GNATHO:
            The victory won
400 By the sweat of another man's brow is often pre-empted
    By the man of wit. As in your case.
THRASO:
            Exactly.
GNATHO:
    The King, I take it, only had eyes . . .
THRASO:
            Too true!
GNATHO:
    . . . For you?
THRASO:
            Precisely. Consigned his armies to me.
    Made me privy to his Grand Designs.
GNATHO:
            I'm agog.
THRASO:
    There's more:

> *When court and the affairs of state*
> *Had taken their exhausting toll,*
> *Had forced him to evacuate*
> *His ... His ...*
>   You know the line?

GNATHO:
              Like this,
     I think:
> *Had forced him to evacuate*
> *His throne and purge his griping soul.*

THRASO:
              That's it.
On such occasions, he'd withdraw with a single
Guest – myself.

GNATHO:
     Imagine. A king with taste.

THRASO:
Earned me no end of envy, of course. Backbiting   410
Behind my back. Couldn't have bothered me less.
Everyone sick with jealousy. One poor chap.
In particular. Fellow in charge of the Indian elephants.
One day, was more of a screaming bore than usual.
Fixed his wagon. 'Tell me, Strato,' I said,
'Are your manners so monstrous because you manage
     monsters?'

GNATHO:
You certainly had him there. Phrasing, point –
Right between the eyes. And what did he say?

THRASO:
What *could* he say? Dead silence.

GNATHO:
     The only reply.

PARMENO [*aside*]:
The gods are just. A fathead paired with a fraud.

THRASO:
Got in a neat stroke under the guard of a fellow
From Rhodes at a dinner once. I ever tell you

420   About it, Gnatho?
GNATHO:
                Never. I'd love to hear it.
        [*Aside*]
        The thousand-and-first performance.
THRASO:
                At a dinner once.
        This fellow from Rhodes I mentioned. Young
                whippersnapper.
        Had a camp follower with me, that started him off.
        Innuendoes at her expense. Cheap cracks at mine.
        Let him have it: 'Show a little respect,
        Sonny,' I said. 'The hare doesn't run with the hounds.'
                [*Hysterical laughter from* GNATHO]
        What's all this?
GNATHO:
                It's witty, whimsical, droll,
        An A-number-one retort. Original with you?
        I thought it was old.
THRASO:
                What? Heard it before?
GNATHO:
                        Again
        And again. It's known as a real crusher.
THRASO:
                It's mine.
GNATHO:
430   It pains me to think of its use on a thoughtless boy.
PARMENO [*aside*]:
        Damn you to hell.
GNATHO:
                Could he make a reply?
THRASO:
                        Wiped out.
        Rest of the party died with laughter. Then panicked.
        Paled at the sight of me.
GNATHO:
                And well they might.

THRASO:
 Hold on. About Thais. She thinks I fancy that girl.
 Best to relieve her suspicions?
GNATHO:
  Just the reverse.
 Do your best to increase them.
THRASO:
  Why?
GNATHO:
   It's simple.
 You know the effect any mention or praise of Phaedria
 On Thais's part produces in you – that sudden
 Heartburn?
THRASO:
  Feel it now.
GNATHO:
   There's only one cure,
 And that's this: Whenever she says 'Phaedria', you   440
 Cut in with 'Pamphila'. Counter her 'Let's have Phaedria
 Over for dinner' with 'Let's have Pamphila sing'.
 Whenever she praises his looks, extol the girl's.
 Match her, tit for tat. Hit her where she lives.
THRASO:
 Might help, Gnatho. Provided she really loves me.
GNATHO:
 She's eager to get your presents, correct? Therefore
 She loves them. Therefore, *she loves you*, too. And
  therefore,
 It's easily in your power to cause her pain.
 She lives in fear of your anger. You just might take
 The harvest she reaps and sow it somewhere else.   450
THRASO:
 Beautifully put. But should have hit it myself.
GNATHO:
 You're joking. You simply chose to expend your mental
 Energies elsewhere. Otherwise, you'd have leaped
 To the same conclusion in a much more brilliant fashion.

Scene 2

THAIS *enters from her house*

THAIS:

Who's here? I thought I heard my Major's voice.
And so I did. Oh, Thraso darling, hello!

THRASO:

Ah, Thais, you luscious morsel. Love me a little
For that girl guitarist?

PARMENO [*aside*]:

Now, there is finesse. The perfect
Amatory preamble.

THAIS:

A lot, and you deserve it,
Every last bit.

GNATHO:

And so to lunch.

[*To* THAIS]

Why aren't you

460   Ready?

PARMENO [*aside*]:

The other master of tact. Can this one
Really be human?

THAIS:

I'm ready whenever you are.

PARMENO [*aside*]:

Time for my entrance. I'd better pretend I've been
Inside.

[*He moves from* DEMEA's *doorway to the group*]

Oh, Thais. Going for a walk?

THAIS:

Er – Parmeno?

[*Improvising*] I won't need you any more today. I was just
Going out . . .

PARMENO:

Out where?

THAIS [*aside to* PARMENO]:

Stop it! You see who's here?

PARMENO [*aside to* THAIS]:
  I do, and it makes me sick.
    [*Loudly*]
      – Phaedria's presents
  Are ready whenever you want them.
THRASO [*to* THAIS]:
      No point in standing
  Around here. Ought to be leaving.
PARMENO [*to* THRASO]:
      Sir, by your leave,
  Request permission for truce and parley with lady.
  Object: Gifts, Presentation of.
THRASO:
      Hmmm. Gifts.
  Magnificent items, no doubt. Equaling ours.
PARMENO:
  Learn first-hand.   470
    [*He moves nearer* DEMEA's *door and calls*]
      Ahoy in there!
  Send that pair
      Out, on the double!
    [*The African maid appears at the door*]
          You first. Right this way.
    [*She moves to him*]
  – Direct from darkest Ethiopia!
THRASO:
      Three *minae*.[6]
GNATHO:
      At most.
  Pure schlock.
PARMENO [*calling to the door again*]:
      Hey, Dorus! Where are you?
    [CHAEREA *appears at the door, dressed as a eunuch*]
      Over here.
    [CHAEREA *moves to him*]
  – Now there, I submit, is a eunuch! Kindly note
  The thoroughbred features, the flawless freshness . . .

THRASO:
     Damnation.
Handsome beast.
PARMENO:
     Well, Gnatho, any observations?
No faults to pick at?
     – Thraso, how about you?
– The ultimate accolade: Silence.
     [*To* THAIS]
     Inspect him, please.
Examine his Literature. Music. Athletics. Guaranteed
Performance in all the pursuits deemed fit and proper
For a well-brought-up young gentleman.
THRASO:
     Know a pursuit
I wouldn't mind trying with him. If forced, of course.
480   Or even sober . . . [GNATHO *jabs him in the ribs*]
PARMENO:
     The man who presents these gifts
Sets no conditions upon you. He does not demand
That you exclude your other friends and surrender
Yourself completely to him. He recites no battles,
He shows no scars, he sets no ambushes for you
On the street – like a certain party who shall be
     nameless.
He rests content if, on such rare occasions
As time, inclination, and circumstance may permit,
You will condescend to receive him.
THRASO:
     Owner of a slave
Like that – must be insolvent. Back to the wall.
GNATHO:
     I couldn't agree with you more. No man would struggle
Along with that if he could afford another.
PARMENO [*to* GNATHO]:
     Shut up, vulture. You've dropped to the lowest rung
490   On Humanity's ladder by bowing and scraping to *that*
     [*pointing to* THRASO]

In cold blood. You'd scavenge your food from a funeral
   pyre.
THRASO:
Time to be leaving.
THAIS:
   Just let me take them inside
And give the necessary orders. I'll be right out.
   [*She conducts the maid and* CHAEREA *into her house*]
THRASO [*highly offended, to* GNATHO]:
Departing. You wait for her highness here.
PARMENO:
   It figures.
The General Staff cannot be seen in public
With its Great and Good Friend. Has a bad effect on the
   troops.
THRASO:
Er – pointless talking to you. Just like your master.
   [*Again hysterical laughter from* GNATHO, *as* PARMENO
   exits into DEMEA's *house*]
What's so funny?
GNATHO:
   Your witty comeback. A winner.
And then I remembered your slash at that boy from
   Rhodes.
– But here comes Thais.
   [THAIS *enters from her house, followed by* PYTHIAS,
   DORIAS *and other women*]
THRASO:
   Run on ahead. Reconnoitre.
See that lunch is ready.
GNATHO:
   Aye, aye. [*He exits left*]
THAIS:
      Now, Pythias,
Be very careful. If that man Chremes comes   500
While I'm out, first try to get him to wait. If that
Won't work, then ask him to come back later. If *that's*
Impossible, well, you bring him along to me.

PYTHIAS:
  All right.
THAIS:
      Now, what else was it I wanted to say?
    [*To* PYTHIAS *and* DORIAS]
  Oh, yes – be sure that the girl is properly cared for.
  Don't leave the house.
THRASO:
      Forward!
THAIS [*to the other women*]:
          You come with me.
    [*General exit:* PYTHIAS *and* DORIAS *into* THAIS' *house;*
    THRASO, THAIS *and the other women left*]

Scene 3

CHREMES *stumbles on right and makes his way to* THAIS'
door, then stops and addresses the audience

CHREMES:
  I'm in danger.
      No doubt about it. I try
  To figure this out, and always get the same answer:
  This Thais is fixing trouble for me. Big trouble.
  Slick as she is, I see what she's doing to me.
  Fattening me up for the kill. It started the very
510 First time she had me over.
      I know what you're thinking:
  'What was between you two?' Search me; I didn't
  Know who she was. But I went, and had to wait.
  Her excuse was, she had some serious business
  To discuss with me, but was busy saying her prayers.
  Well, now. Right then, I began to be suspicious;
  All this was a trap. She sat down to dinner with me,
  And pushed herself at me, sort of, and tried to start
  A conversation. It died. She changed the subject: How long
  Had my mother and father been dead? A long time, I told
      her.
  Did I have a farm at Sunium? How far from the sea?

(She likes my farm, I bet. She probably wants   520
To steal it.) Finally, did I have a little sister
Who drowned down there, and was anyone with her when
  she died,
And what was she wearing, and who could identify her?
– Now, why would she ask all that, unless she was
  planning
To pass herself off as my sister, back from the dead?
Of all the nerve!
          If my sister's still alive,
She's only sixteen; this Thais she's older than I am.
Not much, but older.
          And now she's sent me another
Invitation. Serious business again. But this time
It's put up or shut up: She tells me what she's after,
Or gives up pestering me. I won't come see her
Again, and that's for sure. [*He knocks at* THAIS' *door*]
          – Hey, anybody home?   530
Chremes is here! [PYTHIAS *and* DORIAS *spring out*]

PYTHIAS:
          Lover, how divine to see you!

CHREMES [*aside*]:
I told you. An ambush, yet.

PYTHIAS:
          Thais is out.
She left you an urgent message: Please come back
Tomorrow.

CHREMES:
          I'm going to the farm.

PYTHIAS:
                    Oh, do it for me.

CHREMES:
I tell you I can't.

PYTHIAS:
          Then wait inside – with us –
Till she comes home, hmmm?

CHREMES:
          Not on your life.

PYTHIAS:
      Why not,
  Lover?
CHREMES:
     You go to hell.
PYTHIAS:
      You seem determined.
  Then please go see her now?
    [*Pointing off left*]
    That way.
CHREMES:
      I'll go.
PYTHIAS:
  Dorias, take him right on over to the Major's.
    [DORIAS *leads* CHREMES *off left.* PYTHIAS *exits into the*
    house]

Scene 4

    ANTIPHO *enters right and stops in front of* DEMEA's *house*
ANTIPHO:
  Yesterday, down at the harbour, a bunch of the boys got
    together
540 And planned a party for today. We left the arrangements to
    Chaerea,
  Gave him our IOU's, and agreed on a time and a place.
  The time's gone by. The place is still there, but nothing's
    ready.
  And Chaerea's nowhere. I don't have the slightest idea
    what happened.
  The rest of the group's given me the job of finding him.
  And so I'll see if he's home.
    [THAIS' *door opens and* CHAEREA *emerges beatific, still in*
    the eunuch's clothes]
    – Who's this leaving Thais's?
  Is it him or not?
    It's him.
        But who's he supposed to be?

Why the disguise? What's wrong?
    I'm floored. I can't even guess.
Unless, of course, I hide over here and find out what's up.
[*He conceals himself from* CHAEREA *in the space between
the house*]

Scene 5

CHAEREA:
    Anybody out here?
    Nobody.
        Anybody follow me?
        Nobody!
Is this the moment to let my rapture erupt?
    O Jupiter,   550
My time has come. I'm ready and willing to meet my
    death,
Before life's little messes debase this total bliss.
– No interruptions?
    Nobody around to poke and pry,
To dog me, hound me, quiz me, pump me to death?
    No questions?
Like, why am I shaking, or why am I happy, or where am I
    going,
Or where have I been, or where did I get this silly costume,
Or what am I leading up to, or am I sane or crazy?
ANTIPHO [*aside*]:
He seems disappointed. I'll go and do him the favour he
    wants. [*Moving to* CHAEREA]
– Hi, Chaerea. Why are you shaking like this? What's this
    costume
Leading up to? Why so happy? What does this mean?
Have you gone crazy?
    Well, why are you looking at me like that?
Why the silence?
CHAEREA:
    Antipho, hello! My day is perfect.   560
There's nobody living I'd rather share this moment with.

ANTIPHO:
    I'd like it if you'd explain this.
CHAEREA:
        I'd love it if you'd listen.
    You know my brother's mistress?
ANTIPHO:
        I know her. Thais, isn't it?
CHAEREA:
    That's her.
ANTIPHO:
        I thought it was.
CHAEREA:
            Today she received a present –
    A virgin. I don't have to list the fine points of her beauty to
        you;
    You know my standing as a qualified virgin-watcher. Just
        say
    She knocked me out.
ANTIPHO:
        You mean it?
CHAEREA:
            The living end. One look'll
    Convince you. I fell in love, that's enough. And was awfully
        lucky:
    We had a eunuch at home. My brother had bought it for
        Thais
570   But hadn't delivered it yet. Well, Parmeno – he's our slave –
    Suggested a plan. I snapped it up . . .
ANTIPHO:
        What sort of a plan?
CHAEREA:
    The stiller you are, the quicker you learn.
        – For me to trade clothes
    With him and go in his place.
ANTIPHO:
        The eunuch's place?
CHAEREA:
            That's it.

ANTIPHO:
>What fun could you get out of that?

CHAEREA:
>>Oh, really. The sight, the sound,
>The physical presence of a girl that I was mad for – is
>>that
>A measly motive, Antipho, a shoddy stimulus?
>>– Thais
>Was thrilled when they put me into her hands. She hustled
>>me in
>And put the girl straight into mine.

ANTIPHO:
>>Your hands?

CHAEREA:
>>>My hands.

ANTIPHO:
>>>>Well, safety
>First.

CHAEREA:
>>She spelled out my orders: No man was allowed to
>>>visit.
>I wasn't allowed to leave the women's quarters. Compelled
>To stay by the girl at all times.
>>I lowered my eyes and nodded
>Assent.

ANTIPHO:
>>Poor boy.

CHAEREA:
>>>'I'm going out to lunch,' she said,   580
>And took her maids along. She left a couple behind
>To tend to the girl . . . but they were young ones, new at the
>>job.
>They start to prepare her for the bath; I urge them to show
>>some speed;
>She sits in her room, in the middle of all this bustle,
>>inspecting
>A picture on the wall. A famous subject: Jupiter launching
>A shower of gold into Danaë's lap. I began to inspect it

Myself. It repaid attention. Encouraging: Here was a god
Long ago, who'd played almost the same game – disguised
  himself
(As a man) sneaked under another's roof (right down the
  chimney)
And seduced a woman. And not just any god, but the one
Who makes the heights of heaven bound
590   *And flounder at his thunder's sound.*[7]
I might be only human, but couldn't I do the same?
And so I decided to do it.
        During my internal debate,
They took the girl to the bath. She went, she bathed, she
  returned.
Lastly, they put her in bed. I stood there, waiting for orders.
'Hey, Dorus,' says one of them, coming up, 'you take this
  fan
And refresh her while we take our baths. Then, when we're
  done,
Take yours, if you want.' I grumble a little, but take the
  fan.

ANTIPHO:
I'd love to have seen you standing there – the look on your
  face.
A great big donkey like you waggling your itty-bitty fan.

CHAEREA:
The words weren't out of her mouth before they ran out of
  the room,
600   Off to the bath with a whoop – when the cat's away, and
  all that.
Meantime, the girl fell asleep. I sneaked a sideways peek
Through the fan, like this. I took a careful look around.
The coast was clear. I locked the door. [*A pause*]

ANTIPHO
        Then what?

CHAEREA:
            Then what,
You moron?

ANTIPHO:

    That's me.

CHAEREA:

        A chance like this, no matter how short –

Do you think I'd miss it? Temptation, aspiration, surprise,
   and passion

All mixed in one?

    Just what do you think I am – a eunuch?

ANTIPHO:

Enough. I'm convinced.

    But meanwhile, what about our party?

CHAEREA:

All ready.

ANTIPHO:

    Good boy. Your house?

CHAEREA:

        The freedman Discus's place.

ANTIPHO:

That's quite a ways. Oh, well, so we hurry faster. Better   610
Change those clothes.

CHAEREA:

    Okay, but oh hell, where? I'm banished

From home, for now; my brother might be inside. Or,
   what's worse,

Dad might be back from the farm already.

ANTIPHO:

    Come to my house.

The nearest place where you can change.

CHAEREA:

    A good idea.

Let's go. On the way, I'd like your advice about the girl:

How do you think I can make her my own for good?

ANTIPHO:

    We'll see.

    [*They exit right*]

ACT IV

Scene 1

DORIAS *enters from the left*

DORIAS:

    God almighty, after what I've seen, I'm nearly scared sick:
    The Major's lost his mind; he's liable to start a riot
    Or make an attack on Thais today.
        It happened at lunch
    Because of that fellow Chremes, our virgin's brother:
    When I brought him over, she pestered the Major to ask
        him in.
    The Major blew up, but didn't dare risk a flat refusal.
    Thais kept digging away: Invite him in. (And I know
    Why she did it – to keep him around till she could tell him
620   All she wanted to about his sister. This wasn't the time.)
    With a very sour face, he invited him in. So Chremes
        stayed.
    And oh, what table talk. The Major thought he'd seen
    A rival installed there right before his eyes. Decided
    He'd like to get some of his own back.
        'Boy,' he said to a slave,
    'Go bring Pamphila here to give us some entertainment.'
    'Pamphila here to lunch? Certainly not!' said Thais.
    The Major insisted. From this, it was only a step to a fight.
    Meanwhile, she slipped her jewellery off and gave it to me
    To bring home. I know that sign: She'll slip out as soon as
        she can.
    [*She enters* THAIS' *house*]

Scene 2

PHAEDRIA *enters right*

PHAEDRIA:

    I was making my way along the road to the farm
630   And started thinking. It's a habit I have when upset.

One worry after another, each worse than the last . . .
To put it briefly, I sank so deep in my thoughts
I missed the house. I blundered a good way beyond it
Before I noticed, then came on back, disgusted.
I reached the turnoff, stopped . . . and started thinking
Again:
  'Now, look – do you really have to stay
Down here for two whole days? Alone. Without her?
And afterward – what happens then?'
  'No worry there.'
'No worry, hell. The policy's "Hands Off" now;
You think it won't be "Eyes Off"?'
  'So touching's out;
At least they'll let me look.'
  'Well, long-range love   640
Is better than nothing.'
  – This time, I missed the house
On purpose. [*Looking off left*]
  – Here's Pythias. What's got her so flustered?

Scene 3

PYTHIAS *enters from* THAIS' *house, followed shortly by an
uncomprehending* DORIAS,[8] *who still carries the jewellery
box. They do not see* PHAEDRIA

PYTHIAS:
Where can I find that savage? Where do I look for that
 thug?
Disaster, catastrophe – how could he have the gall to *do*
A thing like that?
PHAEDRIA [*aside*]:
 Whatever this is, I'm scared of it.
PYTHIAS:
When he'd had his fun with the girl, he did stop? Oh, no –
 atrocity
Wasn't enough for him; he shredded her dress and ripped
 out
Her hair in handfuls!

PHAEDRIA [*aside*]:
>   He what?

PYTHIAS:
>   Just let me at him – I'll take
> These nails and scoop his eyeballs out, that . . . ooh, that
>   *poisoner!*

PHAEDRIA [*aside*]:
> It's not too clear, but I'd say there'd been a disturbance in
>   there

650
> While I was away. I'll go see.
>   – What's up, Pythias? Why this
> Rushing around? And who are you hunting?

PYTHIAS:
>   Well, well – Phaedria.
> Will you kindly take your pretty present and go to hell?
> Or anyplace else that'll take you?

PHAEDRIA:
>   What do you mean?

PYTHIAS:
>   You know
> What I mean! You and your eunuch – you didn't bring us a
>   gift,
> You brought us to rack and ruin! You know that girl from
>   the Major?
> Your eunuch raped our virgin!

PHAEDRIA:
> He which? You must be drunk.

PYTHIAS:
> Whatever I am at the moment, I wish it on all my enemies.

DORIAS:
> Pythias, please! This thing you said – it's just not natural!

PHAEDRIA:
> I say you're crazy. He was a eunuch; how could he rape?

PYTHIAS:
> I don't know what he *was*; but, as to what he *did*,
> The evidence speaks for itself. The girl can't speak for hers;

660
> She's crying, too shaken to talk when you ask her what
>   happened.

And Nature's Nobleman's nowhere around to be found.
   Which makes
Another worry: It's likely he lifted some little items
On his way out of the house.

PHAEDRIA:
      I'd be surprised if he got
Very far away. A pretty sad specimen. Probably came back
Home to us.

PYTHIAS:
      Please do me a favour. Go see if he's there.

PHAEDRIA:
   I'll let you know in a minute.
   [*He exits into* DEMEA'*s house*]

DORIAS:
      But darling, this is awful.
I never even heard of such an unspeakable act!

PYTHIAS:
I have to admit I'd heard that, where women are concerned,
Eunuchs are very lecherous types, but completely . . .
   unable.
I never gave it the slightest thought. If I had, I wouldn't
Have put him in charge of the girl; I'd have locked him up
   somewhere.

Scene 4

PHAEDRIA *enters from* DEMEA'*s house, dragging after him
the frightened and confused eunuch* DORUS, *who is
dressed, quite badly, in* CHAEREA'*s clothes*

PHAEDRIA:
Outside, goon! Stop dragging your heels and move,
You rotten runaway! Forward, you waste of money,
March!

DORUS:
      Mercy!

PHAEDRIA:
         Eccch, what a face he's making.   670
Scare you to death.

[*To* DORUS]
 – Why the return to our house?
Why the change of clothes? Let me have the story.
– If I'd been just a little later, Pythias,
I wouldn't have caught him inside. He'd already put on
A disguise to escape in.

PYTHIAS:
 Oh please, have you got the man?

PHAEDRIA:
Of course I've got him.

PYTHIAS:
 Wonderful!

DORIAS:
  I'll say it is!

PYTHIAS:
 Where is he?

PHAEDRIA:
  Where *is* he? Don't you see him?

PYTHIAS:
  See him?
See who?

PHAEDRIA:
 This fellow here.

PYTHIAS:
  What fellow is that?

PHAEDRIA:
The one they delivered to you today.

PYTHIAS:
 Oh, no,
Phaedria. None of our girls has ever laid eyes
680 On this one.

PHAEDRIA:
 They haven't?

PYTHIAS:
  Honestly, did you believe
They delivered *this* to us?

PHAEDRIA:
 It's the only eunuch

I had.

PYTHIAS:

Oh, dear. There's no comparison here
With the one we received. He was very handsome.
Distinguished.

PHAEDRIA:

He only appeared that way because he was wearing
Those gorgeous clothes. Now that he's changed, he looks
Disgusting.

PYTHIAS:

Please stop this nonsense. You talk
As though the difference were tiny; it's not. The gift
Delivered to us today was a boy. Youngish.
And handsome? – You'd be happy to see him, Phaedria.
This one's decrepit, dilapidated, desiccated – and *old*.
His skin looks like a weasel's.

PHAEDRIA:

Dammit, what sort
Of a fairy tale is this? You trying to reduce me   690
To confusion? I know what I bought.
    [*To* DORUS]
    – Did I buy you?

DORUS:

You did.

PYTHIAS:

My turn. Have him answer one for me.

PHAEDRIA:

Ask it.

PYTHIAS [*to* DORUS:]:

Were you at our house today?
    [DORUS *shakes his head. She turns to* PHAEDRIA]
        – Negative.
The other one came. A boy of about sixteen.
Parmeno brought him over.

PHAEDRIA [*to* DORUS]:

Come on, you. Give me
Some answers. First, those clothes you're wearing: Where
Did you get them?

Well?
         Look here, you freak, are you going
To tell me or not?
DORUS:
         Uh . . . Chaerea came . . .
PHAEDRIA:
                My brother?
DORUS:
  Yup.
PHAEDRIA:
         Well, when?
DORUS:
                Today.
PHAEDRIA:
                        How long ago?
DORUS:
  A little.
PHAEDRIA:
         Who with?
DORUS:
                Parmeno.
PHAEDRIA:
                        You knew him before?
DORUS:
  Nope. I'd never even heard of him.
PHAEDRIA:
700   Then how did you know that he was my brother?
DORUS:
         Parmeno
Said so. Your brother gave me these clothes.
PHAEDRIA:
         Oh, hell.
DORUS:
  He put mine on. And then they both went out.
PYTHIAS:
  I hope you're satisfied. Now was I drunk? Now was I lying?
  Now do you believe what happened to the girl?
         Rape!

PHAEDRIA:
  Calm down, now; don't go wild. Would you take the word
    of *this?*
PYTHIAS:
  What's with taking words? The evidence speaks for itself.
PHAEDRIA [*aside to* DORUS]:
  Come over this way a little. Got me? And just a bit more . . .
  That's good.
    [*The two converse privately, out of range of* PYTHIAS *and*
    DORIAS]
      Now, let's go through these answers once again:
  Chaerea stripped your clothes off?
DORUS:
    Yup.
PHAEDRIA:
        And put them on
  Himself?
DORUS:
    Yup.
PHAEDRIA:
      And got delivered in your place?
DORUS:
        Yup.
PHAEDRIA [*loudly*]:
  Oh, god, of all the harebrained delinquents![9]
PYTHIAS:
    Oh, no, not again!
  We were the victims of a sneak attack – won't you believe
    it?   710
PHAEDRIA:
  I know that you'll believe whatever this cretin says.
    [*Aside*]
  I don't know what to do.
    [*Aside to* DORUS]
    – Now, get this: This time, answer
  No.
    [*Loudly*]
    – I'll tear the truth out of you if it takes me all day.

Did you or did you not see my brother Chaerea?

DORUS:
  Nope.

PHAEDRIA [*to* PYTHIAS]:
See? Need torture to make him confess.
    [*Aside to* DORUS]
  – Stick right with me.
    [*To* PYTHIAS]
– First it's Yup and then it's Nope.
    [*Aside to* DORUS]
    – Now beg for mercy.
  [*He hits* DORUS]

DORUS:
Phaedria! Mercy!
  I mean it!

PHAEDRIA [*loudly, as he kicks* DORUS]:
    Get back in there, and hurry!

DORUS:
Ouch!
  [*He exits into* DEMEA's *house*]

PHAEDRIA [*aside*]:
    It's the only way I can see to get out of this
And save my standing. [*Loudly, after* DORUS]
  – All right, you hoodlum, any more fooling
Around with me and you have had it!
  [*He exits into* DEMEA's *house*]

PYTHIAS:
    As sure as I'm living,
I know that this was one of Parmeno's tricks.

DORIAS:
    You're right.

PYTHIAS:
I swear I'll find some way to pay him back. Today.
720   An equal favour.
    What do we do now, Dorias?

DORIAS:
      You mean
About our virgin?

PYTHIAS:
    Yes. Do I tell Thais or keep it quiet?
DORIAS:
Good lord, if you've got any sense, you don't know a
    thing.
The eunuch, the rape, nothing. That way, you're out of this
    mess
And build up thanks with *him*.[10]
    [*Indicating* DEMEA's *house, home of* PHAEDRIA]
    Just say that Dorus has disappeared.
PYTHIAS:
That's what I'll do.
DORIAS [*looking off left*]:
    Oh, look. It's Chremes. Thais'll be back
Any minute.
PYTHIAS:
    How do you know?
DORIAS:
        She'd already started
A fight with the Major before I left.
PYTHIAS:
    Well, take that jewellery
Back in the house. I'll find out how things stand from
    Chremes.
    [DORIAS *exits into* THAIS' *house*]

Scene 5

    CHREMES *enters left, very drunk*
CHREMES:
Behold the victim of a wicked trick. Undermined by wine –
I'm blind.
    'S odd. At table I seemed to be able to stay
Impossibly sober. But when I got up to go, my feet
Defected. My brain refrained from performing its usual
    function.
PYTHIAS:
Chremes?

CHREMES:
    Who's there?
        If it isn't Pythias. What a quick change.
    Yum. How lovely you've gotten.
    [*He embraces her. She works loose*]
PYTHIAS:
    God. How lively you've gotten.
CHREMES:
    I exemplify the proverb:
    Without Demeter and Dionysus
    Aphrodite a lump of ice is.[11]
    – Did Thais beat me
    Back by much?
PYTHIAS:
    Has she already left the Major's?
CHREMES:
        Long since.
    Years. There arose a rift. A rupture. A ruckus. A rhubarb.
PYTHIAS:
    Didn't she tell you to follow her?
CHREMES:
    Not in the least. The merest
    Hint of a nod as she left.
PYTHIAS:
    What size of a sign do you need?
CHREMES:
    I protest. I hadn't the least idea of her meaning. The Major,
    However, rectified my regrettable lack of experience.
        He threw
    Me out. [*Looking off left*]
        – Oh, here she comes. How did I beat her back?

Scene 6

THAIS *enters right and addresses the audience*
THAIS:
    He'll turn up here to reclaim her in a minute. I know he
    will.

Just let him try! If he so much as touches that girl
With his little finger, I'll rip his eyes out, right on the
    spot.   740
Stupidity I can endure, conceit I can stand – but only
As long as he sticks to words. If he translates his
    shortcomings
Into action, he'll pay with his skin.

CHREMES:
        Thais, I've been here for hours.

THAIS:
    – Chremes, darling, just the person I wanted to see.
    Do you know that you were the cause of that fight? that
        you're the focus
    Of this whole affair?

CHREMES:
        Who, me? Impossible. How?

THAIS:
                    Because
    Of your sister. My attempts to return her to you safe and
        sound
    Involved me in this mess, and lots of others like it.

CHREMES:
    Where is she?

THAIS:
        There, in my house.

CHREMES:
            In *there?*

THAIS:
                Don't be worried;
    She's a decent girl. Quite worthy of you.

CHREMES:
        How do you mean?

THAIS:
    These are the facts: Your sister's my present to you,
        Chremes;
    I ask no payment in return.

CHREMES:
        I thank you, Thais. I assure you   750

That you shall receive suitable expression of my
appreciation.

THAIS:

Good, but you'd better watch out: You may lose my gift
before

You get it. She's the girl the Major's coming to abduct.
– Pythias, go get the evidence. The box of things that prove
Her identity.

CHREMES [*looking off left*]:

Thais, look! Here comes . . .

PYTHIAS [*to* THAIS]:

Where *is* the box?

THAIS:

It's in the chest. Please hurry!

[*Exit* PYTHIAS *into* THAIS' *house*]

CHREMES:

. . . the Major! He's brought an army
Along. An attack – help!

THAIS:

Now don't tell me you're scared.

CHREMES:

Perish the thought – me scared? Don't know the meaning of
fear.

THAIS:

Just what we need.

CHREMES:

I'm afraid . . . that you don't know the sort
Of man I am.

THAIS:

760   But I do, I do. Now, think this over:
Remember that you're an Athenian citizen dealing with an
alien.
You've got influence, reputation, friends. He hasn't. He's
weak.

CHREMES:

I know all that. But isn't it stupid to borrow trouble
When you can avoid it? Prevention is better than
vengeance,

Isn't it? Why get hurt?
    Look here, you go on inside
And bar the door, while I take a quickish run downtown.
    [*He points off left to downtown, checks, and points off
    right*[12] *to the harbour and the country*]
We require reinforcements to fight this battle.
    [*He starts off right.* THAIS *grabs his arm*]

THAIS:
    Stay here.

CHREMES:
    My plan is better.

THAIS:
    Stay here.

CHREMES:
        Leggo. Be back in a minute.

THAIS:
    Chremes, we don't need help. Just tell him that she's your
        sister.
    You lost her when she was little, and today you identified
        her.
    And then you show him the evidence.

PYTHIAS [*entering from the house with a box*]:
        And here's the evidence.

THAIS [*taking the box from* PYTHIAS *and thrusting it on*
    CHREMES]:
    Keep this.
    Oh. If the Major resorts to force, just take him to court.
    Have you got all this?

CHREMES:
        Oh, perfectly.

THAIS:
            When you say your piece,
    Don't be nervous.

CHREMES:
        Depend on me.

THAIS:
            Let's gird up those loins!

770   [*Aside*] Oh dear. Where can I find a defender to protect my
        champion?
        [*Exeunt into* THAIS' *house*]

                              Scene 7

        THRASO *and* GNATHO *enter left, followed by the motley
        army of* DONAX, SIMALIO *and* SYRISCUS. *They bear an
        assortment of household tools*
THRASO:
        Flagrant dishonour, Gnatho. Escutcheon grossly
        besmirched.
        Accept it? Never. Death were better.
            – Forward, men!
        Simalio, Donax, Syriscus – this way!
        [*The group shambles to a stop in front of* THAIS' *house*]
        Now, strategy: First –
        House, Assault on.
GNATHO:
            Brilliant.
THRASO:
                    Virgin, Plunder of.
GNATHO:
                            Breathtaking.
THRASO:
        Thais, Reprisals Against.
GNATHO:
        A positive master-stroke.
THRASO:
        – Donax, you and your crowbar form the centre, here.
        – Simalio, take the left wing.
            – Syriscus, take the right.
        – The rest of you men . . . [*He realizes that there is nobody
            left*]
                Where's Sergeant Sanga and his thieves' platoon?
        [SANGA, THRASO'*s cook, runs on bearing a dishmop*]
SANGA:
        All present and accounted for, sir.

THRASO:
You goldbrick, why aren't you armed
With regulation gear? You thought that battles were fought
with mops?

SANGA:
No, sir. I knew my general's valour and the might of his
men:
I figured there'd have to be blood. So this is to swab out the
wounds, sir.

THRASO:
Where are the others?

SANGA:
The others? Just what the hell do you mean, sir?
There's only Sannio left, and he's looking after the house.   780

THRASO:
Draw up the troops. Posting myself in the second rank.
Spot where I can command the entire field of battle.
[*The slaves, under* SANGA'*s direction, move towards the
house.* THRASO *moves away from it, followed by*
GNATHO]

GNATHO:
Tactical genius!
[*Aside*]
A formation which keeps him safe in reserve.

THRASO:
A manoeuvre made famous by General Pyrrhus.[13]
[THAIS *and* CHREMES, *unseen by the others, appear at*
THAIS' *upper window*]

CHREMES:
You see what's happening,
Thais? That was an excellent plan, barricading the house.

THAIS:
One thing's certain: That may look like a hero to you,
But it's just a fraud. Don't worry.

THRASO [*to* GNATHO]:
Any suggestions?

GNATHO:
I wish

That you had a sling. It's time for long-range fire from
   cover.
You'd cut them to pieces. The rout would be on.

THRASO:
   There's Thais. In person.

GNATHO:
How soon do we sound the attack?

THRASO:
   Not yet. Exhaust all other
Avenues before resorting to passage of arms. The mark
Of a wise commander. Conditions gained without the use
790   Of force, if possible.

GNATHO:
   Heaven preserve us, what a blessing
Is wisdom! I never come near you without departing
   improved.

THRASO:
   – A question, Thais, before we begin: On receipt of that
   girl,
You promised me your complete attention through
   tomorrow – yes?

THAIS:
   So what if I did?

THRASO:
   So what? Introducing your lover inside
My house right under my nose . . .

THAIS:
   What business is it of yours?

THRASO:
   . . . Sneaking away from me to join him . . .

THAIS:
   That's what I felt like.

THRASO:
Then give back Pamphila now. Or else I take her by force!

CHREMES:
You won't get her back. You won't even touch her, you . . .

GNATHO:
You shut up!

THRASO [*to* CHREMES]:
　　Just what do you mean? She's mine; I'll touch her.
CHREMES:
　　Yours, you bastard?
GNATHO:
　　Be careful, youngster. You obviously don't know whom
　　　you're addressing.
CHREMES [*to* GNATHO]:
　　Get out of here!
　　　[*To* THRASO]
　　　　– Do you know how you stand at present?   800
　　You start the least little fuss here now, and I'll give you a
　　　reason
　　To remember this day, and this place, and me, as long as
　　　you live.
GNATHO:
　　Boy, it grieves me to see you making an enemy of such
　　An important person.
CHREMES:
　　Get Out of Here, or I shall personally
　　Knock your block off.
GNATHO:
　　　You will, will you? Where's your manners,
　　You sonofabitch?
THRASO:
　　　Who *are* you? What are you aiming at?
　　What possible concern is this girl of yours?
CHREMES:
　　I shall inform you.
　　Point One: She is a freeborn . . .
THRASO:
　　Pah!
CHREMES:
　　　　. . . Athenian citizen . . .
THRASO:
　　Tchah!
CHREMES:
　　　　. . . Also, my sister.

THRASO:
   Insolent puppy!
CHREMES:
    Major,
I therefore enjoin you from any show of violence against
  her.
— Thais, I'll go get the nurse, Sophrona, and bring her
  back
To see the evidence here.
THRASO:
  You'd really prevent me from touching
A girl that belongs to me?
CHREMES:
   Exactly. I will prevent you.
I have spoken.
  [*He disappears from the window, leaves* THRASO' *house and
  stalks off right*[14]]
GNATHO [*to* THRASO]:
Hear that? He as good as confesses to theft. That's all you
  need.
THRASO:
810 You agree with that fellow, Thais?
THAIS:
   Find somebody else to answer
Your questions. I'm through.
  [*She closes the shutters.* THRASO *turns to* GNATHO]
THRASO:
What now?
GNATHO:
   Well, let's go home. She'll come there soon enough
On her own. And on her knees.
THRASO:
   You really think so?
GNATHO:
    Certainly.
I know the female mind: Say yes, and they say no.
Say no . . . and they suddenly find that there's nothing they
  want so much.

THRASO:
  Excellent thought.
GNATHO:
    Should I dismiss the army now?
THRASO:
  Whenever you like.
GNATHO:
    – Sanga, as befits a soldier in the field,
  Turn your thoughts to the fires of home.
SANGA:
    My heart has never
  Left my broiler.
GNATHO:
    Good boy.
THRASO:
      – This way, men. Forward, march!
  [THRASO, GNATHO *and the army straggle off left*]

ACT V

Scene 1

  THAIS *and* PYTHIAS *enter from* THAIS' *house*
THAIS:
  Oh, damn you, Pythias, please stop talking in riddles.
  'I know . . . but no, I don't know . . . he's gone . . . I
    heard . . .
  I wasn't there . . .' Unravel this tangle of words
  And tell me straight – what *is* all this?
      I've got
  A virgin in there in tears; her dress is in tatters;   820
  She won't say a thing. And what I haven't got
  Is a eunuch. Why? What happened?
      Well, say something!
PYTHIAS:
  Oh, dear. How do I start?
    People are saying

That wasn't a eunuch.
THAIS:
    What was it, then?
PYTHIAS:
        Uh . . . Chaerea.
THAIS:
    What's a Chaerea?
PYTHIAS:
    Phaedria's teenage brother.
THAIS:
    Don't gossip, you witch. That's a poisonous thing to say.
PYTHIAS:
    It's true. I checked it out.
THAIS:
        But what could he want
    In our house? Why did they bring him?
PYTHIAS:
        I don't know . . .
        [*A threatening gesture from* THAIS]
    But I *think* that he might have been in love with Pamphila.
THAIS:
    Oh, hell. If what you're telling me is true,
    You jinx, my reputation's dead and buried.
            This can't
    Be the reason the girl's in tears?
PYTHIAS:
        I think it can.
THAIS:
    It can't have happened. You're lying.
        I warned you against
830   That very thing when I left!
PYTHIAS:
            And what was I
    Supposed to do? I followed your orders to the letter:
    Put him in charge, you said, alone. I did.
THAIS:
    You set the wolf to watch the lamb. Oh, damn you!
    It nauseates me to be taken in like this.

What sort of a man can he be?

PYTHIAS [*looking off left*]:

    Oh, mistress, shhhh!

Please shhhh. We're saved.

    We've got the man in question.

THAIS:

    Where is he?

PYTHIAS:

    Look over there to your left. You see him?

THAIS:

    I see him . . .

PYTHIAS:

    Quick, now, have him arrested!

THAIS:

        Idiot.

What would we do with him then?

PYTHIAS:

    Do you have to ask?

What do you see when you look at that face? Impudence,

No?

    You agree?

        Oooh, what a cocky type!

Scene 2

CHAEREA, *still wearing* DORUS' *clothes, enters left*[15] *and
stops. He does not immediately see the women*

CHAEREA:

Antipho's father and Antipho's mother were both   840

At home. You'd think they'd planned it, placing themselves

Just where I couldn't get in without being seen.

So, while I was standing outside their door, an

   acquaintance

Began to move in my direction. At this,

I tore out of there as fast as I could and ducked

Down an alley. Nobody around. And then from there

To another alley, and then another, running

Away. And more than half out of my mind with fear

That someone who knew me might see me wearing these
  clothes.
– But isn't that Thais?
     It is.
          I'm stuck: What shall
I do? No matter – what will she do to me?
THAIS [*to* PYTHIAS]:
850   Let's go meet him.
     [*To* CHAEREA]
      – Greetings, Dorus. Delighted
To see you. Tell me, now: Did you run away?
CHAEREA:
  Yes, ma'am. It comes to that.
THAIS:
     You're pleased with yourself?
CHAEREA:
  No, ma'am.
THAIS:
     You think you'll get off easy, perhaps?
CHAEREA:
  Please pardon this first offence. If I ever commit
Another, put me to death.
THAIS:
     But why did you do it?
Did I look like such a vicious mistress?
CHAEREA:
     No, ma'am.
THAIS:
  Then what was the reason?
CHAEREA [*indicating* PYTHIAS]:
     Her. I was afraid
She'd go to you and accuse me.
THAIS:
     What had you done?
CHAEREA:
  It's nothing, really.
PYTHIAS:
     Nothing Really? That's

Too much! You raped a freeborn Athenian virgin –
You call that Nothing Really?
CHAEREA:
    I thought that she
Was one of us slaves.
PYTHIAS:
    Was one of us slaves! Of all
The unnatural . . . I'm using all my control, or I'd tear   860
Your hair out.
    – All this, and he comes to laugh at us!
THAIS:
You're raving; get out of here.
PYTHIAS:
    Why should I? What sort
Of damages would I have to pay for assaulting
A thug like him – a self-admitted slave?
THAIS:
Let's drop this nonsense.
    – Chaerea, what you've done
Is horribly wrong. I may deserve an affront
Like this in the highest degree; regardless, you had
No right to commit it. And now I swear to god
I don't have the least idea what course to follow
About this girl. You've overturned all my planning.
How can I give her back to her people the way
She should have gone, the way I wanted her   870
To go? And tell me, Chaerea, what becomes
Of the tangible thanks I hoped to get out of this?
CHAEREA:
At least I hope it's the start of a permanent bond
Between us, Thais. In affairs like this one, appalling
Beginnings often lead to lasting friendships.
There may be a god behind it all – who knows?
THAIS:
Yes. There's an interpretation I'm happy to accept.
CHAEREA:
Please do. There's one thing you can be sure of. I didn't
Do this to cause you any affront; I did it

For love.

THAIS:

    I know you did, and that's what makes me
All the more disposed to forgive you. I'm not
880 Exactly a stranger to human nature, Chaerea,
Or inexperienced. What love can do, I know.

CHAEREA:

    I swear to heaven, Thais, I love you, too.

PYTHIAS [to THAIS]:

    Better watch out for him; it's your turn now.

CHAEREA:

    I wouldn't dream . . .

PYTHIAS:

    I don't believe a word.

THAIS [to PYTHIAS]:

    Stop it!

CHAEREA:

    And now I humbly beg your assistance
Out of this mess. I commend and commit myself
Into your keeping, I name you my advocate. Thais,
Help me: I'll die if I don't marry that girl.

THAIS:

890 Yes, but your father . . .

CHAEREA:

    I guarantee he'll say yes.
As long as she's a citizen.

THAIS:

    If you can wait
A little, her brother should be back in a minute.
He went to get the nurse she had as a baby.
You can be there when she's identified, Chaerea!

CHAEREA:

    Fine; I'll stay.

THAIS:

    Then wouldn't you rather wait
Inside for him, instead of out here in the street?

CHAEREA:

    I'll jump at the chance.

PYTHIAS [*to* THAIS]:
>   And what, may I ask, do you think
> You're doing?

THAIS:
>   What's wrong now?

PYTHIAS:
>   Do you have to ask?
> Letting him in your house after what he did!

THAIS:
>   Why not?

PYTHIAS:
>   You take it from me, he'll start a nice, fresh
> Fracas.

THAIS:
>   Please do shut up.

PYTHIAS:
>   You refuse to realize   900
> Just how much of a menace this man is!

CHAEREA:
> I'll be quite harmless, Pythias.

PYTHIAS:
>   I know you will,
> Unless they let you get your hands on something.

CHAEREA:
> Well, then, Pythias, take me in charge yourself.

PYTHIAS:
> Not me. Take you in charge or put you in charge . . .
> I wouldn't dare.
>   Now, *git!*

THAIS [*looking off right*]:
>   Here comes her brother.
> Just in time.

CHAEREA:
>   Oh, hell. Oh, *No!* Please, Thais,
> Let's get inside. I couldn't stand to have him
> See me wearing these clothes on the street.

THAIS:
>   Why not?

Modesty *now?*

CHAEREA:
     I'm afraid so.

PYTHIAS:
          Afraid so? A veritable
     Virgin!

THAIS:
          You go ahead. I'll follow.
          – Pythias,
     You wait here for Chremes and bring him inside.
     [*Exeunt* CHAEREA *and* THAIS *into* THAIS' *house*]

Scene 3

PYTHIAS:
910 Idea, inspiration, hot flash – I need one now:
     Some way to pay back the slick pathological liar
     Who fobbed that bogus eunuch off on us. How?
          [CHREMES *and* SOPHRONA *enter right, very slowly*]

CHREMES:
     A little more speed, nurse. Come on, move.

SOPHRONA:
          I'm moving.

CHREMES:
     Which direction?

PYTHIAS [*running up*]:
          Have you shown the nurse
     The evidence yet?

CHREMES:
          Every last item.

PYTHIAS:
               Well,
     What did she say? Could she identify them?

CHREMES:
     By heart.

PYTHIAS:
          That's marvellous news. I do so like
     The girl.

Go right on in; my mistress has been
Waiting for you for hours.
[CHREMES *and* SOPHRONA *exit into* THAIS' *house.* PAR-
MENO *enters from* DEMEA'S *house and stops, not seeing*
PYTHIAS]
– Lo and behold,
A noble soul advances . . . Parmeno. Such
A leisurely pace. Please god, I think I've found
A personal method for bringing this crook to book.   920
First, I'll go inside and make quite sure
The identification's secure; then back out here,
To scare that scoundrel out of his scheming skin.
[*Exit* PYTHIAS *into* THAIS' *house*]

Scene 4

PARMENO:
Back for a check on Chaerea's progress. I hope
He's managed the matter with some acumen; if so
Imagine the praises accruing to Parmeno's account –
So *rightly*.
        Just what have I done?
            I omit from mention
The sheer achievement involved in effecting an affair
As potentially clumsy and costly as this – the procural,
From a hardened, tight-fisted pro, of the girl he loves –
Without trouble, toll, or expense of any sort.
Let all that pass. I pride myself on my second
Success, my masterpiece, my moral breakthrough: 930
I have developed a device whereby an innocent
Youth can learn the true nature and mores of whores
At an early age, and acquire a disgust to last him
The rest of his life.
        To see these broads abroad
From their houses, daintily nibbling away at lunch
With a lover, at intimate suppers, this is to conclude
That no more tasteful, better-dressed, or sweeter
Creatures exist.

But a stay inside those houses
Shows *Truth*: The filth, the overall bathless squalour
Of these soiled doves, their underlying ugliness,
The greasy greed with which they slosh their hunks
Of black bread in leftover soup and slobber it down.
940   Such an education can be a boy's salvation.

[*During this set piece,* PYTHIAS *has entered from* THAIS'
house and overheard]

PYTHIAS [*aside*]:
Heel. I'll make you eat those words . . . and your deeds
As well. You've had your fun with us. You'll pay.

[*Loudly, pretending not to see* PARMENO]
– God save us, what a revolting development! Ohhh, the
poor boy,
And so young, too! It's criminal, criminal – and Parmeno's
guilty!
He brought him here.

PARMENO [*aside*]:
What's up?

PYTHIAS:
He's such a pitiful sight,
I couldn't bear to watch. I ran out here before
They started that sickening punishment. How can they
inflict such pain?

PARMENO [*aside*]:
Oh god, what's all this uproar? Have I sunk myself
somehow?
I'd better go see.
– What's happened, Pythias? What's this mean?
Who's having such sickening pain?

PYTHIAS:
What, *you?* And you need to ask?
In your single-minded zeal to put one over on us,
950   You have destroyed the boy you tried to pass off as a
eunuch.

PARMENO:
But how? Tell me what happened!

PYTHIAS:
    I'll tell you, but first you tell me:
    The girl that Thais received as a gift today – who is she?
PARMENO:
    H-how should I know?
PYTHIAS:
    You didn't know that she's a citizen,
    The sister of one of the best-connected men in town?
PARMENO:
    Er – no.
PYTHIAS:
    She is. They just found out. And that is the girl
    Your unfortunate young man happened to rape. I say
      unfortunate:
    Her brother heard about it – a violent man, and given
    To shocking outbursts of . . .
PARMENO:
    What did he do?
PYTHIAS:
             Well, first he trussed
    Your fellow up in a fashion that must be appallingly
      painful . . .
PARMENO:
    He trussed him up?
PYTHIAS:
    He did. In spite of Thais's prayers for mercy.
PARMENO:
    He didn't!
PYTHIAS:
    And now he's threatening him with the usual treatment
    Reserved for convicted rapists.[16] Ugly, disgusting business;
    I've never seen it, and I never want to.
PARMENO:
    He can't do that – it's
    Preposterous!
PYTHIAS:
    Preposterous? Pray tell me why.

PARMENO:
        What else can you call it?
960   Whoever arrested a man for rape inside a whorehouse?
PYTHIAS:
  H-how should I know?
PARMENO:
      Well, here's an item you'd better know,
Pythias, all of you: I hereby proclaim that that boy
Is my master's son . . .
PYTHIAS:
      My goodness. Is he really?
PARMENO:
      So Thais
Had better take care that no harm comes to him.
      Matter
Of fact, why don't I go in myself?
    [*He starts for* THAIS' *door, but* PYTHIAS *stops him*]
PYTHIAS:
      Parmeno, think:
What can you accomplish? You won't help him and you'll
  ruin yourself;
They've already got you down as the cause of the whole
  affair.
PARMENO:
Then what the hell do I do? Is anything worth a try?
    [*Looking off right*]
Now look at this – the old man, on his way home from the
  farm.
Do I tell him or not?
      Oh god, I tell him. I know it ensures
Destruction for me, but I've simply got to do what I can
To help that boy.
PYTHIAS:
      Quite sound. I'll retire and leave him to you.
970 Do relate the events in sequence.
      And don't leave anything out.
    [*She exits into* THAIS' *house*]

Scene 5

DEMEA *enters right, and stops in front of his house*

DEMEA:

There's one advantage in having a farm close in:
City or country, I'm never bored with either.
Whenever one locale begins to cloy,
I switch.

[*He sees* PARMENO *in front of* THAIS' *house, and moves to him*]

Hel-lo, isn't that Parmeno? Sure.
– Hey, Parmeno, why are you standing around over here?
Who are you waiting for?

PARMENO [*stalling*]:

Why, how can this be?
Oh, boss. I'm glad to see you got back safe and ...

DEMEA:

Who are you waiting for?

PARMENO [*aside*]:

Oh, hell. My mouth's
Gone dry.

DEMEA:

What say? You're shaking – why? Are you
All right? Come on, speak up.

PARMENO:

The first thing, boss,
I want you to know is the truth, and this is the truth:
Whatever happened, it wasn't my fault that it happened,   980
And that's the truth.

DEMEA:

Eh?

PARMENO:

A very intelligent question.
First, I should have told you what happened. Phaedria
Bought a eunuch to give as a gift.

[*Pointing to* THAIS' *house*]

To her.

DEMEA:
  To who?
PARMENO:
    To Thais.
DEMEA:
      He *bought* it? Tarnation. How much?
PARMENO:
  Twenty *minae*.
DEMEA:
    I'm bankrupt.
PARMENO:
      Then Chaerea fell
In love with a girl in there who plays guitar.
DEMEA:
  He what? In *love*? At his age, he knows about whores?
  I thought he was still on the farm. Trouble breeds trouble.
PARMENO:
  Don't look at me, boss. I didn't force him to do it.
DEMEA:
  Let's not talk about you, you bastard. *You*
990 I'll attend to, provided I live through this. But first
  An explanation: What is going on?
PARMENO:
    Well, Chaerea
Got delivered to Thais. She took him for a eunuch.
DEMEA:
    For a *eunuch*?
PARMENO:
      That's right. And then they caught him in there
And trussed him up. They took him for a rapist.
DEMEA:
  Murder!
PARMENO:
    Whores are very unprincipled people.
DEMEA:
  Is that the lot? Perhaps you missed a disaster?
  Or maybe a small foreclosure?

PARMENO:
> That's it.

DEMEA:
> Then there's
> No need to wait. I'll break my way in now.
> [*He hurriedly exits into* THAIS' *house*]

PARMENO:
> No doubt about it, this business can only end
> In punitive measures against me. Not puny ones, either.
> But it had to happen, and I do have this consolation:
> I'll be the cause of measures just as unpleasant
> Against that nest of whores. The old man's been sniffing   1000
> Around for a long time to find an excuse
> For lowering the boom on them. And now he's found it.

Scene 6

PYTHIAS, *laughing, enters from* THAIS' *house. She does
not immediately see* PARMENO

PYTHIAS:
> Never, for longer than I can remember, has a happy ending
> Made me as happy as the ending that just turned out inside,
> What with the old man stumbling in, a bundle of blunder.
> I was the only one who saw anything funny – I knew what
> he
> Was afraid he'd see.

PARMENO [*aside*]:
> What's up this time?

PYTHIAS:
> And now to go
> See Parmeno. Where can he be?

PARMENO [*aside*]:
> She's hunting me down.

PYTHIAS:
> Oh, there
> He is. I'll go right over.
> [*She moves to him, and breaks into whoops of laughter*]

PARMENO:
>What is it, stupid? Why the chuckles?
>What's so damned funny?
>>Stop it!

PYTHIAS:
>>Do spare a poor girl some pity –
>I've laughed at you till I'm pooped.

PARMENO:
>And why, may I ask?

PYTHIAS:
>>Do you need to?
>On my honour, I have never seen, nor do I expect
>To see, a more consummate knucklehead. The innocent
>   amusement

1010
>That you've supplied us inside is simply too great to relate.
>I actually used to believe that you were cool and shrewd . . .
>*You!* A man who'd swallow whatever I said without
>   checking.
>A man who was so ashamed of turning a lad to crime
>That he'd double the young man's troubles by telling his
>   father about it.
>How do you think that Chaerea felt when his father saw
>   him
>Wearing those clothes? Well?
>>Admit it, you are *through*.

PARMENO:
>You slut, you mean that you were lying? And now you can
>   laugh?
>It gives you some twisted pleasure to make a joke of my
>   life?

PYTHIAS:
>Pure bliss.

PARMENO:
>Provided you get home free.

PYTHIAS:
>>Really?

PARMENO:
>>I swear

I'll pay you back for this.

PYTHIAS:
>Doubtless. But Parmeno, threats
>Like yours are likely to be deferred for a bit; meanwhile,   1020
>You'll hang, on each or both of two counts: First, you led
>Your nitwit boy to a life of crime, and then you turned
>The same boy in. They'll get you either way.

PARMENO:
>I'm dead.

PYTHIAS:
Which constitutes your reward for services rendered.
>'Bye.

>[*She exits into* THAIS' *house*]

PARMENO:
Finished. Tangled and trussed in my very own vocal cords.

Scene 7

>GNATHO *and* THRASO *enter left. They do not see* PAR-
>MENO, *and he doesn't see them*

GNATHO:
And now? We're on the march, Thraso – but what's the
objective?
What's the strategy? What do you hope to win?

THRASO:
>Er – me?
Surrender, mine. To Thais. Her terms.

GNATHO:
>You mean . . . ?

THRASO:
>No less
Than Hercules. Slave to a queen in his time. Omphale.[17]

GNATHO:
>A most
Impressive prototype.
>[*Aside*]
>I'd love to see her soften your skull
With her shoe.

[*Up*]

– There goes her door.

[CHAEREA, *still dressed as a eunuch,*[18] *bursts from* THAIS'
house]

THRASO:

Damnation. Another reversal.

1030   Never saw him before – a new one? Why such a rush?

Scene 8

CHAEREA [*to no one in particular. He doesn't see* THRASO
and GNATHO]:

Friends, neighbours, I ask you: Breathes there a luckier man
Than I?

The answer is No – nobody at all.

Today

The gods have made me Exhibit *A* of their might, a
showplace

For their powers, a dumping ground for the greatest
number of boons

In the shortest possible time.

PARMENO [*aside*]:

Now, why should he be so cheerful?

CHAEREA:

– Parmeno, friend and buddy – detector, director, and
perfecter

Of all my joys! Do you realize how happy I am?

Do you realize they've found that Pamphila's really a
citizen?

PARMENO:

So I heard.

CHAEREA:

Do you realize that we are engaged?

PARMENO:

Thank god and congratulations!

GNATHO [*aside to* THRASO]:

Did you hear what I heard?

CHAEREA:
  And that's not all; I'm happy for Phaedria, too. His affair
  Has finally found snug harbour. Just one big happy family:
  Dad's taken Thais under his wing; now we're her official
  Patrons, protectors, and sponsors.[19]
PARMENO:
  And your brother's her only lover?   1040
CHAEREA:
  Of course.
PARMENO:
  That means more cheer: The Major will get his
    discharge.
CHAEREA:
  Go find Phaedria fast as you can and tell him the news.
PARMENO:
  I'll see if he's home.
  [*He exits into* DEMEA's *house*]
THRASO [*aside to* GNATHO]:
  No doubt about my predicament, Gnatho?
  Annihilation, utter?
GNATHO [*aside to* THRASO]:
  I quite agree. No doubt at all.
CHAEREA:
  Whom should I put at the top of the list? Whom should I
    load
  With the greatest praise?
      Parmeno the planner, who formed the design?
  Or myself the actor, who had the guts to try it out?
  Or Lady Luck the conductor, who brought so many
    blessings
  To bear on one short day? Or dear old Dad, for his
    gladness,
  Good humour, and general zest?
      O Jupiter, hear my prayer:
  Stand by your bounty. Don't let our windfalls blow away.

Scene 9

PHAEDRIA *enters from* DEMEA's *house.*

PHAEDRIA:

    God save us all, what a staggering story Parmeno told me.

1050   But where's my brother?

CHAEREA:

       Present.

PHAEDRIA:

          I couldn't be more delighted.

CHAEREA:

    I'm not surprised. No one deserves love more in this world

    Than Thais does yours. Given the favours she's done for
      the family,

    That girl's a positive philanthropist . . .

PHAEDRIA:

       Whoa! You really don't need

    To praise her to *me.*

    [THRASO *and* GNATHO *converse apart*]

THRASO:

       Damnation. Lost. Yet passions swell

    As prospects shrink. Gnatho, appeal to you. Last hope.

GNATHO:

    Just what would you like me to do?

THRASO:

       Secure me a beach-head – size

    No matter – in Thais's household. Use cash, cajolery,
      whatnot.

GNATHO:

    A rather large order.

THRASO:

       Motive all you need; know you.

    Upon successful completion of mission, will undertake to
      supply

    Reward. Your choosing. Ask and receive.

GNATHO:

       You mean it?

THRASO:
> Just so.

GNATHO:
My conditions are these: If I succeed, I will receive
Carte blanche at your house whether you're home or not –
a permanent
Place at table.

THRASO:
> My absolute guarantee.

GNATHO:
> I shall gird my loins.   1060

[*He and* THRASO *approach the brothers*]

PHAEDRIA:
I hear somebody – who?
> Oh. Thraso.

THRASO:
> Good day to you both.

PHAEDRIA:
You are, perhaps, in ignorance of what has happened here?

THRASO:
Er . . . no.

PHAEDRIA:
> Then why do I descry you in this vicinity?

THRASO:
Relying on you . . .

PHAEDRIA:
> I'll give you something to rely on, Major.
Now hear this: If, after today, I should ever chance
To meet you on this street, even if you should say,
'Just passing through; I have an appointment and this is a
shortcut' –
You are a dead man.

GNATHO:
> Now, wait a minute. That's not a very nice
Thing to say.

PHAEDRIA:
> It's said.

GNATHO:
        This arrogant air – it's just
Not *you*, somehow.

PHAEDRIA:
        It's me, all right; the way I do things.

GNATHO:
Before you do them, I have a few words I'd like you to
    hear.
Just let me have my say, then do whatever seems best.

CHAEREA:
Let's listen to him.

GNATHO [*pointing left*]:
        Thraso, clear off that way a little.
    [THRASO *obeys, and the three converse out of his hearing*]
I definitely want to establish one point with both of you
Before I begin: Whatever action I propose in this matter,
1070   I do it entirely out of enlightened self-interest. *But*,
If my proposal should prove to be to your interest, too,
It would, I believe, be folly for you to refuse it.

PHAEDRIA:
        What is it?

GNATHO:
I advance the view that you should admit the Major as a
    rival.

PHAEDRIA:
What? *That I should admit . . .*

GNATHO:
        Now, don't be hasty. Reflect:
This life which you enjoy with Thais, Phaedria – or rather,
This good, high living in which you rejoice with Thais –
    how
Is it maintained? By give and take. As it happens, of money.
But you have little to give, while Thais is so constructed
That she must take a great deal.
        Problem: How to afford your affair
Without undue expense to you. Solution: The Major,
Than whom there exists no source of funds more useful, or
    less

Inconvenient. *Item:* The Major is loaded, and throws the
   stuff
Around with unmatched abandon. *Item:* The Major is
   brainless,
Witless, and senseless, a dull hebetudinous clod who passes
His days and nights in snoring, and thus will afford you no
   worry
As a possible object of Thais's affections. Besides, you can
   always   1080
Kick him out; it's easy.

PHAEDRIA [*to* CHAEREA]:
   Well?

GNATHO:
            One final *Item*,
To my way of thinking the most important: The Major
   stands
Alone as a host, and sets a table that knows no equal
For quality or for quantity.

CHAEREA:
   It may mean stretching a point,
But I think we ought to work him in.

PHAEDRIA:
   I tend to agree.

GNATHO:
You're making no mistake.
   Oh, one thing more – a personal
Favour: Please let me join your crowd. I'm sick of rolling
That boulder uphill.

PHAEDRIA:
   You've joined, as of now.

CHAEREA:
            And welcome aboard.

GNATHO:
By way of requital to you, Phaedria, and you, Chaerea,
I present the main course, a bountiful source of
   nourishment and laughs.
Eat hearty.
   [*He indicates* THRASO]

CHAEREA:
   A dainty dish.
PHAEDRIA:
      Receiving its just deserts.
GNATHO:
   – Thraso, come back. Any time.
THRASO [*running up*]:
      Well? Victory or defeat?
GNATHO:
   We won, of course. Our friends didn't know the real you.
   I had only to show them your inner nature and way of life,
1090 To tally up your achievements and appraise your peculiar
      virtues,
   And I carried the day.
THRASO:
      Beautifully done. Extend my heartfelt
Thanks.
      The whole world over, have always attracted unalloyed
Love.
GNATHO [*to* PHAEDRIA *and* CHAEREA]:
   I told you. Finesse to the core.
PHAEDRIA:
      He's just as advertised.
   [*Conducting the rest to* THAIS' *door*]
   All right, men, this way.
      [*To the audience*[20]]
      – To you, farewell. Applause, please.
   [*Exeunt into* THAIS' *house*]

                     Translated by Douglass Parker (1974)

Notes

Aristophanes, *The Birds*
(notes by Alan Sommerstein, selected by Erich Segal)

1. *Tereus, the hoopoe*: According to legend, *Tereus* married *Procne*, the king of Athens' daughter. He later met her sister Philomela, raped her, then cut out her tongue to prevent her from revealing the secret crime. But she was still able to send a message to her sister in the form of a woven garment. Procne took revenge for herself and her sister by killing Itys, their only child, and cooking him for a banquet. Tereus, realizing the further horror being performed, chased the two women intending to kill them. Miraculously they were saved by the gods, who transformed Procne into a swallow, Philomela into a nightingale and Tereus himself into a hoopoe. And yet Aristophanes seems to have forgotten the gory details, for here he presents this blood-soaked family as a happy household.

2. *obol*: Silver coin (three obols was the daily wage of a juryman).

3. *to birdition*: An appropriate pun on perdition.

4. *Sacas*: A nickname for the tragic dramatist Acestor, who, though an Athenian citizen, was widely accused of being of foreign birth.

5. *basket, a pot ... myrtle-wreaths*: Specifically a ritual-basket, containing the knife and other requisites for the sacrifice to be offered upon the foundation of a new city; a pot containing live coals; wreaths for the participants in the sacrifice to wear on their heads.

6. *stage-house*: The ever-present building that varies from play to play, being a castle or a hovel.

7. *Just you ask my lower half*: In Peisetaerus' fright, his bowels have involuntarily emptied themselves.

8. *jurorphobiacs*: Greek *apeliasta*, probably coined by Aristophanes to mean people who avoid jurors.

9. *a woolly mantle*: A cloak made of goatskin or sheepskin with the hair or fleece left on.

10. *the Cranaans*: A poetic name for the Athenians, derived traditionally from a mythical king Cranaus.

11. *the Salaminia*: One of the two 'sacred' triremes which formed part of the Athenian navy.

12. *you live the life of newly-weds*: There are three layers of meaning: (1) the birds' life is, as it were, one long honeymoon of carefree joy; (2) several of the plants mentioned are associated with weddings – the bridal couple were garlanded with water-mint and sesame-seed cakes, and perhaps also poppy-seed cakes were eaten; (3) several of the plant-names are also common expressions for the female genitals or various parts thereof.

13. *halcyons*: The halcyon was a mythical bird believed to build its nest on the surface of the sea.

14. *prosecutors*: The Greek is *sukophantai*, 'sycophant'. These were Athenian con men that were addicted to bringing relentless lawsuits against one and all, usually for blackmail.

15. *to run in the four hundred*: More precisely the 'four hundred' refers to the *diaulos*, a foot race of twice the length of the stadium.

16. *bringing owls to Athens*: The proverbial reference is like 'bringing coals to Newcastle'.

17. *I have welcomed here two men who are enamoured of our society*: There are distinct erotic overtones.

18. *Nicias*: The celebrated general and statesman, one of the more moderate Athenian political leaders.

19. *Foot by foot*: A military technical term for looking back at the enemy as you withdraw slowly.

20. *A passionate desire . . .*: Some of the words Tereus uses have erotic overtones.

21. *I swallowed an obol*: Greeks habitually carried small coins in their mouths.

22. *Lysicrates*: Nothing is known of this man; the scholia say he was 'an Athenian general, a thief and villain'.

23. *by Goose*: A comic corruption of 'by Zeus'. Cf. French *parbleu* for *par Dieu*.

24. *debauch*: The Greek word is severely critical.

25. *their Alcmenas . . . Alopes . . . Semeles*: Alcmena was seduced by Zeus and became the mother of Hercules. Here, for once in his life, the object of the seducer's affections was totally faithful and Zeus had to disguise himself as her own husband to get into bed with her. Alope, the daughter of Cercyon, became pregnant by

Poseidon and is the mother of Hippothoon. Semele, the daughter of Cadmus, became the mother by Zeus of Dionysus.

26. *five human ages lives the raucous crow*: Adapted from Hesiod (fragment 304).

27. *Ammon*: An oracular shrine of the Egyptian god Ammon, equated by the Greeks with Zeus.

28. *Erebus*: The deity of primeval darkness.

29. *In the beginning . . .*: This has a biblical ring to it – like the book of Genesis.

30. *Tartarus*: The darkest lowest region of the Underworld, as far below the earth as earth was to the sky.

31. *wind-gotten egg*: This sustains the belief that certain female birds could be impregnated by the wind.

32. *Orestes*: The nickname of a man who for some reason had the reputation of being a clothes-snatcher – a grave offence in ancient Athens.

33. *Delphi . . . Dodona*: Famous Greek oracles.

34. *Phrynichus*: One of the oldest Greek tragedians.

35. *a Phrygian*: Phrygians at Athens would normally be slaves.

36. *phylarch . . . hipparch*: Commander of one of the ten tribal divisions of the Athenian cavalry . . . commander of the whole cavalry corps.

37. *not at the hand of another, but by our own feathers*: Adapted from Aeschylus fragment 139.4 (= *Myrmidons* 231.4).

38. *Athena Polias*: Athena of the Citadel, who dwelt on and protected the acropolis.

39. *Phythian cry*: Properly the music of a hymn sung to the accompaniment of the pipes, in honour of Phythian Apollo.

40. *Hestia*: Goddess of the hearth.

41. *a word of Pindar's*: A poem by Pindar in honour of Hieron (fragment 105b).

42. ORACLE-MONGER: The Greek designates a person whose collection of alleged oracles just happens to be extremely relevant to the current situation.

43. *Meton*: The renowned contemporary astronomer, here presented as decidedly sophomoric. Informed that our heroes are debating how to 'bash up' all quacks, he quickly decamps. This is typical of how all applicants for citizenship to Birdland are treated.

44. *The man's a Thales*: I.e an intellectual genius. Thales of Miletus, who lived in the first half of the sixth century, was and is generally regarded as the earliest of Greek philosophers.

45. *Diagoras the Melian*: A notorious atheist.

46. *A most splendid . . . piece of work . . . hundred fathoms*: The vast dimensions of the walls seem to parody Herodotus' description of the ramparts of Babylon (1.178.3–179.3). The fathom was six feet.

47. *already the sound can be heard . . . of an airborne god*: The first god to test their sovereignty arrives – the haughty messenger Iris – and is condemned to death; despite her protestations that she is immortal and cannot be killed, Peisetaerus retorts with supreme comic illogic.

48. *and the halls of Amphion*: An irrelevant tragic tag added purely for effect.

49. *Porphyrion*: King of the Giants who once made war on the Olympians.

50. *I'm still hard enough to stand three rammings*: Iris will be amazed at Peisetaerus' boast. In fact Peisetaerus shows a growing sexual urge when he threatens to rape her not once but three times.

51. *quail-tapper*: Referring to a common gambling sport.

52. *Corcyraean ones*: An allusion to the whips carried by certain officials at Corcyra (present-day Corfu).

53. *Enter PROMETHEUS*: Traditionally the god who took the side of mortal man against the divine hierarchy, most notably by his gift of fire, and for this earned terrible punishment from Zeus. He arrives to advise the mortals on how to topple the Olympians, urging them to demand *everything* from Zeus, not least of which, although it does not say so by name, must be the prize woman Hera herself.

54. *Zeus is finished*: Prometheus means that Zeus has no chance of avoiding defeat in his conflict with the birds. Peisetaerus apparently takes him as meaning that Zeus is dead – but instead of expressing astonishment, he calmly asks for further details as if this was a perfectly ordinary event.

55. *Thesmorphoria*: An important festival, normally celebrated by women alone, in or around October.

56. *Triballians*: The Greeks regarded them as the lowest form of humanity, savages who apparently spoke no known language.

57. *Princess*: The translator's choice of 'Princess' is too mild. At this daring moment the rebels come as close as possible to saying explicitly that she is Hera herself. To emphasize this still further, the play concludes with a paean to the (former) Queen of the Universe (1720–65): the chorus all but spells it out. After all, in the grand finale who else could Zeus' constant companion be? As we dance to a conclusion, they sing of 'Olympian Hera and

the Great One who ruled over the gods' and now must give way. Thus the play concludes – as all comedies should – in a wedding. But there is no doubt that Peisetaerus has won the supreme bride – which must be Hera herself. [ES]

58. *thanks to you ... we can eat broiled sprats*: Literally, we broil food on coals (sprats in particular were often cooked in this way) – a comical way of saying 'we possess fire'.

59. *a downright Timon*: I.e. one who hates other gods as much as Timon, the notorious misanthrope, hated other men. He was later believed to have been an actual Athenian of the fifth century, but is probably a legendary figure.

60. *Peisander*: Son of Glaucetes of the deme Acharnae, a significant figure in Athenian politics. Comedy satirizes him as a coward.

61. *just like Odysseus*: Odysseus sacrificed a ram and a ewe (*Odyssey* 10.527) rather than a young female camel.

62. *Chaerephon*: The context suggests he is a living ghost.

63. *Laespodias*: A politician, satirized principally for having mis-shapen calves which he concealed by letting his cloak hang down to his ankles.

64. *Silphium*: An ancient drug, used here with cheese and oil to garnish the birds Peisetaerus has killed, a practice he has earlier denounced.

65. *phratry*: A religious guild whose members were considered to be descended from a common ancestor.

Menander, *The Girl From Samos*
(notes by Norma Millar, augmented by Erich Segal)

1. *I was treated ... good family*: The text is uncertain, but the point seems to be that Moschion, though adopted, was treated exactly as a son of the house.

2. *festival of Adonis*: According to the myth, Adonis was a beautiful boy, loved by Aphrodite, the goddess of love. After his accidental death, he was allowed to spend part of the year on earth, but had to return to the Underworld for the rest. The Athenian festival was held in the spring, and consisted of mourning for death followed by celebration of rebirth. Quick-growing seeds were planted in trays (the 'gardens'), symbolizing the renewal of life. The festival was an especial favourite of women.

3. The text is uncertain.

4. *ritual basket*: This contained barley, garland and knife, for the preliminary sacrifice.

5. The general sense of two damaged lines.
6. *Tereus, Oedipus, Thyestes*: Notorious rapists and murderers of
    their own families. For Tereus, see n. 1 to *The Birds*; Oedipus
    killed his father and Thyestes his three sons.
7. *Amyntor's rage . . . blind your son*: Amyntor was jealous of his
    son Phoenix's attentions to his (Amyntor's) mistress, cursed him
    and sent him into exile. According to Euripides' *Phoenix*, he also
    blinded him.
8. *Zeus . . . steam of gold . . . locked up*: To seduce various
    mortals, Zeus had to take on different shapes. To reach Danaë,
    locked in a tall tower, he entered her chamber as a shower of
    gold.
9. *Chairephon*: A notorious hanger-on of the generation before
    Menander.
10. *Androcles*: Nothing is known of him.
11. *to the Foreign Legion*: Moschion says he will go to Bactria or
    Caria, the two areas where a mercenary soldier of the time could
    most easily find employment. Bactria (on the borders of modern
    CIS and Afghanistan) was in turmoil after Alexander's partial
    conquest, and Caria (now in south-west Turkey) was fighting off
    Persian claims to sovereignty.
12. There are a few small gaps in the text of the speech, but the
    general sense is clear.
13. *Dionysus*: Patron god of the theatre.

Plautus, *The Brothers Menaechmus*
(notes by Erich Segal)

1. *Epidamnus*: Port city on the Adriatic coast.
2. *in every play*: Plautus criticizes other Roman playwrights for
    boasting of their 'authenticity', their fidelity to the Greek models,
    a practice which evidently had some snob appeal (to judge from
    Terence's prologues, in a later age). Plautus, as he here ironically
    proves, preferred mob appeal.
3. *the very same*: This 'explanation' is also calculated to add some-
    thing to the comic confusion about which Menaechmus twin is
    which.
4. *he owes a debt*: The text is uncertain. This is the translator's
    guess.
5. *Metre by metre*: The Latin *pedibus* could mean human feet or
    feet of verse. A pun.
6. *was all he had*: There was a pun in the Greek original which

Plautus has not succeeded in rendering in Latin. The same Greek word, *tokos*, means both children and money.

7. *and on and on*: Plautus' prologue is incomplete, lacking at least one verse. The translator has added this line, which at least has the virtue of giving the prologue-actor something to say as he strolls off-stage.

8. *festivals*: The Latin refers specifically to the festival of Ceres, a holiday in April, when public banquets were held in Rome.

9. *ungrateful too*: This is the first 'lyric' in the play. There will be four more (lines 351ff., 571ff., 753ff., 966ff.).

10. *the city prophets*: The text is fragmentary. Peniculus seems to be referring to the College of Augurs, official prophets of Rome.

11. *odours quite unwashable*: Never a praiser of women, Plautus none the less stoops very, very rarely to jokes this unsavoury.

12. *rub-a-dub dubbing*: The Latin is 'furtum scortum prandium'. This triad has never been rendered into English with all its assonantal splendour. An attractive suggestion is 'purloin, sirloin, her loin', although the reference to the steak seems anachronistic. Perhaps the reader can concoct a thrilling threesome.

13. *outtop*: Erotium's sexual innuendo that Menaechmus will always be *superior* as far as she is concerned, recalls Martial's wry epigram advising that a wife should always be *inferior* (8.12.3–4): 'Inferior matrona suo sit, Prisce, marito / non aliter fiunt femina virque pares' ('Priscus, a woman should always be beneath her husband, / Otherwise they won't be equal in relationship').

14. *stole the girdle from that Amazon Hippolyta*: Hercules stole the golden girdle the queen of the Amazons had received from Ares.

15. *duties with such diligence*: Menaechmus calls his mistress *morigera*, a dutiful epithet usually reserved for Roman wives.

16. *along those lines*: All foods 'along those lines' were forbidden to Romans by various censorship rulings, especially the puritanical food prohibitions put forth by the Elder Cato.

17. *tell me, please*: One of the all-time obvious cue lines.

18. *exotic Greece*: Greece beyond the mainland; most specifically, Magna Graecia, the Greek settlements in southern Italy. The precise area is hard to define. According to some, 'exotic Greece' might extend as far north as Naples.

19. *no kin ... bro-kin*: This pun renders Plautus' play on *geminum*, 'twin brother', and *gemes*, 'you'll groan'.

20. *undamaged*: Plautus puns on the name of the town, Epidamnus, and *damnum*, which means 'financial ruin'.

21. *my back is dead*: Non-clever slaves in comedy (especially Plautine

comedy) are always worried about whiplashes on their backs –
the reward for misbehaviour.

22. *for sacred pigs*: As the context suggests, pigs were used as ex-
piatory animals, offered up to cure diseases, especially mental
ones.

23. *the party's parts*: Cylindrus talks grandiloquently, as comic cooks
were wont to. The Latin says, in stately fashion, that he is about
to bring delicacies to Vulcan, the fire-god – a fancy way of saying
'stove'.

24. *King Phintia*: There is enough historical accuracy here to suggest
that Plautus *might* have found these names in his Greek model.
On the other hand, the names would be well known to the
Romans who had fought in Sicily during the Punic Wars.

25. *given me today*: In a modern production, this would seem an
ideal moment for the intermission.

26. *this tradition*: Menaechmus talks a great deal about 'tradition',
mos in the Latin, leading many scholars to believe that this is a
'Roman song', for the benefit of the *patroni* and *clientes* in the
house (i.e. almost everybody). This is likely, for the word *mos*
was a very important one. The Romans, as anyone who has read
Cicero will know, constantly harped upon *mos maiorum*, their
forefathers' tradition.

27. *step into court*: To make all this litigation intelligible to the
modern reader, the translator has merely given the gist of
Menaechmus' legal manoeuvring, which involves a procedure
per sponsionem, a type of out-of-court arbitration. The important points are that (*a*) Menaechmus was forced to defend a
client, (*b*) the client was clearly guilty, and (*c*) notwithstanding
his guilt, the client was an idiot, who spoiled all of Menaechmus'
efforts on his behalf.

28. *pretending*: Line 639a omitted.

29. *I didn't give it to her*: The emphatic *non dedisse* in the Latin has
much the same double entendre as the English phrase. We recall
Ovid's plea to his mistress, urging her to reject her husband's
amorous advances (*Amores* 1.4.69–70): 'Sed quaecumque tamen
noctem fortuna sequetur / cras mihi constanti voce dedisse nega!'
('And yet, whatever chances to happen this night, tomorrow –
/ In unshaking tones, deny you gave him anything').

30. *universally kicked out*: Perhaps not an adequate rendering of
exclusissumus, a Plautine coinage based on the adjective
exclusus, 'kicked out'. Most literally, I suppose, we could say
'kickedest-out', but the word does not play very well.

31. *Hecuba ... female dog*: Hecuba, queen of Troy, was taken prisoner at the fall of Troy; she suffered so many woes thereafter that she was ultimately transformed into a bitch.

32. *father-in-law of Hercules*: Plautus, showing off his erudition, refers to Porthaon, grandfather of Deianira, wife of Hercules. The aim, of course, is mytho-hyperbolic: 'I don't know you from Adam', or some such.

33. *friend of Agamemnon*: Plautus uses Calchas, prophet of the Greek army at Troy. The translator has substituted Calchas' employer, King Agamemnon.

34. *big-dowry wives*: Plautus abounds in jokes about the pains which accompany dowried wives. Here even the woman's own father complains of the convention.

35. *what his business is*: The old man advises her to be *morigera*, as the ideal Roman wife should be.

36. *with perjury*: It may seem odd to the modern reader that, after calling your antagonist a smelly goat, you then call him (merely) a perjurer. But we must remember how the Romans praised plain-dealing and honesty; by their standards, how you reek was less important than how you speak.

37. *compared to him*: Reading *Tithonus* for W. M. Lindsay's *Titanus* (Oxford Classical Text). Tithonus was Aurora's lover, immortal but not immutable. With time he became a mere wrinkle.

38. *horses' hoofbeats*: In 'see the sound of horses' hoofbeats', Menaechmus anticipates the nonsensical outburst of Shakespeare's Pyramus: 'I see a voice!' (*Midsummer Night's Dream*, V.1.194).

39. *hauls me from the car?*: Needless to say, Menaechmus II is making all this up as he goes along. The Romans revered their elders; any assault on an old person, even on the comic stage, was unthinkable.

40. *Enter OLD MAN*: The old man does get back with the doctor rather quickly. And he complains of having had to wait, at that. Perhaps there was a musical interlude. Or perhaps, counter to the comic spirit, we are being too literal in noticing.

41. *or is he frantic?*: 'Depressed' and 'frantic' in the Latin are *larvatus*, literally, 'haunted by ghosts', and *cerritus*, 'out of his head'.

42. *his royal patron*: The Latin is *rex*, 'king', the title by which a parasite would refer to his benefactor.

43. *tons of hellebore*: An ancient tranquillizer.

44. *like a Nestor now*: Nestor, elder statesman of the Greeks at Troy.

Homeric legends were just becoming fashionable at Rome, which
may explain Plautus' frequent references to them.

45. *All's well*: Plautus too is tampering with a proverb.

46. *for me, that's best*: A few lines of dubious authenticity have been
omitted here.

47. *for something nice*: The meaning of this line is unsure. I have
made a conjecture.

48. *and help me as well*: The absurdly logical process that Messenio
now undertakes has puzzled many. Why are they so hesitant?
Isn't it clear that the brothers have found each other? Why this
detailed investigation? There is a simple explanation: Plautus
never stops until he gets the nth laugh out of his audience. And
he does wring quite a few more jokes out of this protracted
recognition dialogue.

Terence, *The Eunuch*
(notes by Douglass Parker, augmented by Erich Segal)

1. *DEMEA*: This is the name given to the old man in the oldest
extant manuscript of Terence, not at this point (none of the MSS
presents a cast list), but in the scene-heading at Act V, Scene 5,
where other MSS give the name Laches. Further, the fourth-
century grammarian and critic Donatus notes that the father in
Menander's *Eunouchos* was named Simon. Inasmuch as the text
proper finds no occasion to name the old man at all, my principal
reason for sticking by Demea is a capricious neatness; I realize
that it might have been supplied from the *Adelphoe*, even as
Laches might have come from the *Hecyra*. Given the old man's
somewhat uncharacteristic behaviour, he might as well be named
Cheeryble.

2. *someone exists*: The someone is Terence's standing literary adver-
sary, the elder playwright Luscius Lanuvinus.

3. *Ghost . . . Contested Treasure*: Terence, victim of countless cal-
umnies, is here accused of plagiarizing plays by Menander.

4. *A street in Athens*: The following frame for the play's presentation balances itself between the requisites of the text and such
facts as we know about the Roman stage. It is a rationalization
of the action, nothing more, and has two principal aims: (1) to
establish with the audience, as the play unfolds, a knowledge of
the pertinent off-stage locations – put as simply as possible, the
exit stage left leads to Thraso's house, while the exit stage right
leads everywhere else; (2) to maintain aim while avoiding

awkward meetings, at entrance and exit, by characters unaware of each other's presence. Such difficulties as arise will be dealt with as they occur. One other point: in common with most translators and commentators, I have opted here for a two-house set, though the presence of three doors on the Roman stage is undoubted. But the three need not always be used, and the physical representation of Thraso's house seems to contribute nothing but an onstage location for what is clearly conceived of as offstage action.

5. *For guard duty there*: This would be part of Chaerea's required service as an Athenian adolescent.

6. *Three minae*: A sum of money.

7. *at his thunder's sound*: According to Donatus, a parody of the Latin poet Ennius.

8. *an uncomprehending DORIAS*: That is, Dorias has been greeted, upon entering the house, with an uproar; she knows that something is wrong, but doesn't know *what*. Another solution is for her to knock at Thais' door at the end of Act IV, Scene 1, wait patiently (and unperceivingly) for admittance throughout Phaedria's soliloquy, and finally receive an answer when Pythias bursts forth.

9. *of all the harebrained delinquents*: The motivation here adopted for this line, and Pythias' reaction, is this: Phaedria has quizzed Dorus privately in the hope of establishing Chaerea's innocence; when that hope is firmly defeated, he shouts in annoyance at his younger brother's stupidity. Pythias, hearing the shout, interprets it as directed against Dorus, an attempt to impugn his testimony.

10. *build up thanks with him*: Or possibly with *her*; the Latin *illi* is ambiguous. The possible candidates and reasons: thanks would be due from (1) Phaedria, for protecting his brother; (2) Thais, for concealing the somewhat shopworn condition of a counter which she hopes to trade for patronage and protection; (3) Pamphila, for hiding her shame. (1) and (3) seem more likely than (2), and (1) more likely than (3).

11. *Aphrodite a lump of ice is*: Apologies are due somewhere for this doggerel, as well as for the retranslation of Latin divinities into Greek that makes it possible. Its only excuse is that it contributes to the general rhetorical inflation marking Chremes' drunkenness – a drunkenness that lasts, incidentally, through all the oscillations of his Dutch courage, until he has departed to get the nurse.

12. *checks, and points off right*: This overful blocking is necessary to reconcile *mise-en-scène* with text, but I believe it has some additional warrant, thus: the conventional downtown exit, stage left, has already been established as the way to Thraso's house, and hence the route by which the army is approaching. Chremes grabs at the first possible excuse to leave the field of honour, does a double-take when he sees that it would lead him into collision with the oncoming enemy, and changes to a direction completely at variance with his suggestion.

13. *General Pyrrhus*: King of Epirus, renowned for winning two battles against the Romans, but losing so many men that his victory was also a defeat (cf. Pyrrhic victory).

14. *and stalks off right*: Alternatively, Chremes might merely disappear from the window, and be presumed, by those for whom such presumptions are necessary, to have left by a back door.

15. *enters left*: The one wing entrance in this play whose direction is definitely specified in the text (by Pythias' line slightly earlier). The fact that it is not the direction by which Chaerea departed is, I think, sufficiently motivated by his remarks immediately after this on his confusion. An analogous confusion ('I've been looking all over and can't find the girl') underlies his first entrance in the play, where (in this version) he has lost Gnatho's procession and debouches into his home street by a different route.

16. *Reserved for convicted rapists*: Probably radical castration, which would under the circumstances be peculiarly (if horribly) appropriate; Pythias has obviously given the matter some thought. 'Adulterers' may be closer to *moechis* than 'rapists', but its use here and later would evoke in a modern audience different attitudes, not to say definitions, from the ones desired.

17. *Omphale*: Lydian queen who once owned Hercules as a slave.

18. *still dressed as a eunuch*: I adopt this stage direction in deference to Donatus' interpretation: 'Chaerea is in the eunuch's costume, but bursts forth in manly self-assurance, frightening the soldier by seeming to appear as a new rival.' Alternatively, of course, if Dorus' clothes are distinctive enough, Thraso might be startled at the appearance of a new eunuch. Or Chaerea just might, at long last, have thrown something on over the costume.

19. *Patrons, protectors, and sponsors*: To the Roman audience this would probably suggest the legally recognized client–patron relationship, though the Athenian institution which it reflects is somewhat different: the sponsorship (*prostasia*) of a resident alien by a responsible citizen.

20. *To the audience*: The Cantor has been omitted as a quasi-character, and the dismissal speech has been given to that actor who is, at the moment, directing the final exits.

PENGUIN CLASSICS

THE BIRDS AND OTHER PLAYS   ARISTOPHANES

THE KNIGHTS / PEACE / THE BIRDS / THE ASSEMBLYWOMEN / WEALTH

'Oh wings are splendid things, make no mistake: they really help you rise in the world'

The plays collected in this volume, written at different times in Aristophanes's forty-year career as a dramatist, all contain his trademark bawdy comedy and dazzling verbal agility. In *The Birds*, two frustrated Athenians join with the birds to build the utopian city of 'Much Cuckoo in the Clouds'. *The Knights* is a venomous satire on Cleon, the prominent Athenian demagogue, while *The Assemblywomen* considers the war of the sexes, as the women of Athens infiltrate the all-male Assembly in disguise. The lengthy conflict with Sparta is the subject of *Peace*, inspired by the hope of a settlement in 421 BC, and *Wealth* reflects the economic catastrophe that hit Athens after the war, as the god of riches is depicted as a ragged, blind old man.

The lively translations by David Barrett and Alan H. Sommerstein capture the full humour of the plays. The introduction examines Aristophanes's life and times, and the comedy and poetry of his works. This volume also includes an introductory note for each play.

Translated with an introduction by David Barrett and Alan H. Sommerstein

PENGUIN CLASSICS

PROMETHEUS BOUND AND OTHER PLAYS
AESCHYLUS

PROMETHEUS BOUND / THE SUPPLIANTS / SEVEN AGAINST THEBES / THE PERSIANS

'Your kindness to the human race has earned you this.
A god who would not bow to the gods' anger – you
Transgressing right, gave privileges to mortal men'

Aeschylus (525–456 BC) brought a new grandeur and epic sweep to the drama of classical Athens, raising it to the status of high art. In *Prometheus Bound* the defiant Titan Prometheus is brutally punished by Zeus for daring to improve the state of wretchedness and servitude in which mankind is kept. *The Suppliants* tells the story of the fifty daughters of Danaus who must flee to escape enforced marriages, while *Seven Against Thebes* shows the inexorable downfall of the last members of the cursed family of Oedipus. And *The Persians*, the only Greek tragedy to deal with events from recent Athenian history, depicts the aftermath of the defeat of Persia in the battle of Salamis, with a sympathetic portrayal of its disgraced King Xerxes.

Philip Vellacott's evocative translation is accompanied by an introduction, with individual discussions of the plays, and their sources in history and mythology.

Translated with an introduction by Philip Vellacott

PENGUIN CLASSICS

THE FROGS AND OTHER PLAYS   ARISTOPHANES

THE WASPS / THE POET AND THE WOMEN / THE FROGS

'This is just a little fable, with a moral: not too highbrow for you, we hope, but a bit more intelligent than the usual knockabout stuff'

The master of ancient Greek comic drama, Aristophanes combined slapstick, humour and cheerful vulgarity with acute political observations. In *The Frogs*, written during the Peloponnesian War, Dionysus descends to the Underworld to bring back a poet who can help Athens in its darkest hour, and stages a great debate to help him decide between the traditional wisdom of Aeschylus and the brilliant modernity of Euripides. The clash of generations and values is also the object of Aristophanes' satire in *The Wasps*, in which an old-fashioned father and his loose-living son come to blows and end up in court. And in *The Poet and the Women*, Euripides, accused of misogyny, persuades a relative to infiltrate an all-women festival to find out whether revenge is being plotted against him.

David Barrett's introduction discusses the Athenian dramatic contests in which these plays first appeared, and conventions of Greek comedy – from its poetic language and the role of the Chorus to casting and costumes.

Translated with an introduction by David Barrett

PENGUIN CLASSICS

LYSISTRATA AND OTHER PLAYS   ARISTOPHANES

LYSISTRATA / THE ACHARNIANS / THE CLOUDS

'But he who would provoke me should remember
That those who rifle wasps' nests will be stung!'

Writing at a time of political and social crisis in Athens, Aristophanes
(*c.* 447–*c.* 385 BC) was an eloquent, yet bawdy, challenger to the
demagogue and the sophist. In *Lysistrata* and *The Acharnians*, two pleas
for an end to the long war between Athens and Sparta, a band of women
and a lone peasant respectively defeat the political establishment. The
darker comedy of *The Clouds* satirizes Athenian philosophers, Socrates
in particular, and reflects the uncertainties of a generation in which all
traditional religious and ethical beliefs were being challenged.

For this edition Alan H. Sommerstein has completely revised his
translation of these three plays, bringing out the full nuances of
Aristophanes's ribald humour and intricate word play, with a new
introduction explaining the historical and cultural background to
the plays.

Translated with an introduction by Alan H. Sommerstein

PENGUIN CLASSICS

MEDEA AND OTHER PLAYS   EURIPIDES

MEDEA / ALCESTIS / THE CHILDREN OF HERACLES / HIPPOLYTUS

'That proud, impassioned soul, so ungovernable now that she has felt the sting of injustice'

Medea, in which a spurned woman takes revenge upon her lover by killing her children, is one of the most shocking and horrific of all the Greek tragedies. Dominating the play is Medea herself, a towering and powerful figure who demonstrates Euripides's unusual willingness to give voice to a woman's case. *Alcestis,* a tragicomedy, is based on a magical myth in which Death is overcome, and *The Children of Heracles* examines the conflict between might and right, while *Hippolytus* deals with self-destructive integrity and moral dilemmas. These plays show Euripides transforming the awesome figures of Greek mythology into recognizable, fallible human beings.

John Davie's accessible prose translation is accompanied by a general introduction and individual prefaces to each play.

'John Davie's translations are outstanding ... the tone throughout is refreshingly modern yet dignified' William Allan, *Classical Review*

Previously published as *Alcestis and Other Plays.*

Translated by John Davie, with an introduction and notes by Richard Rutherford

PENGUIN CLASSICS

ELECTRA AND OTHER PLAYS   SOPHOCLES

AJAX / ELECTRA / WOMEN OF TRACHIS / PHILOCTETES

'Now that he is dead,
I turn to you; will you be brave enough
To help me kill the man who killed our father?'

Sophocles's innovative plays transformed Greek myths into dramas featuring complex human characters, through which he explored profound moral issues. *Electra* portrays the grief of a young woman for her father Agamemnon, who has been killed by her mother's lover. Aeschylus and Euripides also dramatized this story, but the objectivity and humanity of Sophocles's version provided a new perspective. Depicting the fall of a great hero, *Ajax* examines the enigma of power and weakness combined in one being, while the *Women of Trachis* portrays the tragic love and error of Heracles's deserted wife Deianeira, and *Philoctetes* deals with the conflict between physical force and moral strength.

E. F. Watling's vivid translation is accompanied by an introduction in which he discusses Sophocles's use of a third actor to create new dramatic situations and compares the different treatments of the Electra myth by the three great tragic poets of classical Athens.

Translated with an introduction by E. F. Watling

PENGUIN CLASSICS

GREEK TRAGEDY

'Man must suffer to be wise'

The fifth century BC saw the fullest flowering of art, literature and philosophy in ancient Athens, and this major new selection brings the masterpieces of the great tragedians of that era – Aeschylus, Sophocles and Euripides – together in one volume. Powerful and devastating, they depict complex characters locked in brutal conflict both with others and themselves in situations that offer no simple solutions. Through the revenge-murder in Agamemnon, the hideous family secret revealed in Oedipus Rex and a mother's slaughter of her children in Medea, we see the wrenching dilemmas of humans living in a morally uncertain world. This volume also includes extracts from Aristophanes' comedy *The Frogs* – a comic satire on tragic playwrights – and a selection from Aristotle's masterful *Poetics*, which presents a philosophical discussion of Greek tragedy.

Simon Goldhill's introduction illuminates the plays' cultural background and place in ritual ceremony, and illustrates their lasting effect on the Western imagination. This edition includes a preface, chronology, further reading and detailed notes on each work, while genealogical tables clarify the complex legends behind each tragedy.

Edited by Shomit Dutta

With an introduction by Simon Goldhill

PENGUIN CLASSICS

THE CONSOLATION OF PHILOSOPHY   BOETHIUS

'Why else does slippery Fortune change
So much, and punishment more fit
For crime oppress the innocent?'

Written in prison before his brutal execution in AD 524, Boethius's *The Consolation of Philosophy* is a conversation between the ailing prisoner and his 'nurse' Philosophy, whose instruction restores him to health and brings him to enlightenment. Boethius was an eminent public figure who had risen to great political heights in the court of King Theodoric when he was implicated in conspiracy and condemned to death. Although a Christian, it was to the pagan Greek philosophers that he turned for inspiration following his abrupt fall from grace. With great clarity of thought and philosophical brilliance, Boethius adopted the classical model of the dialogue to debate the vagaries of Fortune, and to explore the nature of happiness, good and evil, fate and free will.

Victor Watts's English translation makes *The Consolation of Philosophy* accessible to the modern reader while losing nothing of its poetic artistry and breadth of vision. This edition includes an introduction discussing Boethius's life and writings, a bibliography, glossary and notes.

Translated with an introduction by Victor Watts

THE STORY OF PENGUIN CLASSICS

Before 1946 ...'Classics' are mainly the domain of academics and students, without readable editions for everyone else. This all changes when a little-known classicist, E. V. Rieu, presents Penguin founder Allen Lane with the translation of Homer's *Odyssey* that he has been working on and reading to his wife Nelly in his spare time.

1946 *The Odyssey* becomes the first Penguin Classic published, and promptly sells three million copies. Suddenly, classic books are no longer for the privileged few.

1950s Rieu, now series editor, turns to professional writers for the best modern, readable translations, including Dorothy L. Sayers's *Inferno* and Robert Graves's *The Twelve Caesars*, which revives the salacious original.

1960s The Classics are given the distinctive black jackets that have remained a constant throughout the series's various looks. Rieu retires in 1964, hailing the Penguin Classics list as 'the greatest educative force of the 20th century'.

1970s A new generation of translators arrives to swell the Penguin Classics ranks, and the list grows to encompass more philosophy, religion, science, history and politics.

1980s The Penguin American Library joins the Classics stable, with titles such as *The Last of the Mohicans* safeguarded. Penguin Classics now offers the most comprehensive library of world literature available.

1990s The launch of Penguin Audiobooks brings the classics to a listening audience for the first time, and in 1999 the launch of the Penguin Classics website takes them online to a larger global readership than ever before.

The 21st Century Penguin Classics are rejacketed for the first time in nearly twenty years. This world famous series now consists of more than 1300 titles, making the widest range of the best books ever written available to millions – and constantly redefining the meaning of what makes a 'classic'.

The Odyssey continues ...

The best books ever written

PENGUIN ✦ CLASSICS

SINCE 1946

Find out more at www.penguinclassics.com